THE MATTER OF BLACK LIVING

The Matter of Black Living

THE AESTHETIC EXPERIMENT OF
RACIAL DATA, 1880–1930

Autumn Womack

•

The University of Chicago Press   Chicago and London

The University of Chicago Press, Chicago 60637
The University of Chicago Press, Ltd., London
Published 2022
Printed in the United States of America

31 30 29 28 27 26 25 24 23 22   1 2 3 4 5

ISBN-13: 978-0-226-80674-7 (cloth)
ISBN-13: 978-0-226-80691-4 (paper)
ISBN-13: 978-0-226-80688-4 (e-book)
DOI: https://doi.org/10.7208/chicago/9780226806884.001.0001

This publication is made possible in part by
the Barr Ferree Foundation Fund for Publications,
Department of Art and Archaeology, Princeton University.

Library of Congress Cataloging-in-Publication Data

Names: Womack, Autumn, author.
Title: The matter of Black living : the aesthetic experiment of racial data,
    1880–1930 / Autumn Womack.
Description: Chicago : University of Chicago Press, 2022. |
    Includes bibliographical references and index.
Identifiers: LCCN 2021030560 | ISBN 9780226806747 (cloth) |
    ISBN 9780226806914 (paperback) | ISBN 9780226806884 (ebook)
Subjects: LCSH: African Americans in literature. | African Americans in
    motion pictures. | African Americans in art. | American literature—
    20th century—History and criticism. | Motion pictures—United
    States—History—20th century. | Photography—United States—
    History—20th century. | African Americans—Social life and customs—
    19th century. | African Americans—Social life and customs—
    20th century. | Social surveys—United States.
Classification: LCC PS173.N4 W66 2022 | DDC 810.9/896073—dc23
LC record available at https://lccn.loc.gov/2021030560

♾ This paper meets the requirements of ANSI/NISO Z39.48-1992
(Permanence of Paper).

In memory of Rosemary Marshall,
my grandmother

Contents

Color plates follow page 144.

Introduction

DATA AND THE MATTER OF BLACK LIFE

Undisciplining Data

Drat statistics . . . these are folks!

W. E. B. DU BOIS, *The Quest of the Silver Fleece* (1911)

You know the formula. There's data, which becomes information,
which becomes knowledge. But the step right after that is wisdom.
Neither one of those first three is sufficient.

TONI MORRISON, "Being or Becoming the Stranger,"
Norton Lecture, Harvard University (2016)

We must become undisciplined.

CHRISTINA SHARPE, *In the Wake* (2016)

The Quest of the Silver Fleece (1911), W. E. B. Du Bois's first published
novel, stages a racial data crisis. An account of the intersecting worlds
of cotton speculation, liberal reform, and post-Reconstruction politics, *Quest*'s fictional territory is populated by a motley crew of reformers, students, farmers, and financiers, all of whom are variously
invested in Tooms County, Alabama, a fictionalization of Lowndes
County, where Du Bois coordinated research for his lost social study
"Negro Labor in Lowndes County, Alabama." In Tooms, Du Bois in-
troduces Bles Alwyn, an enterprising boy who arrives to attend the local all-black school, and Zora, a "heathen hoyden of twelve untrained

years" who is as captivating as she is categorically confounding.[1] *Quest's* data dilemma comes into focus against the background of the late nineteenth century's racial, technological, and disciplinary particularities, all of which were crucially concerned with the matter of free black life. As the century came to a close, and the political and social aftershocks of Reconstruction's failures intensified, questions swirled around African Americans' relationship to the nation. Rechristened "the Negro Problem," and outsourced to a burgeoning class of social scientists, race theorists, and reformers, black freedom was formulated as a perplexing problem best addressed through data-driven analysis and empirically grounded research. As they endeavored to order the seeming disorder of free black life and mitigate the deep anxiety about incorporating African Americans into the national landscape, race theorists harnessed sociological studies, statistics, photographs, and literary texts as novel data sources. What ensued was nothing short of a "data revolution," one that authorized the visual and racial schemas that determined whose life mattered, regulated a color line that emancipation threatened to destabilize, and streamlined the technologies that converted black people into statistical integers, mere data, and the subject of a national racial problem.[2] Certainly, the violent process that sought to order, control, and systematically quantify black life are not particular to the turn of the twentieth century. The revolutionary nature of racial data at this moment, then, is owing to the particular ways that innovations in data technologies met the specificity of the post-emancipation landscape to produce a frenetic outpouring of racial data in the name of addressing and resolving the "Negro Problem."

Against the compulsion to isolate, atomize, and apportion black life as an object of knowledge and a problem that could be measured, classified, and contained, in *Quest* Zora emerges as an inscrutable force who defies the moment's taxonomic compulsions and evades even the best attempts at social ordering. A swamp-dwelling girl who earns her living in a brothel and rejects the purported value of both formal education and narrowly defined domestic duties, Zora is stationed outside of normative social and gender categories, rejecting the social legitimacy and sociological legibility that her status as either a student or participant in a capitalist economy would afford. Simultaneously poised as the ideal candidate for social reform and exploding the social containers that seek to define her, Zora materializes at the intersection of Du Bois's commitment to an empirically driven approach to the "Negro Problem"—what he summed up in 1898 with the mantra "if we would solve a problem we must study it"—and the realization that, when it came to studying social life, "facts . . . were elusive things" that could not be easily converted into actionable information.[3] In the pages of *Quest*, Zora *is* ultimately transformed into a bourgeois subject who renounces her morally questionable, if economically independent, life, first as a pupil in the "Negro" school and ultimately as Bles's partner in life and business. Nevertheless, the slippage between Zora's incalculability and her susceptibility for reform deserves pause. For even as *Quest* manifests the Victorian-inspired reformist vision that Du Bois was never quite able to shake, it also articulates the productive oscillation between data's instrumental horizons and the "elusive" nature of free black life. This interplay is at the heart of *The Matter of Black Living*'s exploration into the aesthetic offspring that are produced when black social life confronts data's disciplinary regimes. Mounted on stages and in photographs, and surfacing in technical missteps and strategic narrative decisions, the dissonant interface between blackness and data is animated by the project of squaring the vitality of black life with data. This data crisis, as it were, finds expression in aesthetic innovation at the historical juncture when racial data was as much an experiment as was black freedom.

To unpack the stakes of this claim, consider more closely *Quest*'s opening vignette. *Quest* does not begin on a plantation or at a school, settings that feature prominently in the text and yet are redolent with disciplinary histories. Rather, the "red waters of the swamp" are the book's entry point.[4] A site of environmental and sexual surplus, the swamp is home to Zora as well as the brothel that is frequented by the local white plantocracy. Along with Bles, the "red swamp" conducts readers into a dark cacophonous soundscape, scored by a "human music" that is also "a wildness and weirdness."[5] "Impelled by some strange power," Bles is drawn to a "ragged and black cabin," a dark and dreamy site of sensory overload where, in midst of white patrons' "hoarse staccato cries and peals of laughter," Zora emerges:

> Amid this mighty halo, as on clouds of flame, she was dancing. She was black, and lithe, and tall, and willowy. Her garments twined and flew

around the delicate moulding of her dark, young, half-naked limbs. A heavy mass of hair clung motionless to her wide forehead. Her arms twirled and flickered, and body and soul seemed quivering and whirring in the poetry of her motion. As she danced she sang. . . . It was no tune nor melody, it was just formless, boundless music. The boy forgot himself and all the world besides. All darkness was sudden light; dazzled he crept forward, bewildered, fascinated, until with one last wild whir, the elf girl paused.[6]

The offspring of "ecological excess," Zora manifests the representational challenges historically wrought by the swamp, a space that Daphne Brooks describes as a symbol of "radical black subterfuge" and the location from which "revolt might gestate."[7] Nurturing Maroon communities and incubating forms of rebellion, swamps were the grounds for a "spectacular opacity" that confused technologies of surveillance and their aspiration to make black life utterly visible, profitable, and manageable. If in its antebellum literary and visual iterations the swamp is a surplus form that, in "obstructing and resituating the spectator's wide and roving gaze," offered refuge from slavery's visual and racial economy, then in its turn-of-the-century expression it confounds post-Reconstruction classificatory schemas that aimed to make black life discernible as either a subject of serious historical inquiry or a social problem that could be (re)solved through scientific study and systematic categorization.[8] *This* is the swamp from which Zora emerges.

An embodiment of sonic, sexual, and choreographic superfluity, Zora elides the disciplining logic that takes black life as eminently knowable and the data regimes that would compel her conversion into evidence of black moral degeneracy. For unlike the sorrow songs that Du Bois describes in *The Souls of Black Folk* as the "the articulate message of the slave to the world," Zora's weird and wild music is neither a gift nor a "sign of development."[9] Instead, its "formless and boundless" nature generates a panic that is as categorical as it is affective: Bles retreats from the cabin in utter terror before fainting. Neither quite girl nor human—she is alternately described as "elflike" and "birdlike"—in *Quest*'s earliest pages Zora wages a blow to social-scientific frameworks that would seek to either fix her on a vertical chain of being or tender her a quantifiable social problem. Instead, she simply disintegrates into a "wild whir."

Zora's eventual assimilation into a progressive historical model, where she transforms from a swamp-dwelling girl to a model of ideal black leadership, ultimately orders and resolves the chaos from which she emerges. Yet in this study I am interested in the way that *Quest*'s formal and generic eccentricity (it traffics in the economic study, social reform manifesto, romance, and political bildungsroman, to name just a few) registers a disciplinary and aesthetic tangle, one that Du Bois was always enmeshed in and that emerges from an effort to reconcile a deep commitment to the transformative potential of data with a keen recognition of its violence.[10] Just as *Quest* is a formal exercise through which Du Bois could exploit the novel's flexible boundaries and order the chaos of postbellum life, the novel also gives voice to a deep anxiety about black life's compatibility with the Progressive Era's structures of (e)valuation, enumeration, and classification. Thus when, in its second chapter and in response to a statistically driven argument against educating African Americans in anything other than industrial labor, the white teacher Miss Smith exclaims, "Drat statistics . . . these are folks!" we hear an echo of a conflicted Du Bois, who was equally concerned that statistics would never account for the elusive nature of blackness and that Zora's weird music and whirring motion would always strain statistics' regulatory boundaries. Even as Zora successfully transforms from a recalcitrant girl who confounds the senses and exceeds perceptual faculties into a subject who is both shaped and purportedly discovered by social science, the opening moments of *Quest* provide the occasion to reconsider the conditions of possibility—aesthetic, epistemological, and racial—that emerge at the interface of black social life and empiricism's regulatory data regimes at the very moment when, as we will see, race and data were affixed to each other in particularly modern ways.[11]

Quest is neither the first nor the last time that Du Bois would try to order the seemingly disordered world of black social life while seeking to express what Vilashini Cooppan describes as his devotion to "a multiple and moving notion of blackness."[12] Indeed, it is safe to say that the work of generating a socially and politically transformative body of racial data without stamping out the complexities of modern black life underpins his entire oeuvre. Here, we can look to the hundreds of photographs that he arranged for the 1900 Paris Exposition, a compendium of black achievement and vitality that Shawn Michelle Smith has argued "dismantle[s] and reconfigure[s] the popular and scientific genealogy of African Americans that inform dominant turn-of-the-century viewing practices."[13] We might also train our attention to the array of "data portraits" he curated during his tenure at Atlanta University, a collection of "charts, maps, and other devices designed to illustrate the development of the American Negro."[14] By summoning data's expressive forms, Du Bois performed what Alexander Weheliye describes as the work of "diagrammatically desediment[ing] the Negro as a 'natural' phenomenon."[15] And in the countless tables and maps that he drew by hand for his sociological study of Philadelphia's Seventh Ward, *The Philadelphia Negro*, Du Bois labored to make visible the class differentiations that normative sociological discourse obscured.[16] Rather than approaching these projects independently or as points of arrival, the location where Du Bois sticks his theoretical landing and, at least temporarily, resolves the seemingly unresolvable, I understand them as iterations of an ongoing engagement with the question of documenting black social life, of finding a medium that can record black vitality without reducing it to mere data or converting it into a seemingly effective, yet inert and undifferentiated, body of information.[17]

Another way into this line of thinking, and one that draws us toward a second conceit of this book, is through Du Bois's foundational query, "How does it feel to be a problem?"[18] Cast as an unspoken question that structures the color line, as well as African American literary scholarship more broadly, this proposition launches *The Souls of Black Folk* and maps multiple routes to a series of answers. As Du Bois names it, to live in Jim Crow America is to be continually assaulted with the knowledge that your very presence is problematic and to confront the "Negro Problem" as juridical, geographic, and social, and also deeply affective.[19] If being a problem is a feeling, then *The Souls of Black Folk* gives shape and structure to the amorphous and abstract terrain of blackness, one that Du Bois reminds us often refuses conventional logic and demands heterogeneous expressive modes.[20] Given the highly visual nature of Du Bois's work, we can also imagine a version of the project that begins with the provocation, "What does a problem *look* like?" This is not so much a question of capturing black life, of holding it up as a problem for examination and study. Rather, this query directs us toward the technical, aesthetic, and epistemological challenges wrought by the task of communicating black life as enlivened and vital, of loosening the clasp that insists on reducing blackness to an object of knowledge, to data, to a racial calculus that always confirms black life's disposability. To ask this question is to also consider the technological and representational forms assumed by racial data. Put another way, what does racial data look like, and what political work can it perform, if any? What kind of technical or aesthetic innovation would yield a dynamic body of racial data, one resistant to visual technology's propensity for capture and arrest? Or, to borrow a useful phrasing from Leigh Raiford, how might we reconcile "movement with medium"?[21]

As it registers the aesthetic possibilities that emerge when the force of black life confronts racial data's regimes, the earliest moments of *Quest* are underpinned by a question that was crucial to late nineteenth- and early twentieth-century African American cultural producers: how to document the sociality of black life? *The Matter of Black Living* places this provocation at the center of its exploration into how African American cultural producers working in the decades on either side of the twentieth century navigated the interlocking domains of racial data, discipline, and visual technology as they endeavored to generate a socially, politically, and epistemologically transformative body of racial knowledge. Documenting sociality, attending to the matter of black living, it would seem, is a paradoxical endeavor. Documentation evokes instrumental forms like maps, birth certificates, photographs, and their utility as tools for social administration and control. Enveloped by the data revolution's "taxonomic enthusiasms," to borrow a phrase from Lindsay Reckson, and harnessed as techniques of racial management, documents and documentation were both data's storehouse and its expressive medium.[22] Documenting, then, presumes (black) life's legibility, a condition that allows its seamless reduction to data. Sociality, however, registers networks of interaction, relationships, and collective energy. Black sociality in particular has been theorized as a disruptive force, one that, Fred Moten explains, "constitutes a profound threat to the already existing order of things."[23] And what is documentation if not an effort to order the order of things? Rather than searching for sites at which the contradiction between documentation and sociality is resolved, this book is attuned to the points at which the irruptive force of blackness and the instrumental workings of data meet, where sociality confronts racial data's desire for atomization, capture, and discipline. It is from here, I argue, that experiments in racial knowledge were forged and projected, experiments that were also deeply aesthetic. Here, we can think of *Quest's* perpetually shifting tone, genre, and political outlook as of a piece with an effort to dislodge blackness from its ostensible status as an object of knowledge. To undertake such aesthetic and formal acrobatics is what documenting the sociality of black life looks like and requires. What I am addressing here is not an easy ideological distinction between documenting and experimenting. Instead, in the face of black life, documenting was always already an experimental process, one that had the potential to reorder and disorder the easy bundling of data and black life.

Over the course of three chapters I situate previously understudied archives alongside seemingly familiar texts and actors to argue that the project of communicating black life's dynamism, which is also the project of making data move, choreographed the work of figures like Kelly Miller, Sutton Griggs, and Zora Neale Hurston, as well as everyday folk. But perhaps most important, it also buoyed public and scientific discourse on the ever-enigmatic "Negro Problem." Working adjacent to and often alongside Du Bois, the cultural and social actors that I spotlight experimented across a range of data-generating technologies as they ventured to rework the equivalence between black life and data. Their encounters produced often surprising aesthetic responses, including experimental novels, kinetic reactions, and new notions of blackness. Knitting aesthetic innovation to social-scientific discourse and technological experimentation with political marginalization, *The Matter of Black Living's* cast endeavored to produce a socially transformative body of racial knowledge while attending to the seemingly impossible task of documenting the dynamism of black social life that normative social-scientific regimes obscured. Put another way, for white and black intellectuals, reformers, performers, and social scientists, above all else, the stakes of the data revolution hinged on the question of black living. For those seeking to restore the fiction of a pre-emancipation landscape, racial data doubled as a regulatory regime that managed and controlled free black life. For the figures and archives that I take as the subject of this book, the task at hand was to render the openness, dynamism, and relationality that constitutes black sociality. Their work's motivation shapes the decision to emphasize black living over the more potentially fixed formulation black life in this book's title.

For Miller, a Washington, DC–based black mathematician and an early advocate of black experimental fiction, proving black vitality in the face of a profuse body of mortality statistics that discounted African Americans' place in the body politic would eventually prompt his embrace of the social survey, a distinctly hybrid form that dominated the Progressive Era's social-scientific landscape and promised to offer a visual account of social movement. To the south of Miller, the Tennessee-based writer Sutton E. Griggs would excavate the social survey's potential for reordering the social, turning its distinct ligaments into a patently black visual praxis. Working in a different register, a motley crew of northeastern reformers who orient chapter 2, including Du Bois and the little-known white reformer Lillian Jewett, would pry apart and reassemble photography's ontology as they worked to produce a record of anti-black violence that was also an account of black livelihood. Out of this history of technological, aesthetic, and social-scientific experimentation, Zora Neale Hurston, chapter 3's anchor, forged a relationship to film as she tried to reconcile the pulse of Southern black life, which she described as "still in the making," with the disciplinary and technological limits of anthropology's mandate to "record, record, record."[24] As these figures cleaved through the formal and epistemological limits of data-producing technologies, they discovered disorienting possibilities that provided the grounds for unsettling the putative relationship between blackness and data. At the heart of their turn-of-the-century project is an effort to not simply register the fact of black life, but the contours, specificity, and rhythm of black living.

The Matter of Black Living emerges against the backdrop of a number of interrelated social and disciplinary formations, namely the postbellum "Negro Problem," and the rise of sociology and anthropology in the final decades of the nineteenth century. To get at the complexity of this atmosphere, in which data is both an organizing principle and an insufficient horizon, I employ the framework of undisciplining data. On one level, undisciplining data calls our attention to social science's modes of containment, classification, and categorization that transposed its subjects into objects of study, what Dorothy Ross describes as the process by which the postbellum sciences "become 'disciplines' in the double sense, specialized branches of knowledge and agencies of regulatory control."[25] Working overtime as systems of racial and social management, the turn of the twentieth century's notional disciplines assuaged moral panic and restored the social order that modernity disrupted and that free black life was believed to have punctured. Social science's construction of black life as a methodological problem underpins this book, particularly my reading of the social survey in chapter 1, but also film's standing as unmediated visual data in early anthropology, which orients my discussion of Zora Neale Hurston in chapter 3. Yet my mobilization of discipline is not confined to academic fields of study, that is, to disciplinarity proper. In *The Matter of Black Living* I also approach the courtroom, the stage, reform, and the law as domains of bodily and political governance that sought to discipline African Americans as national subject and reformed individuals.[26] Attending to the disciplining and disciplinary workings of fields like social science and locations like the courtroom is only a fraction of this project, however. This book is primarily concerned with how embodied individuals and material forms are incorporated into and as data regimes that could generate knowledge. Or more simply put, how, this book asks, in the context of the turn of the twentieth century, do bodies and forms get perceived as data? As we will see, to raise these questions means approaching data as a dynamic process that can be unsettled, disturbed, and ultimately undisciplined, rather than as an abstract concept. Moreover, scholars of African American history and black literary studies have underscored the force of a racial calculus, one that, as Eddie Glaude has argued, risks hampering our reading of African American cultural life, and that, as Saidiya Hartman has shown, continues to shape the material and structural conditions of black living.[27] Building upon these important interventions, this book insists that any discussion of a racial calculus within the context of the turn of the twentieth century—a moment that was conditioned by the proliferation of data, numerical and otherwise— must consider how a racial calculus turns upon the making of data, the transmutation of black life into an integer that could yield surplus value and negation. Throughout, data is not this book's antagonist; nor does it assert that "correct" or "good" data is going to save us or course correct our murky political future. Instead, each chapter maps a terrain of negotiation, experimentation, and entanglement where data are unruly, unpredictable, and rarely behave according to the disciplinary regimes that attempt to harness and metabolize them as institutionalized knowledge.

By unraveling the social practices, attitudes, and disciplinary methods through which material and embodied forms become data and, in turn, reconstitute the very meaning of data, this book reads sites where data is undisciplined—the stage, the photography studio, the novel, to name just a few—as the meeting ground for theories of black studies, literary history, and critical data studies. This book's critical mattering map knits black studies' attention to the disruptive force of blackness, what Moten describes as its status as both "ordering and disordering movement," to literary history's focus on what Maurice Lee has recently called literature and data's deeply entangled stories.[28] In the case of the latter, this body of scholarship insists upon the semantic world of numbers and the aesthetic nature of data, ultimately refusing the distinction between aesthetics and data that orients contemporary defenses of the literary arts. Within this terrain, data emerges as its own kind of disruptive force, one that agitates seemingly hard-and-fast divisions between the literary and the empirical. And yet African American cultural productions and literary texts have largely evaded the attention of scholars interested in exploring the convergence of literature and data. This elision certainly owes to what Lee describes as nineteenth-century writers' general inability to imagine racialized characters as participants in an "informational modernity," the proliferation of systems of classification and the "superabundance of data and documents" characterizing the nineteenth century and infiltrating its literary landscape.[29] And yet the fact remains that African Americans in particular and race in general were central to the formation of data regimes and informational systems.[30] One of the goals of this book is to wed important insights from black studies to the humanities' interest in data. By taking up data and blackness as co-constitutive, even as they wage powerful disruptions to disciplinary order and racial epistemologies, my readings take inspiration from critics working under the banner of black studies who have excavated the distinct ways that, in the words of Katherine McKittrick, numerical data might be put to "differently work blackness as a category."[31] While McKittrick finds her center of gravity in an antebellum transatlantic context, this book looks toward the late nineteenth century, the very onset of the data revolution. In so doing, I think with and build upon the work of interdisciplinary scholars such as Jacqueline Goldsby, Saidiya Hartman, Khalil Muhammad, and Alexander Weheliye, work that carefully attends to the social, political, and archival particularities of the turn of the twentieth century and all of its complications and contradictions. Joining them in this rigorous and archivally driven analysis, I show how undisciplined data is what is produced at the contentious nexus where black life and data-producing technologies meet but do not necessarily harmonize; it is the errant, the excessive, and the elusive. It is what, this book argues, cannot get composed into data and what emerges when registering black living is at stake. Not only can tracing efforts to document the sociality of black living draw our attention to data's racial refuse; it also can alert us to data's insufficiency as a calcifying process.[32] The practices, forms of life, and strategies that refuse incorporation into data regimes provide the blueprint for aesthetic practices and the road map for knowing and seeing black life outside of social-scientific categories.

In what follows, I detail the historical and social conditions under which race, data, and visual technology intersect in order to carve out the specificity of these terms within the context of the turn of the twentieth century's racial data revolution. In so doing, I detail the book's intervention into the field of race and data studies, a field that curiously bypasses the turn of the twentieth century even as questions of literature, race, and empiricism dominate recent scholarly work. And at the risk of undermining this project's commitment to undisciplining, I outline the aesthetic stakes of this project, arguing for the importance of mapping a genealogy of black creative production according to flash points in the history of data production before sketching the book's particular case studies and methodology.

The Social Life of Racial Data

In this study, "data" is both an interventionist strategy deployed by African American cultural workers and a disciplining regime. Tracing moments in which black life's conversion into data is suspended, I highlight aesthetics as a key route through which data's meanings are consolidated and contested. In tracking data and aesthetics together through the prism of racial blackness, my readings always return to the materiality of blackness in ways that acknowledge and push against the risky overreliance on theorizing data as abstraction(s), as a fixed object of study that finds its home in a database or archive, or as mere representation. As a result this book is conversant with recent work that gathers around "data politics," an approach to data that considers it a site of struggle over power and knowledge. As Evelyn Rupert, Engin Isin, and Didier Bigo assert in their polemic "Data Politics," in addition to being concerned with how data is gathered and to which uses it is put, we must also query "how data is generative of new forms of power relations and politics at different interconnected scales."[33] Dismantling the idea that data is raw, abstract, and neutral, data politics is a reminder that data is iterative and performative, the site at which social and political practice intersect to "generate forms of expertise, interpretation, concepts, and methods that collectively function as fields of power and knowledge."[34] *The Matter of Black Living* is not primarily concerned with debates and questions that gather around big data and digital humanities. And although this book shares contemporary scholars' investment in querying the interface of data and black life, it also does not take decolonizing data or producing anti-racist algorithms as its primary charge, crucial work that exceeds the historical contours of this study. However, in the spirit of data politics, this book puts pressure on the enduring notion that data is abstract, a view that continues to underpin theoretical approaches to data. Certainly, all data are abstract insofar as they require material expression. For proof of this we need only skim the expansive array of maps, charts, graphs, drawings, and imagery that Johanna Drucker assembles in *Graphesis: Visual Forms of Knowledge Production*, a testament to the frank visuality of knowledge and its reliance on material things. The issue, however, is how exactly data is made visible and iterative, how it is asked to perform in the service of knowledge and power. The point that *The Matter of Black Living* cycles through is that thinking about data as always abstract inherently obscures the process by which bodies and material objects become data. Put another way, this book takes as its starting point the idea that data's material expressions depend on the abstraction of black life itself.

To scholars of the nineteenth century, my focus on data over, say, information, empiricism, or even epistemology might come as a bit of a surprise, even as these terms are crucial to this book's arguments. Although African American intellectuals, cultural producers, and writers regularly theorized and deployed terms like *facts* and *evidence*, *data* was used far less frequently and consistently only toward the end of the 1920s. Recently, scholars working to unfurl the complex way that empiricism and data crafted life and literature have reached for a related set of terms. Maurice Lee, for instance, describes "the informational" as a domain of meaning making characterized by "instrumentalism, calculation, and reconfigurable data" that is inextricably bound up with nineteenth-century literary production.[35] Tracking the methods that transformed persons into bodies of information at the turn of the twentieth century, and working with a sociologically inflected agenda, Colin Koopman offers *infopower* as a productive term for naming the process by which data is violently fastened to individuals in the name of biopolitical regimes.[36] Mapping the intimacy of black life and data's regimes in a way that comes closest to my own set of interests, Simone Browne offers a sweeping genealogy of what she describes as *sousveillance*, the mode of surveillance that is both conditioned by and conditions racial blackness and that is conducted through data collection.[37] These three examples are far from comprehensive, but they do begin to register how data is simultaneously pivotal to their working definitions and on the outskirts of their analysis.

As are Koopman, Browne, and Lee, I am interested in data's iterative forms, but I am just as interested in data's role as the building block of information and racial knowledge, what Lisa Gitelman and Virginia Jackson describe as its "morsel like" nature.[38] Importantly, this perspective begins from an enduring formula in which data becomes information before being consolidated and institutionalized as knowledge. It is this well-rehearsed framework that Toni Morrison evokes in the question-and-answer portion of her 2016 Harvard University Norton Lecture. Positioning data as the starting point of an insufficient "formula" that can only ever produce an incomplete historical record, she explains, "You know the formula, there's data, which becomes information, which becomes knowledge."[39] The schema by which data is transformed into information and then knowledge is, of course, an oversimplification. Indeed, one of the arguments to which this book is indebted is that data and black life were co-constituted in the service of producing a racial regime, what

McKittrick metaphorizes as the process by which a violent arithmetic gave birth to New World blackness. But what this schema *does* encourage is a productive slowdown, an invitation to pry apart the very mechanisms, forms, and practices that authorize data and reproduce it as a particularly racialized terrain. For if the endeavors that I track are fortified by a quest to locate a representational mode and a visual epistemology that can both recognize and render a transformative body of racial knowledge, then any such project must reckon with data, epistemology's smallest unit of meaning. From this point, and returning to Morrison's invocation of a data-driven formula that paves the way for a defense of literature and imagination—after all, her answer responds to a question about the role of history in her oeuvre—her provocation opens another fruitful line of thinking that is central to this book. To follow Morrison's consideration of data as part of a formula generative of an incomplete body of knowledge is to understand the "formula," that is, the grammar that always denotes black life as both immanently knowable and disposable, as one that can be unsettled and reassembled.

Over the course of this book, I am particularly attentive to the relationship of data, information, and the material forms that aid in its transformation from abstract morsel to communicative knowledge. The question is not whether data is abstract, in other words, but how it is deployed, shaped, and framed through its material expressions, be it through the grammar of sentence structure, the regime of aesthetics, or a photographic pose. Rather than a fixed calculus that will never hold the excessive, the intransigent, the remainder, and the "folk" who Du Bois argued could not be contained by statistics, I follow the lead of the texts and individuals I explore and approach the "formula" as mutable, flexible, and open for revision so as to produce alternate ways of knowing and apprehending black life.

As a framework for approaching African American intellectual and cultural production of the late nineteenth and early twentieth centuries, this book has particular stakes for visual studies, as many visual technologies were co-opted into data regimes but also deployed to produce social knowledge through visual terms and mediums. The three modes that I spotlight—social survey, photography, and film—are, on the one hand, components of data's regimes, which at the turn of the century were called to comport racial data as information that would solve black life. In their investment in reconciling the vitality of black life with data-producing technology's insistence on capture, and arrest, the practices that I spotlight try to produce a visual document of black living. Here, social surveys, the multidisciplinary mode that I take up in great detail in chapter 1, were commissioned by local and national reform institutions to produce a comprehensive picture of social problems and to shape everything from public policy to philanthropic giving. At the same time, and to varying degrees, the social survey, photography, and film all promised to visualize data in "real" and "accurate" dimensions, to produce a living and moving picture of black life. Even as a robust body of scholarship has alerted us to a form like photography's dual frequency of freedom and repression, in its promise to index life and living, visual technology was a fertile ground for staging new racial formulas.[40]

Racial Data, Visual Revolutions

The production of postbellum black life as a problem of and for data took shape alongside the social sciences' consolidation into discrete fields like anthropology and sociology, the production of visual technologies that claimed to order an unruly modern landscape, and a heightened state of crisis concerning the future place of blacks in the nation-state, or the "Negro Problem." Yet long before these three realms intersected to produce the conditions for what Khalil Muhammad describes as the "racial data revolution," race and data were conjoined under the auspices of race science and the transatlantic slave trade. If, as it is generally agreed upon, slavery and modernity are mutually constitutive, then modernity's investment in submitting the knowable world to systems of classification meant that the enslaved were subject to what McKittrick describes as a "violent arithmetic."[41] Here, ledgers, shipping manifestos, and plantation maps transformed the living into the exchangeable commodity, recomposing "historic blackness" into "the list, the breathless numbers, the absolutely economic, the mathematics of unliving."[42] Scaled according to a racial calculus that always yielded a negative value, black life was evaluated as inventory, capital, and labor.[43] Just as this racial calculus ensured the success of the slave economy, it also provided the conditions through which black life was perceived as an interchangeable unit of meaning making, whether it be in the service of producing profit or of authorizing a narrative of black criminality. Equating blackness with data was not confined to the plantation. As Simone Browne has shown, fugitive slaves and free blacks were also recorded and coded as knowable through practices like branding and lantern laws, both of which enforced a state of total legibility. Such modes of corporeal management and structures of racial knowledge, Browne argues, render the body biometrically knowable.[44] Data's ontological impositions were sustained by the domain of race science, a domain that was equally concerned with categorizing racialized bodies in taxonomic terms. Intent on classifying the steadily diversifying population of blacks, Native Americans, and European settlers, comparative anatomists in the United States turned to regulatory schemas to fabulate racial hierarchies. In his comparative cranial studies, for instance, Samuel Morton insisted that skull cavities could provide a valid measure of the brain, which he argued was the true index of a race's place in the vertical hierarchy of life. In Morton's racial laboratory, "one-eighth-inch-diameter lead shots" became the measure of humanity, a violent allegory for the processes of atomization that were required to transpose bodies into data.[45] The creative strategies that race scientists like Morton undertook to produce data did more than just authorize a racial chain of being where blacks were positioned on the lowest order; they also graphically flattened black life. Importantly, such studies were certainly not limited to Africans and African Americans, what he called "ethiopians"; whites and Native Americans were also included in his taxonomy. Yet race science's affiliations with antebellum debates surrounding slavery meant that such scientific efforts could justify an economic system that relied on positioning black life as disembodied labor.

If the production of racial data was encouraged and enforced by New World slavery, then it was also aided and abetted by visual technology. As Gitelman and Jackson remind us, "surveying the world with data, at some level, means having data visibly before one's eyes, looking *through* the data if not always self-consciously looking *at* the data."[46] Indeed, visual technology has a long and overlapping relationship with racial data, and a central conceit of this book is that the forms that we normally think of as strictly enumerative or taxonomic are also highly visual and deeply discursive, a position that is indebted to the insights of scholars such as Drucker and Nicholas Mirzoeff. For Drucker, maps, bar charts, diagrams, graphs, and statistics produce visual epistemologies. As she elaborates, knowledge shares a deep kinship with vision so that "ordering and classification serve intellectual work" and "the formal systems in which visual forms have been classified and characterized" construct ways of knowing and seeing.[47] Echoing this position, Mirzoeff takes graphic forms like maps, journals, and portraits as a piece of a network of visuality that structures the terms on which reality is known.[48] As the nineteenth century wore on, photographic technologies quickly emerged as the revered mode for visually producing and constructing social reality. For race scientists seeking to maintain a racial order that was fiscally beneficial to the nation, photography's status as an indexical medium that purported to objectively record the visible world was especially appealing. And as a mode of currency that could ascribe and efface value, the photograph, Alan Sekula has argued, operated within a system of classification and comparison.[49] Scholars of visual studies have shown how photographic portraits—from the bourgeois family photograph to the criminal mug shot to the ethnographic image to nominally scientific studies—engendered new ways of imagining subjectivity in the nineteenth century while also offering ostensibly unmitigated records of racial difference.[50] Thus the family photographs that Shawn Michelle Smith explores in her foundational study *American Archives* give substance to the lie that "true" and racialized interior essences were manifest as bodily difference. "Systems of photographic documentation," Smith explains, "were being designed to record and codify the body as the ultimate sign of racial essence."[51] And in the adjacent field of visual ethnology, the now-canonical daguerreotypes of seven enslaved individuals taken by Louis Agassiz banked on photography's status as an indexical medium, providing an archival clearing ground for his theories of polygenesis.

The conflation of race and data was not sequestered to the realm of pure subjection, however. Black cultural producers also labored to breathe life into racial knowledge's violent arithmetic. Insisting, in the words of Fred Moten, that the "object could speak," African Americans have persistently refused the self-evident nature of blackness, its status as an object that could be consumed, dissected, and treated as data.[52] In his 1855 autobiography *My Bondage and My Freedom*, Frederick Douglass recounts the value he provided on the abolitionist lecture circuit as an object lesson of slavery. "I was generally introduced as a *'chattel'*—*'a thing'*—a piece of southern *'property'*—the chairman assuring the audience that 'it' could speak. . . . I had the advantage of being a *'brand new fact.'*"⁵³ Rendered evidence and instructed to skip the philosophy and simply "give us the facts," Douglass would spend his life refusing the terms of objecthood by continuously remaking himself in autobiographies and photographic portraits.⁵⁴ And as Britt Rusert's recent work on race and science has shown, across the antebellum era African American cultural workers like Benjamin Banneker and James McCune Smith, to name just a few of the extraordinary figures she takes as the subject of her book, took up scientific idioms and methods to create a body of knowledge in which black life wasn't easily subject to empiricism's eviscerating protocols.⁵⁵ We can also look to Ida B. Wells and her decision to produce a record of lynching statistics in *A Red Record* as both a radical social-scientific act and a formal experiment that was as much about producing a counter-archive as it was an attempt to animate numerical evidence. Here, "record" surfaces as documentary strategy and a mode of accounting, but also as a performative action that indexes emerging phonographic technologies that purported to keep the voice alive; that is, Wells's red record of racial violence remains open and ongoing, and refuses to relegate black death to a past tense.⁵⁶

But if acts of undisciplining data in the service of accounting for black living have a long history, then in the decades following Reconstruction and through the onset of the Great Depression, race, data, and visual technology cohered in ways that were, on the one hand, highly inflexible and, on the other, deeply ambiguous. The paradoxical and continually shifting relationship had everything to do with the ever-changing terms of the "Negro Problem" itself. Social scientists, writers, and ordinary people engaged in vigorous debates not only about the "Negro Problem" as such, but also over the very idioms used to make sense of its shifting contours, even as they were inventing new ones. While Reconstruction offered legislatively backed and federally funded initiatives aimed to support black businesses, education, and leadership, Reconstruction's reversal, along with landmark legal decisions like *Plessy v. Ferguson* and shifting economic patterns that encouraged migration to Northern cities, generated a conceptual panic. In his 1884 *Atlantic* essay "The Negro Problem," the social scientist and reformer Nathaniel Shaler warned that, given what he insisted was African Americans' innate biological and moral inferiority, "there can be no doubt for centuries to come the task of weaving these African threads of life into our society will be the greatest of American problems."[57] Particularly anxious about how to manage black collectivity that might transform into black political solidarity, Shaler outlined a schematic plan of action that included a federally funded desegregation program to prohibit the "gathering of negroes into large unmixed settlements."[58] While Shaler's fear was in large part buoyed by the worry that an all-black, "un-mixed" settlement would, like the swamp, simply remain opaque to an investigating eye, Shaler's view was one of countless propositions that cropped up to address what he finally, and ironically, dismissed as the "wonderful social endeavor" of emancipation.[59] African American intellectuals like Booker T. Washington, Charles Chesnutt, Anna Julia Cooper, Paul Laurence Dunbar, and T. Thomas Fortune also offered competing views of how best to secure access to the nation-state. Frances Harper's 1892 novel *Iola Leroy*, for example, staged the multiple dimensions of the "Negro Problem" in the context of a postbellum historical romance. When in the chapter "Open Questions," itself a reflection on the degree to which black intellectuals considered problems of black life to be flexible and multitudinous, a white Southern doctor asserts that "the Negro has always been and will always be an element of discord in our country," a chorus of African American professionals emerges to systematically deconstruct the argument. Such competing postures only begin to convey the heterogeneity of this political climate in which intellectual labor was always already experimental.

What endured across these prospects, whether in the name of black civil rights or the retrenchment of slavery's social customs, was a deep commitment to political and social transformation—whether toward citizenship or beyond it—through the production and circulation of racial data. Together demographic information from the newly expanded US census, a rapidly growing cohort of white settlement workers' findings, and a budding cohort of sociologists and anthropologists, produced an overwhelming amount of data that was mobilized to justify everything from black criminality to institutional funding for sites like Chicago's Hull-House settlement house. As Khalil Muhammad has argued, "these pioneering post-emancipation writers set out to lead the way in analyzing this brand-new situation while producing new knowledge about the true nature of black people."[60]

The production of racial data was not relegated to the terrain of social science proper, nor was it the sole property of liberal reformers. Innovations in photography and motion pictures were also quickly adopted into a new regulatory grammar through which they were mined for bodily and social data.[61] In this context, data took on a new shape and currency as it cloaked itself even tighter around black life. Given the proliferation of data produced in the name of knowing and solving the "problem" of blackness, for African Americans the commitment to, or at the very least the engagement with, data became nonoptional.

Scholars have been eager to excavate an archive of the fugitive, furtive, and dissenting practices that antebellum African Americans mobilized to rework and refute science and visual technology's disciplining gaze.[62] Likewise, as they turn toward the twentieth century, critics like Roderick Ferguson and Avery Gordon have charted the intimate bonds between sociology and literary production, asserting how the latter also intervenes and rescripts sociology's logics.[63] But more often than not, studies of "radical" black engagements with social science, data, and visual technology either pull up short of the postbellum period or gloss it altogether. This book dwells in this chronological lacuna. From this historical outpost I argue that postbellum practices were equally experimental, even if the scholarly record has not always framed them as such. I maintain that even as novel technologies contributed to an expanded and expansive domain that could render black life legible as a problem to be studied and solved, the very newness of these technologies also created loopholes that black and white cultural producers encountered with enthusiasm and curiosity. It is the improvisational character of these encounters that this book is crucially concerned with. From the decision to deploy and then modify a form like the social survey, the subject of the first part of this book, to the choreography that upends the temporality of the photographic record, the focus of my second case study, these practices resonate with what Daphne Brooks describes as acts of "afro-alienation."[64] Such acts, Brooks writes, "provide a fruitful terrain for marginalized figures to experiment with culturally innovative ways to critique and disassemble the conditions of oppression."[65] But whereas Afro-alienation is chiefly interested in anti-realist productions, the methods and technologies that I explore, from statistical graphs to photography to early motion pictures, can be classified as deeply realist in their orientation. Even as they were tendered in the service of the consolidation of a new bio-political order, this study argues that the new and experimental nature of these technologies provided the grounds for innovation and nego-tiation and pinpoints the field of aesthetics as the prime battleground from which the meanings and implications of (racial) data were as-sessed and reconfigured.

The Aesthetics of Data

Having outlined this book's historical and cultural musculature, I want to turn to the place of aesthetics in the "Negro Problem" and its utility for theorizing data technologies and documentation strate-gies. In *The Matter of Black Living*, I uncover the aesthetic contours of a variety of evidentiary and data-producing modes: social surveys, photography, and motion pictures, but also numbers, lists, and charts. But what does it mean to think aesthetics and data together? In his meditation on photography in *In the Break: The Aesthetics of the Black Radical Tradition*, Moten speculates on Mamie Till-Mobley's decision to publish a photograph of the open casket of her murdered son, Em-mett Till, on cover of *Jet* magazine. Tracking what he describes as its sonic substance, Moten reads the photograph as an aesthetic object, writing:

> You lean into it but you can't; the aesthetic and philosophical arrange-ments of the photograph—some organizations of and for light—anticipate a looking that cannot be sustained as unalloyed looking but must be accompanied by a listening and this, even though what is lis-tened to—echo or a whistle or a phrase, moaning, mourning, desper-ate testimony and flight—is also unbearable. The difficulty, however, unlocks an emotional surfeit that ultimately rewrites photography's temporality. The looker is in danger of slipping, not away, but into something less comfortable than horror—aesthetic judgment, denial, laughter, some out and unprecedented reflection, movement, murder, song. So that there is an inappropriate ecstatics that goes along with this aesthetics—one is taken out, like in screams, fainting, tongues, dreams. *So perhaps she was counting on the aesthetic.*[66]

Here, the aesthetic is not a regulative discourse rooted in West-ern philosophical values, but, like blackness, it is a disruptive force that cuts through and dissembles photography's status as either an evidentiary technology or an indexical medium, a documentary record or proof of capacity for life. In this regard the aesthetic appeals to the senses, not to activate a politics grounded in either grief or (dis)identification with black suffering, but to inspire sensory overload, what Moten names as an "inappropriate ecstatics." Cloaked in a web of non–sense making, the photograph cannot render death a known quantity, a data point, or an entry in a statistical table. Instead, Till's murder overwhelms, it confuses, it shifts our relation to our own bodies. When photography's veridical standing is suspended and its temporality rewired, Moten suggests, new political and social ontologies can emerge. From this stance, approaching the photograph of a violently violated black corpse as an aesthetic object and not an exercise in mere documentation produces a disruptive visual and sensorial encounter. Rather than being merely horrified or shocked, the aesthetic fights the containment and control reproduced by the photograph as it "rewrites the time of the photograph, the time of the photograph of the dead."[67]

The various data technologies considered in this book—statistical graphs, photography, and motion pictures—also afford aesthetics that can disrupt and reroute the control they purport to exert on black life while advancing blackness as an aesthetic category with the capacity for disruption. As we will see, this often requires rewriting data's temporality (making it move and breathe) and its materiality (making it pulse and vibrate). But, if as Moten imagines it, Till-Mobley was counting on the aesthetic, counting on its capacity to push past and disorder photography's regulative functions, might we invert this paradigm and consider the aesthetics of counting? Phrased another way, what are the aesthetics of counting and (ac)counting? And which aesthetics count? Here we can think of documentary technologies precisely as modes of (ac)counting that aimed to simultaneously manage, control, and produce transformative information about black life toward solving the "Negro Problem." At the very same time, (ac)counting names an effort on the part of black cultural producers to harness data-producing technologies in the name of making black life count as more than mere information, facts, or numbers. This second position signals a way of working with racial data without discounting black life as always abject or socially inert, to borrow a phrase from Du Bois.

Moten's attention to photographic objects as aesthetic ones invites a consideration of the aesthetic workings of other documentary technologies and data modalities. To think of the aesthetics of (ac)counting, then, is to suspend the impulse to approach numbers as a pathway to truth and reason and is to instead be overwhelmed by them. This is certainly what Kelly Miller's work performs as it inundates readers with statistics, an approach I consider in chapter 1. It is also what Hurston's films produce for viewers who are confronted with an overflow of visual cues, considered in chapter 3. Focusing my attention on the aesthetic labor of these forms attunes us to moments of irruption and disruption, moments when the racial logic that data claims to secure was reordered, upended, and totally undisciplined. And while these disruptions are technical and epistemological, just as often they are performative, as with Hurston's films and like Lavinia Baker's improvisational dances that she stages on an anti-lynching lecture circuit that get recovered in chapter 2.

Although I am concerned with the aesthetic as a disruptive category, the explicitly aesthetic terrain of literature is also a crucial way of thinking of the "ecstatic" force of data in this book.[68] One of *The Matter of Black Living*'s central contentions is that approaching postbellum experiments with data technologies as practices that were concerned with suspending, disrupting, or reimagining the forms of knowledge produced by social-scientific forms can guide us toward a new genealogy of black literary production. It is by now a well-known paradox that the "nadir" of African American political life corresponds with a vibrant black literary landscape.[69] The explosion of novels by writers such as Frances Harper, Pauline Hopkins, Charles Chesnutt, and Sutton Griggs was joined by the proliferation of African American newspapers and periodicals, the political writing of figures like Mary Church Terrell, Anna Julia Copper, and Kelly Miller, and a general enthusiasm for collecting, archiving, and printing. Yet curiously, this material abundance has not corresponded with scholarly attention. I suggest at least two ways to account for this asymmetry: periodization and the aesthetic work that we imagine these texts can perform.

The period known as the postbellum/pre-Harlem is bookended by the end of Reconstruction (1877) and the end of World War I (1919).[70] Secured by firmly established anchors—Charles Chesnutt and Jean Toomer, or Frances Harper and Langston Hughes—these historical markers have unwittingly hardened the boundaries of periodization, even as we increasingly accept that emancipation was a "nonevent" and that progressive history is a fiction.[71] Consequently, literary history's attempt to account for black creative movement has arrested the organic routes linking writers and thinkers across generic, disciplinary, and temporal boundaries. At the same time, far too often we read this period's literary activity through a narrow political purview, one in which accessing citizenship and correcting post-Reconstruction's legal rollbacks is the ultimate horizon. What this has meant is that the full range of black intellectual activity has remained obscured and the questions we ask of it limited, even as Caroline Gebhard and Deborah McCaskill implore us to approach the postbellum/pre-Harlem as a "period of high aesthetic experimentation and political dynamism."[72]

Moving across and between literary history's standard zones of periodization, *The Matter of Black Living* offers an approach to aesthetics that stands to reorient the work that we think of as literary and the political labor that we imagine it can do on either side of the turn of the century. Although the aesthetic productions I study get anchored in their historical and cultural moment, I also argue that, when oriented toward the practice of documenting social life and engendering racial data, writers and cultural producers of the 1920s have more in common with those of the 1890s than we have been made to believe. If the aesthetic can cut across and disorder forms of knowledge production, like the photograph, then it can also reroute the sense of literary periods and generic boundaries. In this spirit, I turn to the literary and the aesthetic as modes of relation that keep the surplus outside the regulatory forms—biopolitical, disciplinary, and historical. In each case that I spotlight, what escapes the universal codification imposed by documentary forms is also the site of new kinds of sense making.

Undisciplining as Method

This book's narrative arc moves in step with the formalization of the social and human sciences in the United States. My study begins in 1880 and ends in 1930, the very moment when sociology, anthropology, and psychology became discrete disciplinary formations.[73]

Although this is a period of exacting control that witnessed the emergence of a biopolitical order that had especially profound implications for people of color, it was also a moment of disorder and contradiction.[74] Neither sociology nor anthropology would be institutionalized as areas of study with distinct methodologies until the first decade of the twentieth century, despite the nation's first sociological departments having formed in the 1890s. It would be even longer before sociology would approach race with any degree of care or nuance. As Amanda Anderson has argued, above all else, turn-of-the-century disciplinarity is marked by a deep affinity with what we would now call interdisciplinarity. As fields struggled to contain competing and overlapping idioms (Anderson notes that the human sciences is itself a contradiction in terms), the disciplines regularly reached across the institutional aisle as they tried to reconcile their structural conflicts.[75] The political and geographic landscape was equally hectic. Debates about the future place of African Americans proliferated at a dizzying rate, creating paradoxical notions of freedom, personhood, and blackness. On the one hand, the contest created the perfect landscape for management. As Hartman explains, the moment's "antagonistic production of abstract equality and black subjugation rested upon contending and incompatible predictions of the freed—as sovereign, indivisible, and self-possessed and as fungible and individuated subjects whose capacities could be quantified, measured, exchanged, and alienated," creating the groundwork for the "invasive forms of social control."[76] But on the other hand, for every disciplinary structure that sought to organize and control modernity's unpredictability, there were just as many cracks, loopholes, and pockets of opacity that at once exceeded disciplinary registers and demanded new structures of knowledge production. These were the locations at which "elusive facts" reigned free. It is this undisciplined side of the turn of the twentieth century that this book dwells in and explores.[77]

The Matter of Black Living's methodology is organically interdisciplinary, an approach that reflects the very character of the late nineteenth and early twentieth centuries. What is at stake is a certain account of disciplinary studies, not just at the turn of the twentieth century but also as we imagine our fields of study now. My analysis of the social survey, for example, brings together the history of science, black intellectual history, and recent theories of data visualization to argue for the social survey's role as a visual technology and a literary modality. Likewise, in the second chapter I bring insights from performance studies to bear on the long history of anti-lynching agitation, photography, and the politics of US reform movements. My method is also premised on careful attention to the historical specificity of each technology, cultural actor, and literary text. In this regard, and in keeping with the work of cultural historians such as Jacqueline Goldsby and Daphne Brooks, I read literary texts themselves as rubrics for and expressions of literary and visual theory. This means that I follow the archival story that the case studies produce, weaving together close textual analysis with historical sources and theory to explain how and why literature and visual technology were put to work in the name of disentangling black life from data's disciplinary regimes. This practice has enabled me to assemble an archive of turn-of-the-century cultural actors and productions that have previously gone understudied or entirely overlooked. This is especially true of chapter 2, in which I reconstruct a lost anti-lynching performance archive that, despite its sprawling size, has never received a holistic analysis, and chapter 3, where I turn my attention to Zora Neale Hurston's filmmaking. First, this method enables us to approach a technology like the social survey as articulating a theory of visuality, black life, and aesthetics on its own terms. Second, this method constellates networks of cultural actors and texts to ultimately construct a new view of black intellectual life at the turn of the century. More than recovery work, however, by revealing previously obscured lines of connection between figures like Sutton Griggs and W. E. B. Du Bois or Ida B. Wells and black female performers, I illuminate the complicated cultural and intellectual landscape in which these figures worked and intervened in the name of rendering a new suite of dynamic racial data.

Overview

The Matter of Black Living is buoyed by three corresponding claims: that black life and data cohered at the turn of the twentieth century, albeit asymmetrically and insufficiently; that African American cultural producers intervened into these debates along experimental lines; and, finally, that these experiments doubled as rubrics for literary and aesthetic practice. To advance this argument, I have structured the book into three chapters, each of which corresponds to a data-producing technology—social survey, photography, and film—and the aesthetic and literary practices that encounters with these technologies cultivate: "social document fiction," "looking out," and "over-exposure." Although other technologies and practices crop up over the course of the book (surveying and the statistical gaze, for instance, feature prominently in the first chapter), these are the book's organizing principles. Structured in this way, each chapter is a framework for rethinking the relationship between black aesthetic production, data, and a particular visual technology. This also means that the chapters tend to be longer than average. Chapter 1, for instance, offers a detailed critical map of the social survey and its relationship to the late nineteenth century's racial, disciplinary and aesthetic concerns. This is a wide and largely unchartered territory, one that demands both a critical practice and a readerly stamina that does justice to the archival materials and methods that I've set forth.

Importantly, I do not aim to offer a complete media history of the social survey, photography, or film; that labor exceeds the scope of this project. In taking up each of these technologies I do, however, work to extend and revise a robust body of scholarship on late nineteenth- and early twentieth-century visual culture that tends to prioritize photography, even as it charts the nuanced ways that African American cultural workers navigated and negotiated its dubious demands. Thus, while *The Matter of Black Living* is in conversation with scholars who spotlight the often ambivalent place of photography in the long history of black freedom movements, I also ask us to think about the myriad ways that other media were being leveraged as visual technologies, sometimes alongside photography, but just as often in lieu of it. Curiously, this work has primarily taken shape in research on the early nineteenth century. Holding up material objects as diverse as the friendship album, the botanical drawing, the photographic portrait, and the microscope, scholars of antebellum African American life have crafted a capacious archive of black visual practices from the antebellum period. Yet far less attention has been paid to the technical and formal dimensions of visual technology, what Tavia Nyong'o has recently described as the idea that "representations must be treated as immanent to the technical apparatus that construct them, especially if we wish to unburden ourselves of their oppressive weight."[78] Taking Nyong'o's claim to heart, and insisting that we begin this work with attention to the 1880s, I argue that any focus on experimental encounters must attend to the technical contours of those technologies, the very facets that would affect and structure those engagements.

Finally, this is not expressly a book about Du Bois, but he haunts every chapter, just as he does this introduction. Sometimes he appears as a direct interlocutor and at other times he skirts the margins of a discourse, practice, or key term. On the one hand, telegraphing questions of data and black life through Du Bois is not entirely surprising. For evidence of this we need look no further than the explosion in literature and scholarship on Du Bois, *The Philadelphia Negro*, and his relationship to social-scientific thought that has emerged in recent years.[79] My decision to move with and through Du Bois also risks repeating what is fast becoming a trope in black literary scholarship and black studies more broadly. Yet as I completed this book, it became clear that it is impossible to write a story about race, data, and visual technology at the turn of the twentieth century without seriously taking hold of Du Bois. What I have hoped to show here is that when we situate the question of (black) social documentation and data at the center of our reading of Du Bois, his intellectual network expands in unexpected angles and directions. From here, Du Bois is less an impresario or singular genius, although the case can certainly be made that he is both. Nevertheless, I am interested in how Du Bois's work orients our gaze away from him and beside him to his collaborators and co-thinkers who are sometimes recognized but just as often not.

The questions of data, blackness, and aesthetics are first taken up in relation to the social survey, the form that has the most recognizable ties to data and yet perhaps surprisingly was proffered as an alternative to the violent limitations of statistical graphs and charts. In chapter 1, "The Survey Spirit," I curate a cast of characters and texts around the social survey, the predominant tool of social scientists and reformers invested in the idea of social transformation through proximity and observation. Made famous by the London reformer Charles Booth in the 1880s, the social survey was quickly adopted in the United States, where it rapidly emerged as a principal method of social inquiry and expression for white progressives like Jane Addams, but also African Americans like Miller, Du Bois, and Alain Locke. In "The Survey Spirit," I theorize the social survey as a modern visual technology, one that conceptualized visuality as a particularly collective endeavor and from which a new observer emerged to challenge Western science's detached, disinterested, and exacting eye. This chapter is grounded in the argument that the social survey was a novel technology that, at least in theory, promised to produce an animate body of social data.

Over the course of this chapter, I follow the survey's emergence at the onset of the Progressive Era to the Harlem Renaissance, when the genre began to fall out of favor. Drawing on contemporaneous reviews and theories of the survey, I argue that despite its instrumental functions, the social survey was nevertheless alluring because it modeled a dynamic visual practice premised on collectivity, multiplicity, and relationality. Pitched as an alternative to narrow social-scientific practices and visual technologies, the social survey's formal properties and methodologies doubled as a model for a visual practice that might convey the vitality organizing modern black life. Through close readings of Du Bois's *The Philadelphia Negro* (1899), *Charities* special issue "The Negro in the Cities of the North" (1905), Locke's edited volume of *Survey Graphic* "Harlem: Mecca of the New Negro" (1925), and Miller's famous critique of Frederick Hoffman's 1896 treatise on black morality, *Race Traits and Tendencies of the American Negro*, I show how the social survey's key features work at two frequencies: loosening the grip of the statistical gaze and yielding new modalities for seeing and writing black life.

As I detail the various iterations of the survey spirit, I track the aesthetic workings of the social survey to explicate how the visual strategies at work in the social survey are intensified, and indeed realized, in the genre of writing termed "social document fiction." First deployed by Locke in a 1928 essay to evaluate *Quest*, social document fiction describes works generally regarded as important sociological treatises but failed aesthetic productions. This chapter locates this genre's beginning in Griggs's 1899 novel *Imperium in Imperio* and argues that in fastening the fantastic to the documentary, as *Quest* did, *Imperium in Imperio* was also assessed for its capacity to act as an ideal sociological document. To make this point, I turn to Kelly Miller's little-known review of Griggs's debut novel and argue that in his choice phrasing, which mirrors the terms Miller used to assess Frederick Hoffman's 1896 book *Race Traits and Tendencies of the American Negro*, Miller suggests that Griggs achieved what strictly statistical studies could not: historicizing and visualizing the "Negro Problem" as a dynamic "plexus" of problems caused by social conditions and institutional racism. Moving out from Locke and Miller's assessments, I maintain that *Imperium in Imperio* adopts the survey's formal conventions but deploys multiple framing devices, anti-realist plots, and episodic chapters to undercut the authority of objective visual observation, the hallmark of the social survey. In place of the detached investigator's gaze, *Imperium in Imperio*'s narrative map offers a multisensory visuality that reconstructs narrow interpretations of the "color line's" spatial and visual architecture. This visual practice re-presents the black body as vital and reassembles the social as a site of dynamic interaction.

Where chapter 1 takes its cue from the discipline of sociology and the social survey as a practice and technology that might unsettle the relationship between data and black life that statistics affixed, in chapter 2 photography, reform, and the courtroom are posited as three interrelated disciplinary terrains. The second chapter, "Looking Out" takes photography as its orienting technology as it explores how it was mobilized as a data-producing medium, and conversely, the various creative strategies that emerged in the name of reconciling black living with photography's deep imbrication with lynching. Like the social survey's focus on urban life, racial violence was also figured as both an explicit component of the "Negro Problem," which could be resolved through visual strategies, namely photography. Alongside statistics and narrative prose, lynching photography expressed lynching's data. Revising the widely accepted views of contemporary scholars who theorize lynching as a theatrical event that is amenable to photographic documentation, I argue that anti-black violence presented a conceptual and representational conundrum for turn-of-the-century anti-lynching activists who, in large part, relied on the conflation of photography and evidence, and by extension, photography's privileged place within data's disciplinary regime. Yet as reformers began to weave photographs into their anti-lynching agenda, they labored to reconcile the medium's logic of arrest and death with their defense of black living. At the heart of this endeavor, I argue, was the task of registering lynching as an ongoing catastrophe that exceeds the scene of the crime and the time of photographic capture.

Offering a new visual praxis that I term "looking out," this chapter recovers and analyzes the visual and performance archive related to a family of lynching survivors: Lavinia Baker and her five children who escaped the infamous 1898 lynching in Lake City, South Carolina, that claimed the life of the black postmaster Frazier Baker and the Baker family's infant daughter. In the aftermath of the lynching, the Bakers were featured in a multimodal anti-lynching performance spectacle that included, among other feats, a musical revue, a motion picture, a photographic portrait session yielding at least seven photographs and cabinet cards, and sold out anti-lynching lectures during which the Bakers put their wounded bodies on display for an at-capacity crowd of three thousand mostly black spectators. The brainchild of an unknown white reformer, Lillian Jewett, the Baker Exhibit ventured to transform the family into "living evidence." Tracking the relationship between the enlivened and the evidentiary, I read three aspects of the Baker Exhibit—the family's testimony at the trial of their accusers, their performance on stage in Providence and Boston, and the commissioned photographs—to argue that in its capacity to exceed and indeed evade visual capture, lynching announces itself in temporal and ontological tension with photography. In the Bakers' refusal to assume the status of political icon or embodied citizen subject, the Baker archive also engenders the practice of "looking out." Rather than simply reversing the gaze, the paradigm that is most often used to theorize a resistant black visuality, "looking out" names a perceptual practice that is attuned to the slow violence that is constitutive of black life. Following a case study of the Baker Exhibit, the chapter ends with an analysis of the publication of lynching photographs in Du Bois's *The Crisis*. Although the role of the National Association for the Advancement of Colored People (NAACP) and *The Crisis* in the anti-lynching movement has been well documented, this chapter spotlights the first time a photograph of a hanging body was published, in the December 1911 issue of *The Crisis*. In his editorial decision to embed the photograph within a line drawing and as the illustration to his speculative short story "Jesus Christ in Georgia," Du Bois also registers a photographic hesitance, that is, a sneaking suspicion that photographs could never communicate the scope of racial violence.

"Overexposure," the third and final chapter of the book, shifts focus to the late 1920s—the period often considered the height of the New Negro Renaissance—considering film as a technology that was simultaneously evoked by anthropologists as an evidence-bearing medium and mobilized by African Americans as a newfangled representational device that could contribute to and revise debates about the "Negro Problem." Like Locke's embrace of the social survey that I address in chapter 1, the project of rendering black life as open and generative persisted well into the 1920s, especially for Zora Neale Hurston. Building on this framework, chapter 3 situates Hurston's 1920s literary oeuvre in relation to the rarely discussed films she recorded between 1927 and 1930 while traveling throughout the American South. Whereas critics most often assess this footage through the terms of ethnography, this chapter argues that Hurston's experiments and encounters with the 16 mm handheld camera indicate her ongoing attempt to capture and convey the continually evolving nature of black folk living. Her experiments, in turn, manifest a visual and aesthetic practice that I term "overexposure." Overexposure engenders a viewing style in which the gaze is lured, but not rewarded, by the promise of unmitigated racial knowledge, narrative resolution, or quantitative documentation. As praxis that is germane to but also exceeds the material bounds of film, as both technical aberration and aesthetic principle, overexposure also finds expression in Hurston's literary works, such as her 1928 essay "How It Feels to Be Colored Me" and the 1924 short story "Drenched in Light," and a cinematic theory of black gestural life. Film thus emerges in dynamic relationship to Hurston's aesthetic theories and racial politics, both of which were rooted in the theory that black life was perpetually inventive, deeply embodied, and thoroughly intransigent.

In writing this book, my goal is to clear a space from which we can recognize a different relationship between race and data, one that might reveal pathways toward new political futures that have, thus far, been obscured by an overreliance on the givenness of data. With this horizon in mind, I conclude with a coda that argues that the tension between the political power of data and the discourse of black life's incalculability that continue to structure twenty-first-century discourse on racial justice attunes us to an understudied aspect of recent scholarly debates concerning slavery's afterlives. Buoyed by the work of critics such as Saidiya Hartman and Christina Sharpe, the thinking that gathers under the heading of slavery's afterlives is meant to critique the fantasy of progress while registering the belated arrival of black freedom. Yet as a strategy for understanding the past's relationship to the present, far too often the currency of afterlives relies on the political value of black corporality, black death, and continues to look for evidence of the past's persistent presence in recognizable forms of data. I intervene in this discourse by arguing that the exercises in undisciplining data that I recover across the book suggest that the past and the present are yoked by a necessarily open question: how do you document black life? That this question continues to underpin debates about political and social life reveals that any attempt to consider slavery's *longue durée* will require addressing the work that evidence is compelled to perform in the name of racial justice and recalibrating the equivalence between data and black living.

If we are living within the long shadow of a racial regime that continues to assess black life as disposable, as proximate to death, as a pathological social body that can be understood only through strident statistical study and the relentless production and interpretation of data and facts, then we are also the inheritors of a relationship to data regimes that, not unlike our turn-of-the-century antecedents, wrestles with their utility at every turn. At this moment, perhaps we can do no better than foreground the matter of black living.

1

The Social Survey

THE SURVEY SPIRIT

*"The Survey Spirit": Origins, Evolution, and the
Radical Operations of the Social Survey*

W. E. B. Du Bois had the social survey on his mind on November 19, 1897, when he delivered "The Study of the Negro Problems" to members of the American Academy of Political and Social Science. Du Bois drafted the speech while he was knee-deep conducting fieldwork among the black population of Philadelphia's Seventh Ward for what would become *The Philadelphia Negro* (1899), his pioneering sociological study of the "social condition and environment" of the "forty thousand or more people of Negro blood living in the city of Philadelphia."[1] Part appeal to major universities to fund social-scientific studies of black life and part endorsement for his forthcoming study, the speech outlined a four-pronged approach to the "systematic study" of the "Negro Problem," or, the "social phenomena arising from the presence in this land of eight million persons of African descent."[2] In contrast to social scientists and race reformers who, in approaching what the racialist Nathaniel Shaler described as the "experiment of making a citizen of the Negro," reduced the "problem" of modern black life to a formula that could be solved through abstracted statistical methods, Du Bois championed an interdisciplinary methodology and an expansive conceptualization of black sociality.[3] Combining historical study with statistical investigation, and anthropological measurement with qualitative interpretation, Du Bois endeavored to produce a framework that would render black life an animate and diverse social body while producing a storehouse of "Truth" that would serve as the basis for re-form.[4] As he reminded his audience, the ever-enigmatic "Negro Prob-lem" "is not *one* problem, but rather a plexus of social problems, some new, some old, some simple, some complex."[5] The methodological answer to the study of "Negro Problems," then, was the equally multi-tudinous social study, two of which Du Bois was already undertaking: the Atlanta University Studies that he began directing the following month and the soon-to-be-completed *The Philadelphia Negro*. In both cases Du Bois employed the research method that was taking shape in the largely female world of settlement work typified by Jane Ad-dams's Chicago-based Hull-House: first-person investigation, detailed daily schedules, and an ethos of influence through proximity. And like his predecessors turned collaborators—both Lucy Salmon and Isabel Eaton worked with him on *The Philadelphia Negro*—Du Bois was con-fident that when published as a social survey, his findings could inter-vene into the experimental world of social science.

If Du Bois had the survey on his mind in the final years of the nine-teenth century, then perhaps it was there to stay. We can also discern the whisperings of the social survey in his debut novel, *The Quest of the Silver Fleece* (1911). Published on the heels of *The Souls of Black Folk*'s success, Du Bois ultimately dismissed his attempt to fiction-ally represent the intersecting lives of white cotton speculators and Southern blacks in the aftermath of Reconstruction as something of a failed novelistic enterprise. In his 1949 autobiography *Dusk of Dawn* he simply noted, "I tried my hand at writing fiction and published 'The Quest of the Silver Fleece' which was really an economic study of some merit."[6] But if Du Bois was unimpressed with his own efforts at fictionally "dramatizing the so-called Negro Problem," then he found refuge in the Atlanta University Studies.[7] Published on either side of *Quest*, the collaborative research projects administered by the histori-cally black college's sociology lab aimed to, in the words of Du Bois, "study the American Negro" by dividing "the various aspects of his social conditions into ten great subjects" that would each be studied for one year "until the cycle is completed," before beginning the "same cycle for [a] second ten years."[8] As Du Bois imagined it, the succes-sively unfolding project would proceed for a century, at the end of which "we shall have a continuous record of the condition and devel-opment of a group of 10 to 20 millions of men—a body of sociological material unsurpassed in human annals."[9] The project folded in 1916, just six years after Du Bois left his appointment at Atlanta University, but not before he had successfully put forth twenty publications, including *The Negro Church* (1903), *The College Bred Negro* (1910), and *Morals and Manners of Negro Americans* (1914). If Du Bois's plan for a century's worth of sociological study is in keeping with Brent Hayes Edwards's classification of him as "the paradigmatic black proponent of centennial logic," then it also reinforces his abiding preoccupation with the social survey in particular and, more generally, the work of locating a form that could record the ongoing development and "continuous" movement of black life.[10]

The social survey was still on Du Bois's mind when he authored a scathing review of Claude McKay's 1928 novel *Home to Harlem*, a critique that is rooted in nostalgia for the kind of social and spatial management that underpins *The Philadelphia Negro* and progressives' agendas more broadly.[11] And the social survey was at the forefront of his consciousness in 1941 when he gathered the leaders of historically black colleges and universities for the first Phylon Institute, where he pitched the idea of the Negro Land Grant, a reactivation of the then-defunct Atlanta University Studies.[12] In fact, of the countless formal, political, and disciplinary undertakings that Du Bois would recruit over the course of his career, the social survey arguably enjoyed the longest shelf life.

Despite the scholarly impulse to read *The Philadelphia Negro* and the early Atlanta University Studies as reflective of a distinct phase of Du Bois's "reformist empiricism," which by the turn of the century would quickly give way to sociological skepticism and an embrace of editorial agitation and literary pursuits, the enduring place of the social survey in Du Bois's oeuvre was neither out of step with nor distinct from his aesthetic and political predilections.[13] Rather, the social survey and the literary were deeply related enterprises whose intermittent interplay is indicative of an understudied epoch in the production of turn-of-the-century black fiction, one in which literature emerged not simply in opposition to social studies but *as* social study.[14] My treatment of social science and black fiction's overlaps resounds with Roderick Ferguson's reading of sociology and African American literature in *Aberrations in Black*. Juxtaposing works from twentieth-century writers like Ralph Ellison, Richard Wright, and

Toni Morrison with canonical sociological treatises, Ferguson illuminates how "African American culture as an epistemological object
produced dialogical relations that both exceeded the formal parameters of its interlocutors and confused the distinctions between factual and fictive enterprises."[15] Where Ferguson concentrates his attention on mid-twentieth-century texts and theories, this chapter argues
that blurring the boundary between fictive and factual precedes the
formalization of sociology. As a result, the late nineteenth- and early
twentieth-century works that are taken as sociological, or at least social scientific, often take shape along the lines of fantasy and formal
experimentation, while the social survey itself was a highly speculative mode. In other words, the supple contours of late nineteenth- and
early twentieth-century social science provide the occasion to reas-
sess the relationship between black fiction and social science's primary modalities, not least of all the social survey.

Du Bois was not alone in his persistent interface with the social survey. Although it has been sequestered to the footnotes of Progressive
Era policy and histories of social work, the social survey was actually
the predominant tool for social scientists and social workers during
the first decades of the twentieth century.[16] The American social survey adopted and adapted the fundamentals of its British predecessors
and reformulated its method and logic to respond to a turbulent postbellum landscape. Mobilized by countless white reformers and social
scientists who, in operating as self-appointed social engineers, sought
to assert order over what they perceived to be a chaotic and disorderly
world, the social survey also took hold in racially distinct sites.[17] As
we will see, the social survey's primary attributes—documenting the
social, with an emphasis on a deeply attached and emotionally con-
nected observer—allowed for a radical rewriting of Western science's
visual and racial epistemologies and, in turn, shaped a new black literary practice that, borrowing from Alain Locke, I call "social document fiction." As the staging ground for the articulation of a new body
of racial data that flew in the face of the statistical status quo, and as
the rubric for formal and aesthetic experimentation, the social survey
existed in dynamic interplay with black literary arts from its emergence in the 1890s to the late 1920s, when it began to be supplanted by
standardized sociological protocols. In this regard, perhaps no other
method encompassed the challenges wrought by reconciling data and

social life or reflected the fundamentally visual nature of this effort more than the social survey.

In what follows, I begin by tracing the emergence of the social survey and outline the key features of the genre. The survey's preoccupation with both conveying and constructing the social landscape required an ever-expanding repertoire of visual methods and metaphors, which ultimately reconstituted the very nature of the social-scientific observer. The latter part of the chapter reconstructs the antagonistic relationship between the insurance agent turned race theorist Frederick Hoffman and the black mathematician Kelly Miller that was staged across their competing texts. In his review of Hoffman's pessimistic analysis of black morbidity statistics, *Race Traits and Tendencies of the American Negro*, Miller summons the social survey while celebrating the value of literary texts like Sutton Griggs's 1899 experimental novel *Imperium in Imperio* for their capacity to manifest the survey's ethos. Reading *Imperium in Imperio* as a text that reworks and ultimately realizes the social survey's promise of dynamic social documentation while issuing a strident critique of an ocular-centric visual methodology, this chapter ends with a consideration of two "standard" social surveys: *Charities*' "The Negro in the Cities of the North" and Alain Locke's 1925 special issue of *Survey Graphic*, "Harlem: Mecca of the New Negro." Despite their ties to social-scientific institutions and regulatory reform projects, each survey supplies the formal and conceptual conditions of possibility for articulating blackness as a geographic and epistemological "elsewhere." This sense of elsewhere signals what Brent Hayes Edwards draws out as a "a shared logic of collaboration and coordination" whose unstable and continuously shifting nature is crucial to imagining a racial community that takes shape beyond the nation-state.[18] In the social survey, this elsewhere is where blackness is coordinated beyond the boundaries of sociological classification and in the asymmetries that supply its expressive force. Thus, both publications position blackness less as the object of study or the pathway to geographically specific information, and more as an invitation to embark on what Fred Moten describes in a different context as the process of "constant searching and research" that emerges at the nexus of aspiration for recognition and refusal to be circumscribed within the production of racial data.[19] Over the course of this chapter, as I move through seemingly disparate sites, I argue for the social survey as a form that made black life visible in new, though not unproblematic, ways.

•

In her 1916 handbook *The Social Survey*, a "guide for social survey work," Dr. Carol Aronovici, Philadelphia's director of the Bureau for Social Research, lamented the "enormous waste of human life and energy that is going on in our midst." Appealing particularly to "social workers and socially minded citizens," Aronovici warned that the social degeneration plaguing the nation would have a far-reaching and irreversible impact. It is not, she reasoned, "merely affecting the individual," but "the loss is clearly social and productive of conditions which are a handicap to the attainment of the high achievement that this democracy is capable of."[20] Likely, the social "waste" that Aronovici had in mind were the tenement dwellers whose living conditions continued to alarm progressives, as well as high unemployment rates and the steady migration of African Americans from the South to major Northern cities. As the title of her project suggests, the social survey was advanced as a tenable solution to the crisis of modernity and to sociology's methodological gaps. Dismissing sociology as a depersonalized "field of speculation," Aronovici encouraged social scientists and reformers to return to the community as a site of inquiry and a methodological guide. "The great laboratories, which are open before us in the midst of the people," she argued, are where we might "gather all the facts." "When the facts are known," she reasoned, "an awakening of the American people is bound to result."[21]

A minor figure in Progressive Era reform, Aronovici's anxious defense of the social survey reflects a broader crisis in knowledge production that characterizes the efforts of turn-of-the-century social reformers and social scientists who, through the dissemination of and investment in incontrovertible evidence and raw data, endeavored to make sense of the period's profound social, political, and industrial upheavals. By the turn of the twentieth century, sociology emerged as a viable solution. But even as social reformers reached for its organizing principles, American sociology was still searching for its methodological center of gravity. When it came to the study of race in particular, writes Mia Bay, the "still forming social science disciplines," particularly sociology, were "based on theoretical speculations rather than on empirical research." For those "bent on creating 'grand theories' of society that could be employed to analyze and solve the social problems of the gilded age," continues Bay, "the founding fathers of American sociology invariably explained racial inequalities with reference to natural laws."[22]

As frustrating as it was, the unstable methodological terrain also provided opportunities for innovation and elaboration. Especially appealing was the power afforded to the accumulation and presentation of objective facts and unfiltered data. For social reformers who, as did Du Bois, often doubled as social scientists, their research agendas were buoyed by what the historian of science Dorothy Ross describes as the "belief that the recital of actual conditions would arouse the civic consciousness and inform public action" and by the desire to take advantage of the cracks in sociology's nascent methods.[23] As Du Bois put it: "There is only one sure basis of social reform and that is Truth—a careful, detailed knowledge of the essential facts of each problem. Without this there is no logical starting place for reform and uplift."[24] Reporting the "facts" was, of course, far from a novel political strategy. This was, after all, what encouraged the wide circulation and wild popularity of the antebellum slave narrative, a genre that repeatedly tried to awaken the nation's moral conscious by proffering eyewitness accounts of the institution of slavery as it really was.[25] The social survey departed from previous reform agendas in its construction of the entire social as an undertheorized laboratory and an untapped scientific resource. As both the problem and the solution, social landscapes—Chicago's West Side immigrant communities, New York's primarily black Tenderloin district, and the American South's Black Belt—would provide the rubric for a systematic reform agenda and a social-scientific praxis.

By the 1880s the social survey had migrated from London, where Charles Booth innovated a seventeen-volume study of poverty, *The Life and Labor of People in London,* to the world of US college settlement houses, where it quickly took root as the primary methodological approach. In domains like Chicago's Hull-House and Philadelphia's College Settlement, and in the hands of mostly female resident reformers, Booth's method of first-person investigation, custom schedules, and an innovative demographic mapping strategy that spatially recorded intersections of race and class, buttressed the general belief that cross-class connection was a key to social improvement. Embodying what Laura Fisher has described as the ethos of "proximity and influence," settlement workers, who "were convinced that earlier reform campaigns had floundered because privileged reformers kept themselves personally and geographically remote from the people they wished to help," stressed the importance of personal experience and social investigation to the production of transformative knowledge and to the process of re-reforming human relationships.[26] As they immersed themselves in their reforming environments—"settling," as it were, among their new neighbors—settlement leaders like Addams, of Chicago's Hull-House, inhabited the Progressive Era's mantra of reform through control by approaching their work as a deeply embodied process. Here, their inner vision would outwardly manifest as a transformed social landscape. In addition to the physical structure of settlement houses, which used spatial design to model aspirational domestic roles and where would-be citizens practiced their role as newly reformed subjects, published findings like the 1895 *Hull-House Maps and Papers* materialized the process and praxis of settling; they were also the earliest expressions of the social survey tradition.[27]

Between the 1890s and the 1920s the social survey morphed as it took root across various ideological agendas and geographic locales. By the turn of the century, the term "survey" was commensurate with settlement workers' collaborative published findings as well as individual research agendas, such as Du Bois's, but it also came to denote progressive publications like *Charities*, which was later rechristened as *Charities and the Commons*, then *Survey*, and finally *Survey Graphic*. Likewise, the social survey's formal and aesthetic contours regularly expanded and were consistently recalibrated. Some works produced in the survey tradition included photographs; others, such as Alain Locke's "Harlem: Mecca of the New Negro," eschewed mimetic visual aids in favor of line drawings and sketches. Still others deployed documentation strategies like maps, bar charts, graphs, and tables. And while some social surveys like *Hull-House Maps and Papers* and the Atlanta University Studies prioritized first-person reportage, it was not uncommon for surveys to include genres like the case study, poetry, or short fiction. Although the term "social survey" would be affixed to the mode only after the publication of Paul Kellogg's landmark *The*

Pittsburgh Survey (before this they were "social studies"), as Martin Bulmer explains, works that fall under the social survey's umbrella share a general set of characteristics. Such studies, he writes, are premised on a commitment to the "investigation, analysis, and coordination of economic, sociological, or other related aspects of a selected community or group" with the express purpose of shaping the views of social theorists or creating a "program of amelioration of the conditions of life and work of a particular group or community." In their attempt to produce "comprehensive rather than haphazard coverage," he continues, social surveys eschewed "reliance upon reports by other pre-existing data" in favor of first-person fieldwork that focused on "individuals, families, and households rather than aggregates."[28] The survey's published findings, in turn, were submitted as a valuable body of research that could activate reform where standard political agitation had failed and as the supplier of new data.

Although the settlement movement gave rise to the US social survey, it quickly moved into the hands of social scientists who embraced the medium and method as a foundational tool for responsible fieldwork and a site where theory and practice intersected. Beginning in 1906 and following the success of similar courses in social survey methods that were taught at the University of Pennsylvania, Robert Park regularly led the popular class at the University of Chicago simply titled The Social Survey. Asserting the social survey as both method and critical orientation, he explained to his class that the social survey was a "new sociological device—a device which, by the way, in its popular form is less method of investigation than a point of view."[29] As Park understood, the point of view was directed toward awakening the public to social problems, what he derided elsewhere as the social survey's debased investment in publicity. Building on Park's assessment of the social survey as methodological "movement," and on the heels of the massive success of *The Pittsburgh Survey*, in 1912 Paul Kellogg attested to the wide appeal of the "survey idea" before the American Academy of Political and Social Science. Armed with "four closely typewritten sheets, thoroughly covered with the names of cities or organizations which either embarked on surveys or are considering surveys, or would like to know more about them," Kellogg proudly boasted its range of influence.[30] Nothing short of a global phenomenon, the social survey, he exclaimed, was being adopted everywhere, from "Minnesota, Missouri, Texas, and Kansas" to the "British Northwest to India."[31] By 1919, the social historian Carl C. Taylor was echoing Kellogg's views in his book-length study *The Social Survey: Its Histories and Its Methods*. Notwithstanding the survey's "rapid rise and immense popularity," Taylor was adamant that the social survey was more than a "fad," and certainly not the unreliable tool of second-rate social workers, as its detractors claimed. Instead, with its "wide revelations and vivid pictures of things previously unknown," the social survey was a "valuable method of social investigation."[32]

The social survey's appeal was at least twofold. First, it constituted an innovation in data production. Framing it as a tool for recording and creating facts, Taylor remarked, "The social survey has, however, to do not only with the gathering and tabulation of social facts, but also with the creation of social facts, so to speak, that is, with problems of creating social consciousness of social situations."[33] Emerging as every bit the social engineer who could manipulate and construct social bodies and restructure public consciousness, Taylor's phrasing also attunes us to the social survey's role as a technology of fabulation, that is, its capacity to construct and imagine social reality. To be sure, the project of social creation, of bringing into being a previously unimaginable terrain, reeked of progressive authoritarian dispositions. Yet as Shannon Jackson has pointed out, the investment in "making something new, in bringing into being something that hadn't been there before" also suggests a "poetics of reform," wherein the final product was subordinated to the process of making itself.[34]

Second, the social survey was appealing because it functioned as a visual technology that could illuminate data that had otherwise eluded the myopic gaze of even the best-trained social scientist. In this regard, the social survey cuts across the field of postbellum visual culture in which visual technologies—from photographs to statistical diagrammatics—contributed to the realist fantasy of social control. Here, what Mark Seltzer outlines as the late nineteenth- and early twentieth-century "imperative of making everything, including interior states, visible, legible and governable," characterizing seemingly distinct productions like Stephen Crane's fiction or the visual exposés of New York City's tenements by photographer–turned–social reformer Jacob Riis, extends to the exacting and penetrating scientific eye that sought to fix social "problems" as knowable objects of study.[35]

But whereas the modes that constitute realism's wheelhouse promised control through demystification, the social survey defined itself according to vague outlines, indeterminate sketches, and broad strokes. The opening pages of *Hull-House Maps and Papers*, for instance, announce the book "not as exhaustive treatise but as recorded observations," whereas *Charities'* landmark 1905 "The Negro in the Cities of the North" extended "a suggestive survey" of black urban life.[36] Far from elusive or vague, the social survey's speculative approach, Taylor remarked, allowed it to register the nebulous world of social and cultural dynamics, and was responsible for its emergence as a transformative technology that would bring focus to otherwise-obscured social conditions. "The social survey" he explained, "appears to be a tool capable of being utilized to isolate facts without sacrificing their social aspects." This intervention, he continued, was largely due to its heterogeneous structure and the wide-ranging chorus of professional voices who contributed as researchers. "Its composite nature retains all of the environing circumstances, which are so much more an essential part of the social fact than they are the historical fact or the fact of exact science," he concluded.[37]

In their quest to find a technological analogue equivalent to this fuzzy and capricious outlook, the social survey's proponents and practitioners summoned an unlikely storehouse of visual metaphors. Thomas Riley, for instance, described the survey's perspective as "wide and deep"; Taylor, building on Park's evaluation of the survey as instrument, imagined it as a cross between a microscope and moving picture.[38] In its full expression, he asserted, "the community surveyed and the social workers and citizens of the country at large will, for the first time, see a social situation under the microscope. A community in miniature will pass before their eyes in order that they may see the actual interwoven, living tensions, forces, and factors of their common life even more distinctly than the experts saw it in their bird's eye view at the beginning of the investigation."[39] In Taylor's two-step process, the sweeping view of the investigator paves the way for a complex tapestry of the social, ultimately revealing what had been previously overlooked: living tensions, or what Kellogg described in his prospectus for *Charities'* 1905 issue as the realm of "dynamic play."[40] Rather than simply spotlighting calcified specimens and fragments, Taylor's augmented microscope animates social patterns while conveying the pulse, dynamics, and rhythms underpinning community life. Yet perhaps cognizant of the technology's atomizing history, by the end of his analysis, Taylor landed on the pageant as the form best suited to communicate the survey's scope. "The ultimate form of the survey exhibit will undoubtedly include the pageant," he forecasted.[41]

More recently, scholars have turned to a new set of visual terms to explain the contradictory potential of the social survey. Jean Converse, for example, begins her expansive *Survey Research* with the following query: "Should it be called a social microscope, perhaps, or a spectroscope, or a demo scope, or a social barometer for recording the ups and downs of political and social tensions all over the globe?" Rejecting these possibilities, Converse ultimately offers the telescope as the most apt descriptor. It is "an image of the 'far-seeing' telescope to scan the rim of the social world, without any real hope of resolving great detail, looking instead for large shapes of social geography, movements of populations, flows of information, opinion, and feeling."[42]

But if the social survey's contours are vague and its resolution is low, then the opportunities it afforded to the visualization of black life are not. For reformers, like Addams and Kellogg, the incentive of a limitless and comprehensive view, even if suggestive and blurry, was the possibility of accumulating more data and extending the already-long arm of unchecked social control. For African American practitioners, the survey's sweeping contours and shadowy boundaries offered both an alternative to the penetrating gaze of normative social scientists and a site from which to imagine new racial epistemologies. The payoff was not simply the emergence of a body of "social data" or new information about the "problem of social life," but also an observer who could tender an animate body of racial information—that is, an observer who could see the "flows" and "movements" constitutive of black social and psychic life, its "opinion and feelings," and the historical underpinnings of "social geography."[43]

In precisely the way the social survey arises from the web of desires to alternatively visualize social life, scholars working at the intersection of visual culture and histories of science have mapped the distinct ways that the modern observer emerges from a matrix of ideological, institutional, historical, and technological factors. Following Michel Foucault and Walter Benjamin, Jonathan Crary, for instance, theorizes the observer as a product of the "techniques for controlling, maintaining, and making useful new multiplicities of individuals" but also of "new urban spaces."[44] Stopping short of the late nineteenth century, Crary admits that he is not interested in the idealized observer's recalcitrant underbelly. Yet I want to suggest that when we look to the turn of the twentieth century and approach the social survey as a visual technology and outlook, a newly constructed observer comes into view, one whose obdurate shadow is productive of new social arrangements and novel visual epistemologies. Picking up where Crary leaves off, we can consider how the field of social science also composed a particular kind of observer, one who in the late nineteenth century found his technological double in photography and his methodological mirror in statistics. Where the detached observer whose disembodied and disinterested calculations on black futures dominated the discourse on the "Negro Problem," the social surveyor was deeply immersed and highly embodied. As Du Bois reflected on his research practice in Philadelphia, "I studied it personally and not just by proxy. I sent out no canvassers. I went myself."[45] Rather than presuming mastery or aiming for a kind of visual evisceration, the social survey's observer skirts along the surface and steadily moves to its itinerant rhythms. As an embodied telescope or social microscope, he understands the social as a dynamic site of relationality. From this orientation, the social surveyor reveals social bodies and relations that are otherwise opaque and loosens the statistical chokehold that renders black life little more than a death toll.

But in addition to its emphasis on visualization, I want to draw out one final aspect of the social survey's ideological architecture to lay bare the aesthetic stakes of its formal eccentricity and imaginative visual horizon—and that is its relationship to fiction. As a methodology, the social survey was deeply invested in stretching the social-scientific gaze to sights and sites previously unknown. This was in large part achieved by shuffling visual and corporeal epistemologies and the technologies of observation that authorize a particularly modern disciplinary gaze.[46] In both stretching science's gaze and unsettling the ideological authority of observation, the social survey consistently grazed against fantasy and imagination.

Granting this dual relation to speculation, Du Bois's preoccupation with the social survey was not simply because of its ubiquity. Rather, as it was for other African American intellectuals, writers, and cultural producers, the social survey was an aspirational mode that, at least in theory, could reorient the narrow and subjectifying gaze of the racial statistician to render black life a dynamic "plexus" rather than an inert body of antisocial data. In the context of what Khalil Muhammad describes as the "racial data revolution"—the moment when new modes of racial accounting were yoked to ever-pressing questions about the future place of blacks in the nation-state—the idea of the responsible study of black life was a challenge as practical as it was philosophical.[47] As black intellectuals confronted the social survey, they exploited its transformative potential and also got tangled in its contradictory web. And just as the survey relentlessly pushed to control and organize the social landscape, African Americans saw in the formally heterogeneous and visually supple form the potential for intervention.

In recent years, and largely owing to a surge in research on W. E. B. Du Bois and *The Philadelphia Negro*, the social survey has reentered scholarly discourse. Du Bois's pioneering social study in particular has been recovered as a foundational sociological document that innovated new methodologies and representational strategies even as it disciplined black life according to its "normalizing discourse of moral standards, gender conformity, sexual hygiene, and capitalist productivity."[48] Drawing out *The Philadelphia Negro*'s significance as an innovator in data visualization, Alexander Weheliye has revealed how its diagrammatics strain against the rhetoric of normative uplift for which Du Bois is best known while also underscoring the centrality of visuality to his racial politics. Rather than merely reproducing black life as numerical figures, a simple equation, or debased data, in the pages of *The Philadelphia Negro*, statistical graphics provide "Du Bois with the means of encoding racial formation beyond phenotype and heredity, instead historicizing the relational materialization of the category Negro in a US American, urban post-emancipation environment."[49] Yet within this exciting and rapidly growing body of research, the social survey as medium, methodology, and technology is rarely interrogated on its own terms. And although *The Philadelphia Negro* is certainly a paradigmatic social survey, readings that solely prioritize Du Bois's Philadelphia labor risk erasing the full scope of African Americans' engagements with the social survey and obscuring the ubiquity of the form itself.

Indeed, in addition to Du Bois's 1899 *The Philadelphia Negro*, his *Negro Labor in Lowndes County, Negros of Farmville, Virginia*, photographic essay *The Negro as He Really Is*, and the dozens of studies he directed for Atlanta University are also social surveys. From here we can also look to the countless contributions that black writers and activists made to survey publications, specifically *Charities'* 1905 "The Negro in the Cities of the North," which included essays by Fannie Barrier Williams, Booker T. Washington, and James Weldon Johnson. The early twentieth-century *Negro Yearbooks* and Charles Johnson's *Opportunity* also stage the aesthetics and politics of the survey, albeit at varying degrees of intensity. We can also read a desire for something like the social survey in the African American mathematician and sociologist Kelly Miller's review of Frederick Hoffman's 1896 treatise on black mortality and criminality, *Race Traits and Tendencies of the American Negro*, while the survey habit of mind underpins Du Bois's enduring critique of the US census and statistical methodologies. And James Weldon Johnson is also moving in line with the social survey tradition when, in the prefatory stunt that opens *Autobiography of an Ex-Colored Man*, the "publishers" assert, "Not before has a composite and proportionate presentation of the entire race, embracing all of its various groups and elements, showing their relations with each other and to the whites been made."[50] More than just a compendium of black-authored documents or sociological evidence that attempts to scientifically and systematically approach the "Negro Problem," engagements with the social survey are, above all else, an attempt to make data move. By this, I mean reassembling the racial schemas that are authorized by data and in turn confirm black life's proximity to abjection, death, and the limits of humanity. To make data move is to realign the presumed equation between black life and data while also insisting on a data regime that might allow us to perceive and receive black social life.

In what follows, I spotlight four sites at which black intellectuals grazed against, flirted with, and summoned the social survey in the service of advancing new racial and visual epistemologies: Kelly Miller's 1897 review of Frederick Hoffman's *Race Traits and Tendencies of the American Negro* (1896); Sutton Griggs's 1899 novel *Imperium in Imperio*; *Charities'* 1905 special issue "The Negro in the Cities of the North"; and Alain Locke's 1925 *Survey Graphic* special issue "Harlem: Mecca of the New Negro." In each instance, the social survey occasions either a radical epistemological overhaul, as in the case of *Imperium in Imperio*, or supplies the conditions from which new racial knowledge can emerge, as is the case of "The Negro in the Cities of the North."

I begin with Frederick Hoffman's statistical treatise on black mortality because this deeply influential text helps us understand the urgency for a form like the social survey and sets up the racial data terrain against which African Americans were working. In doing so, I run the risk of reproducing an oppositional paradigm in which African Americans were simply responding to the work of specious white statisticians and racial scientists. However, in characterizing this period as one of active experimentation, when racial knowledge was simultaneously deeply focused and completely unwieldy, and in focusing on the exploratory undertakings that emerged in sites like the social survey, I highlight how these endeavors were primarily concerned with invention and imagining rather than with simply correcting. Though sometimes intentional, just as often the outcome of the confrontations with the social survey were inadvertent, owing more to the survey's formal and structural workings than to the contributor's or editor's goals. These encounters can be understood as articulations of a "survey spirit," a phrase I borrow from Thomas J. Riley's 1911 essay "Sociology and Social Surveys." As in Du Bois's oeuvre, over the course of the chapter the survey spirit comes in and out of focus, sometimes taking shape as a novel and other times as an explicit derision of statistics. Other moments see the survey spirit emerging from the cracks between competing claims and arguments, as is the case in *Survey Graphic* and *Charities*. In each case the survey spirit's political horizon coheres around the task of loosening the relationship between data and black life, a relationship that visual technologies cemented and that the social survey appeared to upend. Importantly, I am not so much interested in offering a celebratory account of the social survey, one that redeems it from the annals of disciplinary reform movements. Rather, these four case studies offer a sense of the intersection of the social survey and black creative practice. In drawing out each text, I highlight their role in a turn-of-the-century project of locating a paradigm that might make black life, in all its plurality, come into focus.

"Ugly Facts" and (Anti)Social Data: Kelly Miller, the American
Negro Academy, and the Call for the Social Survey

On March 5, 1897, Kelly Miller stood before eighteen leading black intellectuals, politicians, and reformers who had gathered for the inaugural meeting of the American Negro Academy (ANA) and prepared to deliver a scathing review of *Race Traits and Tendencies of the American Negro*, Frederick Hoffman's book-length treatise on black mortality. Although *Race Traits* was published just one year earlier, by the time the ANA convened, Hoffman's thesis on black Americans' pending extinction was firmly established as a touchstone for black and white postbellum thinkers who were desperate to find a solution to the persistently enigmatic "Negro Problem." Armed with data gathered from the 1890 census—the eleventh in the United States— Hoffman pitched his project as an exploration into the "longevity and physiological peculiarities among the colored population that was free from the taint of prejudice and sentimentality."[51] Stitching together charts, graphs, and descriptive prose, Hoffman concluded that "race traits" (innate biological deficiencies) rather than conditions (institutionalized racism, crowded housing, poor access to medical attention) were impeding African Americans' capacity for progress, confirming their inferior racial status, and consolidating the color line. By affixing blackness to morbidity, Hoffman's text authorized a theory of black antisociality, forecasting what Susan Mizruchi would later name a "drama of nullification."[52] The "[black] race," Hoffman deduced, is "on a downward grade, tending towards a condition in which matters will be worse than they are now."[53] To put matters plainly, black life, he predicted, was heading toward "gradual extinction."[54] Characterizing African Americans as a "hopeless problem" and "economic hindrance" who would never enter the fold of civilization and would continuously thwart American progress, Hoffman entreated his readers to patiently wait for blacks to naturally disappear. After all, he cautioned, "of all the races for which statistics are obtainable . . . the negro shows the least power of resistance in the struggle for life."[55]

Following its release, racial theorists immediately seized on the 328-page document as a blueprint for everything from educational policy to theories of criminality to insurance rates. For those eager to make scientific sense of the rapidly changing national landscape, Hoffman's foreign-born status and his deployment of statistics produced a foolproof template for dispassionate and impartial race science. As Frederick Starr put it in his laudatory review: "Much has been said, on both sides, regarding the present condition and outlook of the Afro American. Most of what has been said has been written by prejudiced observers. It is much, then, to have a thoughtful work by an unbiased foreigner, dealing with a wide range of reliable statistics."[56]

The publication of *Race Traits* was certainly timely. As the nineteenth century came to a close, social scientists found themselves clamoring for new methods to theorize racial difference. In the aftermath of what pundits were describing as the "experiment" of emancipation, fields like ethnology, along with the authority attached to the monogenesis versus polygenesis debates, were rendered highly subjective and ineffective modes of knowledge production.[57] With African Americans no longer legally confined to the plantation, the geographic dichotomies (North-South) and categories of personhood (enslaved-free) that had long organized antebellum racial logic desperately needed updating. What emerged was a brand of scientific racism that sought to deny the fundamental claims of black vitality while imagining a racial landscape in which black Americans would quietly retreat to the role of laborers or, worse, simply die out. As Muhammad explains, "The new social scientific imperative of the late nineteenth and early twentieth centuries was to save the nation by measuring black inferiority through any sign of African Americans' failure to dominate or to lead or even to survive in modern society."[58] With its focus on the statistical representation of black life-span data, namely birth and death rates, *Race Traits* emerged as the balm that desperate racial scientists had been searching for.

Importantly, neither Hoffman's motivating question on the future of blacks in the nation nor his data set—the census—was particularly unique. Throughout the nineteenth century racist and anti-racist arguments regularly turned to the census to legitimate their positions. When the 1840 census suggested that free blacks not only had higher mortality rates than slaves but also were more prone to physical and mental disabilities, pro-slavery advocates quickly mobilized the information to argue that African Americans were unfit for freedom.

Meanwhile, black intellectuals like Frederick Douglass and Benjamin Banneker crafted careful counterreadings of those very census returns in the name of black freedom. And beginning in 1859 Thomas Hamilton's New York–based literary magazine the *Anglo-African Magazine* printed a series of anonymously authored essays titled "A Statistical View of the Colored Population of the United States, 1790–1840." Possibly authored by James McCune Smith, who, as Maurice Lee has shown, had a track record of "putting statistics to abolitionist ends," the series argued that the census's inability to imagine the vicissitudes of free black life had the consequence of producing faulty information.[59] But in revealing what black life was not—reducible to mathematical schemas—the politically driven statistical missteps nevertheless reveal what black life is: a dynamic force that always moves in excess of statistical operations.

That said, the novelty of Hoffman's venture was twofold. First, the 1890 census on which he based his work was itself an innovation in demographic data gathering. The 1870 and 1880 censuses had produced valuable information about post-emancipation black life, but the 1890 census promised the first data on the generation of blacks born after slavery. Further contributing to an anticipatory atmosphere was the introduction of an electronic tabulation system that allowed statisticians to "attempt much more complex tabulations of information on the schedules" for the published bulletins.[60] On the whole, analysts were chiefly concerned with whether the African American population was growing at a faster rate than the white population and, more precisely, whether "the mulattoes, quadroons, and octoroons are disappearing and the race [is] becoming more purely negro," as the labor commissioner Carroll D. Wright put it.[61] At stake in the results was the justification of repressive measures that would continue to legitimate the institutionalization of white supremacy, namely the *Plessy v. Ferguson* decision, as well as potential revisions to the popular Darwinist view of racial progress or lack thereof. That is, could African Americans survive outside of the plantation economy? To thus "secure accurate information . . . regarding the Negro race," writes Melissa Nobles, the eleventh census expanded the schedule's racial categories to include "Negros, mulattos, quadroons, and octoroons, as well as more detailed information about mortality rates."[62] Casting the "Negro Problem" as a problem of and for statistics, Wright exclaimed that "it must be settled by statistics and the sooner the statistics are collected, the better."[63]

Second, *Race Traits* boasted what Hoffman described as the "exclusive use of the statistical method."[64] For Hoffman this meant relying on preexisting information and avoiding historical contextualization to create a seemingly new compendium of racial data. In contrast to a previous generation of race scientists who innovated their own methodologies, Hoffman claimed to be neither a creator nor an interpreter.[65] Instead, the statistics, he promised, "speak for themselves."[66] In no uncertain terms, Hoffman explained: "In the field of statistical research, sentiment, prejudice, or the influences of pre-conceived ideas have no place. The data which have been here brought together in a convenient form speak for themselves. From the standpoint of the impartial investigator, no difference of interpretation of meaning seems possible."[67] Channeled through an "exclusive use of the statistical method," Hoffman emerged as a disinterested vehicle of statistical expression whose account of racial morbidity was impenetrable to detractors. Yet Hoffman was far from "impartial." As Muhammad has outlined in great detail, despite being born in Germany, Hoffman had personal and professional stakes in a narrative of black moral and physiological degeneracy. In addition to marrying into a family with deep connections to the slaveholding South, Hoffman was an agent of Prudential Life Insurance, a profession that by nature trades on the value of death and bets on the subprime value of black life.[68] Even without these personal investments, he was not so far afield when he advanced the inevitability of his findings. If, in the words of Mizruchi, "the burden of *Race Traits* is the definitive association of Black culture with death," then the association is aided and abetted by statistics' organizing logic and representational strategies, what Hoffman named as the very "forms" through which data purport to "speak for themselves."[69]

By design, statistics organize and discipline social life through the work of compulsory visibility and categorization, work that is both the condition for recognition as a citizen subject and the pathway to social nullification. As the logic of the census reveals, to count as a person is to comply with certain categories of identification, whereas the ability to be classified simultaneously predicts and provides the conditions that determine whether one's life is deemed valuable, whether it is worth accounting for. If, as Foucault has long alerted us, individuals become legible as meaningful liberal subjects through their capacity for enumeration and statistical tabulation, then these are also the very mechanisms that render them invaluable and anti-social. Thus, when in the beginning of Du Bois's *Quest of the Silver Fleece* a liberal white reformer proclaims, "I want to live in a world where every soul counts—white, black, yellow—all," she simultaneously articulates a political agenda grounded in an ethics of mutual recognition and identifies enumeration's deleterious workings. This is what Avery Gordon describes as the "relationship between accountability and accounting that slavery establishes." Here "those who do not count are those whose worth is literally measured by their price," a violent ethics that compels us to "contend not only with those who do not count but are counted."[70] Relatedly, in its commitment to establishing a norm through the effacement of specificity and difference, statistical labor lubricates the transposition of life into data. As Ida B. Wells took up statistics in her fight against white supremacy, she operated under the knowledge that statistics "condense[s] the complex histories of social encounters gone awry into an abstraction of mere numbers."[71] As she understood, and as I address in chapter 2, working with statistical enumeration, making numbers signify differently, required attention to their forms, figures, and aesthetics, what I described in the introduction as the aesthetics of counting.

Thus, any consideration of the violence wrought by the statistical imaginary necessarily requires attending to the forms used to present data, what Du Bois characterized as the "shape" that information takes on and what Johanna Drucker has recently designated as data's visual form.[72] In *Race Traits* Hoffman used rudimentary tables that he described as "concise tabular statement of the facts" as his preferred representational form.[73] Unlike graphs or bar charts, which "make relations among aspects visible," tables, writes Drucker, merely "hold information."[74] As strategies of containment, tables present their findings as immutable and definitive truths. Tables also erase the complex networks of social relations, patterns, and historical factors that are crucial to information's production and reception. With tables as his preferred representational mode, what emerges from *Race Traits* is a grim and ahistorical tale of racial stagnation and degeneracy whereby statistics' morbid logic structures a narrow gaze that perceives and produces racial stratification. Far from illuminating the nuances of nineteenth-century black social life, Hoffman's statistical maneuvers and representational forms (tables) could only ever communicate a death toll.

In addition to its shapes and forms, *Race Traits'* limited horizon was also a product of Hoffman's shoddy statistical methods. Although Hoffman claimed to simply follow the story that statistics told, as Megan Wolff explains, he made the amateur mistake of failing to disaggregate his data, a move that "had the damaging impact of obscuring any relationship between cause and effect other than the single commonality of race itself," even as it effectively yielded an aggregative racial type.[75] It is possible that eliding historical conditions and skipping over a cause-and-effect paradigm might simply have been Hoffman embracing the descriptive approach to statistics dominating late nineteenth-century methodologies. But Hoffman was also simply a bad statistician. "Such failings indicated that Hoffman had not adhered to the scientific methods on which he prided himself, and on the basis of which the work claimed special credibility," Wolff writes.[76] The task for Hoffman's detractors, then, would not simply be insisting on black vitality or countering the grim statistical data with accounts of black success. It would also be locating a method and practice, a form and shape, that would imbue statistics with the capacity to communicate nuance, ambiguity, and uncertainty, while also advancing a habit of sight that would undercut the authority of the statistical gaze and its narrow purview.[77] More simply put, if Hoffman's "exclusive use of the statistical method" was the primary problem, then challenging his summary would require an inclusive use of the statistical method and a new form that would allow the numbers to tell a different story, a means to "count it out differently."[78]

Armed with the desire not to merely critique Hoffman's argument but to use it as an occasion to identify new social-scientific shapes and forms, Kelly Miller fashioned a review of *Race Traits* that cut through each of Hoffman's central conceits. *Race Traits'* thesis about blacks' "low and anti-social" nature was the very kind of charge that the ANA had set out to dispute.[79] Founded in early 1897 by Alexander Crummell, the ANA's goal was to "bring together men of science, letters, and arts, or those distinguished in other walks of life" in order to promote the "publication of literary and scholarly works" and to establish a line of defense against the "vicious assaults" hurled at black Americans.[80] The ANA remained active until 1928. During this time, it published twenty-two editions of *Occasional Papers* (the organization's official news organ) and counted some of the most influential race theorists and activists as members. In addition to Miller, Du Bois, Francis Grimké, William Scarborough, John Hope Franklin, Carter G. Woodson, Alain Locke, and James Weldon Johnson were also members. Although the March 5, 1897, meeting was largely concerned with hammering out a mission statement, the gathering boasted an impressive roster of attendees and speakers. Over the course of two days the founders committed themselves to the "civilization of the Negro race in the United States, by the scientific processes of literature, art, and philosophy."[81] To this end, attendees listened intently as a subcommittee (which included Miller) reported on the efficacy of publishing a journal, ratified the organization's constitution, and presented a series of papers including Du Bois's "Conservation of Races," Albert P. Miller's "The Development of the Negro Intellect," and Kelly Miller's "A Review of Hoffman's *Race Traits*." Although "Conservation of Races" was praised by the ANA and has since secured a place in the canon of African American letters, Miller's speech arguably had the most immediate impact.

When he arrived on stage, Miller was perfectly poised to take Hoffman's book to task. Six years earlier he had accepted a position at Howard University, his alma mater, where he would remain for the duration of his career, first as a professor of mathematics and later as dean of the College of Liberal Arts. Miller never achieved the posthumous fame of Du Bois or Booker T. Washington. Yet over the course of his career, he published countless essays and books, and drafted plans for a National Museum of African American History. Although Miller was a founding member of the ANA, he was added to the program only at the last minute, after two scheduled speakers canceled. In the end, the substitution proved fortuitous. His remarks prompted hours of debate, leading the ANA to print the "Review" as the first essay of the *Occasional Papers* debut issue. At twenty-five cents apiece and a digestible thirty-eight pages, five hundred copies of the "Review" were printed and circulated nationwide to members and nonmembers alike.[82]

Within weeks, the press took note of the essay. The *New York Age* and the *Washington Bee*, two African American newspapers with extensive readerships, advertised the pamphlet, and the *Washington Times* and *Boston Transcript* dedicated substantial print space to its review. Following his appearance at the ANA, Miller commenced a small speaking tour during which he reprised his comments at Washington's Bethel Literary Society and Historical Association and the Hampton Institute Summer Conference.[83] Upon the success of Miller's circuit, the *Southern Workman*, the official journal of Hampton University, printed a full review of Miller's speech and encouraged readers to purchase a copy for their personal libraries.

Alone, the "Review" levels a powerful attack on Hoffman's claims of blacks' moral and biological inferiority. That Miller, a highly educated black man, could even author a critique of Hoffman undercut the heart of *Race Traits'* thesis. The public's embrace of the review, or at the very least the ANA's support of it, also registers demand for an alternative to the exclusively statistical approach that energized Hoffman's work. The review deftly disproved Hoffman's thesis, offering a new framework for perceiving black life while loosening the stranglehold of statistics. With a combination of wit and sarcasm, Miller positioned himself as a social scientist and a public intellectual who could go head-to-head with the most trenchant racialists in a written debate, all while casting Hoffman as an inconsistent novice who, just four years earlier, had praised blacks for their social development.[84] As he piled up counterevidence, dismissing *Race Traits* as the product of "disputed facts" and "insufficient data," Miller issued a quiet call for an alternative interpretive "point of view" and a "new device" through which Hoffman's claims could be redirected and reinterpreted.[85]

Across seven chapters, the review meticulously dissects each of Hoffman's hypotheses, shattering the central claim that blacks were on the brink of extinction. Each chapter begins by pairing a "subject" of Hoffman's work—"social conditions," "amalgamation," "anthropometry," "vital statistics," "population," and "economic conditions"—with his corresponding takeaway, what Miller terms the "gist." Miller also reprinted *Race Traits'* tables, charts, and particularly salient passages. With this rubric in place, Miller bobs and weaves through Hoffman's claims and data, crafting an alternate reading of the information that had been celebrated as indisputable. In place of "race traits," for instance, Miller offers a host of explanations, from nativism to migration, before making the case that the vitality of black life is, above all, owing to "conditions." In the brief section addressing "economic conditions," for instance, Miller counters Hoffman's finding that "as a general conclusion it may be said that the Negro has not yet learned the first element of Anglo-Saxon thrift" with an excerpt taken from a public complaint made by eight hundred white factory workers from South Carolina who forcefully replaced black employees.[86] Tapping into well-rehearsed rhetoric that positioned black men as a threat to the sanctity of white domesticity, the letter proclaimed, "We affirm, by our physical powers and brave hearts, not to sit supinely by and witness this Negro horde turned loose upon the pursuits of our mothers, our wives, our widows, our daughters, our sisters, and rob them of their living."[87] For Miller, the petition reveals the economic underpinnings of racist fantasies that equate black presence with criminality while drawing out an unmistakable contradiction: if African Americans had yet to master the art of economic independence, as Hoffman suggests, then why would white South Carolinians view them as a financial threat worthy of a public letter?

By briefly and strategically setting aside the statistical here, Miller amplifies the structural conditions that determine black futures while reversing Hoffman's foundational logic. He bluntly writes, "If the alleged low industrial efficiency of the Negro is to be chargeable to race traits, it should attributed to the domineering and intolerant race traits of the white workmen who are not disposed to give the colored man a fair chance."[88] But perhaps most important, Miller's textual performance produces a counterreading of the data that claims to "speak for itself." Far from articulating an objective stance, the numerical narrative mutates according to its agent.

To tackle the general fallacy of Hoffman's claim that "race traits" were moving blacks along an unalterable path to extinction, Miller necessarily addresses the legitimacy of the 1890 census and statistics, the two aspects of Hoffman's work that most excited his supporters. Like many of his peers, Miller dismissed the 1890 census as a flawed enterprise that more frequently than not produced "disputed data."[89] Perhaps anticipating charges of "sympathy" or prejudice, Miller conducts his critique of the census through a damaging review by Texas senator Roger Mills published in the well-established journal *The*

Forum, in which Mills points out inconsistencies in the reported rates of population increase across returns from the South. Such fallacies, Miller reasons, would stand to have an especially damaging impact on African Americans: "Whatever force there may be in the protest of the eloquent Texas Senator, applies with special emphasis to the colored element; for it goes without saying that errors in enumeration in the South would be confined mainly to the Negro race, and since the bulk of the race is confined to this section such errors would have a most disastrous effect upon its rate of increase as shown by the census reports."[90] Miller concludes with the bold statement that, because Hoffman proudly admits to gathering most of his data from the census, in light of critiques, from a Southerner no less, the entire force of *Race Traits* is compromised. "Since the author relies mainly upon the eleventh census for facts to establish his conclusion, and since the accuracy of this census is widely controverted," Miller deduces, "we may fairly call upon him to prove his document before it can be admitted into evidence."[91]

Even if his reliance on the census had been enough to demote Hoffman's tour de force from the realm of evidence to mere conspiracy theory, Miller went on to discredit his "exclusive use of the statistical method." Writing with an unmistakably sarcastic tone, he reflects, "It is passing strange that it escaped the attention of a statistician of Mr. Hoffman's sagacity that, even granting the accuracy of the eleventh census, the natural increase of the Negro race is greater than that of the whites during the last decade."[92] As Miller well knew, Hoffman was not a trained statistician, and what little experience he had derived from his work as an insurance agent. Relatedly, Miller casts Hoffman as the unavoidable victim of statistics' stunted outlook, especially as applied to insurance's investment in the valuation of mortality. At the same time, Miller's phrasing draws attention to the slippery nature of enumeration. Together, statistics' social logic and the broader classificatory systems from which Hoffman extracted his data were structured by erasure, evasion, and obfuscation. Thus, for Miller, the exclusive use of the statistical method was unsatisfactory and insufficient because it allowed Hoffman to overlook the range of factors that affected the data while simultaneously disguising his own racist thinking under a mask of objective empiricism. Miller summed up, "It would seem that his conclusion was reached from *a priori* considerations and that the facts have been collected in order to justify it."[93]

In response to Hoffman's methodological shortcomings, Miller staged multiple (re)readings of the data, insisting that "facts" are always the product of subjective interpretation best expressed with the help of descriptive prose. Far from speaking for themselves, Miller reasoned that numbers demand a range of explanatory documents and can produce countless narrative routes. Funneled through this interpretive schema, Miller submitted the decline of more than 10 percent in the percentage of blacks among the total population as evidence of white immigration patterns, and not, as Hoffman suggested, of "race traits." Driving this point home, he rebuked, "It would be as legitimate to attribute the decline of the Yankee element as a numerical factor in the large New England centers to the race degeneracy of the Puritan, while ignoring the proper cause—the influx of the celt."[94]

Collectively, Hoffman's refusal to account for a range of social conditions, his reverse engineering of facts to fit a predetermined outcome (one that would have benefited Prudential Life Insurance), and his reliance on a faulty data source (the eleventh census) produced what Miller described as "ugly facts": "To the Negro I would say, let him not be discouraged by the ugly facts which confront him. The sociologists are flashing the searchlight of scientific inquiry upon him. His faults lie nearer the surface and are more easily detected than those of the white race."[95] Like many of his contemporaries, Miller regarded "ugly facts" as those relating to crime, poverty, "low standards of family life" and as ones that did not comport with the standards of middle-class respectability that he understood as signifiers of blacks' aptitude for citizenship.[96] Miller was careful not to define "ugly" as a permanent or immutable state, however. Instead, he theorized ugly facts as the product of intense statistical scrutiny and the inevitable result of the sociologist's visualizing techniques that only ever amplify the statistical subject's aberrations from national and racial fictions of progress.

To be sure, Miller's argument laments the willful elision of black middle-class social and economic success from Hoffman's statistical report, a position that confirms his commitment to turn-of-the-century uplift politics. As he explained in his reprisal of the review at Hampton University, when it came to his discussion of class, Hoffman was not entirely off base. "In the main the accuracy of Mr. Hoffman's statistics in regard to immorality, and lack of thrift and business ability" is undisputed, he explained.[97] Yet might we also read his final entreaty as less an expression of his conservative class politics and more of a call for a methodological practice that would illuminate the "beauty" of black life—its vitality, variegation, and futurity? To move in this direction is to understand ugly facts as the defense of white supremacy, the view that black life is inherently antisocial. But it is also to understand how ugly facts authorize an aesthetic arrangement whereby black life is always subject to quantification, classification, and objectification, a position that assumes black life's eminent legibility and perpetual visibility. Going one step further, if in Hoffman's hands statistics generate a narrative of black death, of frustrated starts and stunted beginnings, then what literary genres and politics—racial, personal, social—do beautiful facts engender?

Incidentally, the earliest moments of the review begin to offer some answers. In noting *Race Traits'* impact, Miller compares Hoffman's statistical text to none other than Harriet Beecher Stowe's *Uncle Tom's Cabin* (1852). Hoffman's work, he explains, "presents by far the most thorough and comprehensive treatment of the Negro from a statistical standpoint, which has yet appeared. In fact, it may be regarded as the most important utterance on the subject since the publication of *Uncle Tom's Cabin*; for the interest which the famous novel aroused in the domain of sentiment and generous feelings, the present work seems destined to awaken in the field of science and exact inquiry."[98] Miller's reference to Stowe has been interpreted as an earnest acknowledgment of Hoffman's deep influence across reform movements and a reminder of Miller's own belief in the causal relationship between quantitative methods and racial uplift, a belief system that Hoffman also shared. As Paul Lawrie argues, Miller directed his energies toward challenging Hoffman's form and method, rather than the "ideological and conceptual frameworks" that underpin *Race Traits*. Here, the nod to Stowe indexes a methodologically conservative Miller who focused his attention on Hoffman's statistical missteps and argumentative fallacies and "fashioned a cogent critique of biological theories of racial degeneracy within the bounds of rational inquiry."[99] Miller was, as Lawrie argues, undoubtedly committed to an embrace of "rational inquiry," and, as we have seen, the power of enumeration and quantification. And yet Miller's turn to Stowe is precisely concerned with taking and renovating the "ideological and conceptual frameworks." By invoking Stowe, Miller stretches the bounds of "rational inquiry" to include both the statistical and the melodramatic. Over the duration of the "Review," he insists that conceptual frameworks and methodology are inextricably linked; that is, the statistical is ideological. Moreover, in its capacity to both regulate and disorder what and who counts as valuable according to the terms of order, statistics are also aesthetic.[100]

On the one hand, citing Stowe would seem to underline the distinction between sentimentality and statistics—matters of the heart versus appeals to the mind—the very bedrock of rational thinking. Indeed, in the months following the ANA meeting, Miller further emphasized the gulf between the literary and the social scientific. In a September 1897 iteration of his comments he clarified: "It is considered the most important book that has been written about the Negros of this country since 'Uncle Tom's Cabin' was published. That book aroused generous impulses toward the Negro, but this one has stirred feelings of an opposite nature."[101] The ability of *Uncle Tom's Cabin* to activate an anti-slavery consciousness, Miller suggests, had everything to do with its status as fiction. On the other hand, pairing Stowe and Hoffman, the one a work of melodramatic fiction and the other an expression of "detached" objectivity, muddies the boundary separating the "fields of science" and empathy. From this vantage point, and contrary to Hoffman's promise that his study was free of sentiment, matters of counting are always matters of feeling; or, as Miller put it, both works have "stirred" and stoked racial feelings. Thus, where Hoffman's "exclusive use of the statistical" finds its literary analogue in *Uncle Tom's Cabin*, ugly facts find expression in melodramatic principles.

Despite Hoffman's claim that he chooses statistics over sentiment, literary melodrama and statistics share strategies of influence. At the most basic level, melodrama is based on structural polarities that illuminate a morally legible universe organized around "intense emotional and ethical drama based on the manichaeistic struggle of good and evil." As Peter Brooks explains in his foundational description of melodramatic principles, the "polarization of good and evil" functions to realize the presence of both as "real forces in the world" that must be confronted, expelled, and purged in order to maintain some semblance of a moral universe.[102] Within the world of anti-slavery melodrama, of which *Uncle Tom's Cabin* is the ur-text, the slave economy was reduced to a battle over good and evil, in which "virtue, virginity, and sanctity of the family" were at stake. In this domain, writes Saidiya Hartman in her insightful reading of the politics of the melodramatic imagination, the black body was mobilized as a "vehicle of dissent and protest," its violation used to awaken a latent national outrage and engender empathetic identification.[103] Just as the black body was figured as the site where a moral battle was staged, melodramatic conventions gained their emotional force by rendering black life a trope, a type, and a racial aggregate. It is precisely its ability to reduce interior life to the merely symbolic that allowed melodrama to achieve its spectacular effect. In literature, theater, and visual culture, nineteenth-century melodrama created a literary world that, Susan Gillman has argued, was simultaneously "heightened and hyperbolic, flat and wooden."[104] Elaborated in this way, the description of melodrama could easily stand in for a statistical overview. Indeed, and to return to the initial discussion of the shape and form of statistics, tables and charts are equally stilted even as they portend negative futures. And just as melodrama doubled as a mode of social reordering, so too were statistics charged with clearing a pathway through which the present could be ordered and the uncertain future made predictable. Read as melodramatic expression, in *Race Traits* the struggle over the future of good and evil is recast as the battle between (white) vitality and (black) mortality.

In the end, Miller's "Review" offers the social survey as an alternative to Hoffman's methodology. Where *Race Traits* depended on the value of the aggregate and refused to contextualize its findings, Miller advocated for disaggregation, attention to historical specificity, and a robustly researched account of the "Negro Problem," one whose data set expanded far beyond the census. Even so, that he punctuates the essay with gestures toward the literary (Stowe) and the aesthetic (ugly facts) suggests that his entanglement with Hoffman and his engagement with a method like the social survey would find resolution not in the social sciences proper but in the related terrain of the literary arts. It is significant in this regard that Miller does not offer an explicit prescription to bad statistics, as Du Bois did in "The Study of the Negro Problems." To be sure, Miller's conclusion reassures its black readers that Hoffman's findings are ill informed and that their presumed "faults" are the object of biased scrutiny. At the same time, Miller's gesture to Stowe also poses an open question: what literary form do beautiful facts take? As it turns out, he had a surprising answer.

A Book to Do Some Good: Kelly Miller, Sutton Griggs, and the Emergence of Social Document Fiction

Kelly Miller was not the only person to route a call for something like the social survey through a critique of Hoffman. One year after the inaugural ANA meeting and just as he was coordinating his Atlanta University Studies, Du Bois completed research for what would become *The Philadelphia Negro*. Although they were choreographed around two distinct geographic zones, both endeavors implicitly responded to and reworked what Du Bois dismissed as Hoffman's "abuse of the statistical evidence" and his hurried conclusions.[105] In his own review of *Race Traits*, Du Bois argued that Hoffman's work succumbed to the dangerous trap of conflating counting with analysis, a misstep that emerged from believing that the volume of numbers accumulated could masquerade as sound qualitative analysis. For regardless of the impressive quantity of figures that Hoffman gathered in the name of proving black mortality, as Du Bois pointed out, he "has by no means avoided the many fallacies of the statistical method," which, when irresponsibly practiced, is "nothing but the application of logic to counting, and no amount of counting will justify a departure from the severe rules of correct reasoning."[106] *The Philadelphia Negro*'s vivid portrait of the "Negro group as a symptom, not a cause; as a striving palpitating group, and not an inert, sick body of crime," revised Hoffman's bleak forecast and offered a response to Miller's implicit call to methodological action.[107] Yoking first-person observation to daily interviews with residents of Philadelphia's Seventh Ward, and fusing statistical tabulation with historical analysis, Du Bois's empirical methodology rejects what Aldon Morris has described as the sociologist's "armchair conjectures and flashes of intuition customary at the time." Equipped with a "multimethods approach" that stitched together "number-crunching, surveying, interviewing, participant observing and field work," and that approached the social as a laboratory requiring steady observation from a close physical proximity, Du Bois filled in and illuminated the gaps that Hoffman simply would not see.[108]

Even as he issued *The Philadelphia Negro* as a rejoinder to Hoffman's exclusively statistical method, Du Bois found himself ensnared
in the social survey's limitations—political, ideological, and, not least,
methodological. Although he would explicitly give voice to sociological doubts in his 1905 essay "Sociologically Hesitant," *The Philadelphia
Negro* bears the trace of a statistically skeptical Du Bois who won-
dered whether his empirically rooted approach was incongruous with
his own aims. Anticipating what he would describe in his 1944 essay
as the realization that "facts, in social science . . . were elusive things,"
as early as the preface Du Bois warned that his signature method,
which combined "house-to-house investigation" with "conclusions
formed by the best trained and most conscientious students," was
no match for the rhythm of black living.[109] In spite of the fact that his
multimethods strategy set out to, in the words of Morris, "ensure accuracy by eradicating undetected errors associated with a particular
method," Du Bois admits that strategic aspects of his approach, especially the observer's biased eye and the "misapprehension, vagueness
and forgetfulness on the part of the persons being questioned," likely
prejudiced the research.[110] And although he assures readers that steps
have been taken to minimize margins of error, he remained deeply
concerned that key features of the neighborhood were being overlooked, were exceeding graphic description, or were simply taking
shape beyond his gaze. Thus, even though there was a high frequency
of "prompt and candid" answers, there was often, he professed, "falsi-
fication" and "evasion."[111] And when residents were not home, he was
forced to rely on the dubious testimony of neighbors and friends.

Du Bois was not entirely discouraged by the elusive nature of facts,
however. The comprehensive scope of *The Philadelphia Negro* is itself
a testament to his commitment to grappling with the lives and figures
that simply refused to be contained. And yet if Du Bois's endeavor was
animated by the principle that "statistical analysis could help us gain
a concrete understanding of the social status of the African American
population," and even more, that an expansive study of black life would
"advance the cause of science more generally," the text itself regularly
stages a confrontation between Du Bois "the surveyor" and black sociality.[112] As *The Philadelphia Negro* unfolds, young women who perform
domestic labor outside the home and the larger number of lodgers living in Philadelphia's Seventh Ward turn out to be as visually obstinate

as they are methodologically mystifying. In the chapter "Size, Age, and Sex," Du Bois laments that even a seemingly rudimentary task like graphically and numerically distributing the black population according to sex and age confronts an insurmountable roadblock: "the unusual excess of females." To be sure, single, employed women were not the only part of the social body to refuse the categories of home and work carved out by the patriarchal status quo. Men also elided the kinds of domestic partnership that Victorian ideals demanded. Yet although he confidently admits that there were "a considerable number of omissions" among the mostly male class of "loafers and criminals without homes, the class of lodgers and the club-house habitues," their exclusion from the final figures is ultimately inconsequential: "These were mostly males and their inclusion would somewhat affect the division by the sexes, although probably not to a great extent," he explains. Where Du Bois could rationalize, or at least imagine, black male "loafers and criminals," he struggles to find either a statistical home or a syntactical structure to account for black women's role as either economically independent or socially defiant. As he wrestles to render what Saidiya Hartman has described as the "possibility and promise of the errant path" of black working women, Du Bois takes refuge in the footnotes.[113]

As the citational shadow to transient black men, the servant girl is the site of miscalculation and methodological mishaps. "There may have been some duplication in the counting of the servant girls who do not lodge where they work," he divulges. And while "special pains have been taken to count them only where they lodge," Du Bois admits, "there must be some errors."[114] The foundation of the error, it turned out, was the inordinate number of women who refused the arm of domestic partnership that would affix them within his carefully measured rows and columns. After all, he rationalized, "the seventh ward has a very large number of lodgers; some of these form a sort of floating population, and here were omissions; some were forgotten by landladies and others were purposefully omitted."[115] Dismissed just a few pages earlier as "unusual excess," the "floating population" of women who lodged where they work and work where they lodged, heave against Du Bois's Victorian sensibilities on gendered labor and domestic life.[116] In their production of unpredictable variables, female lodgers posed a conceptual and epistemic challenge that statistics' methodological protocols were unprepared to address. Moving from workplace to home and back again, this "floating population" traveled according to unpredictable routes, ultimately alighting beyond the boundaries of the sociological description itself. Unrestrained by either prose or table, it is only in the footnotes that Du Bois is able to perform a kind of numerical negotiation—that is, an accounting for the unaccountable—as he attempts to make sense of the excessive, the mercurial, and the morally askance.

The Philadelphia Negro is replete with moments in which its populace strains against the social study's formal limits. As do working domestics, divorced persons also trouble the categories allowed by the statistical table and moral grammar of sociology. In one especially telling moment Du Bois writes: "The number of actually divorced persons among the Negros is naturally insignificant; on the other hand, the permanent operations are large in number and an attempt has been made to count them. They do not exactly correspond to the divorce column of ordinary statistics and therefore take something from the married column. The number widowed is probably exaggerated somewhat, but even allowing for errors, the true figure is high."[117] Overwrought with qualifying modifiers, Du Bois's performance of failed statistical management instantiates a subtle critique of what he calls "ordinary statistics," allowing him to mount a case for statistical experiments, the extraordinary methods that he crafts over the course of the study. And yet it is difficult not to read his turn to the paratextual here as expressive of his Victorian moral judgment, the "gendered oldness" that Vilashini Cooppan has noted is paradoxically at the center of the "racial newness" on which Du Bois's sociology relies.[118] After all, he explains in the footnoted passage on divorce, the difficulty of counting owes to the "lax moral habits of the slave regime" that "still show themselves in a large amount of cohabitation without marriage."[119] Likewise, the line between statistical production and gendered reproduction is impossible to ignore. And yet what interests me here is how Du Bois's self-conscious attention to what cannot be enumerated, to the demand for extraordinary statistical tools that might begin to hold the surplus populations, highlights the limits of the surveyor's methodological toolkit while drawing attention to the survey's flexible formal boundaries. Du Bois ultimately allows that neither the pen nor the eye of the neutral social scientist could arrest the transient lives of the black servant girl, the lodger, or the divorcée. Conceding that within the Seventh Ward there is often more than meets the eye, Du Bois struggles to embody the surveyor who is both proximate and distant, a difficult liminality that he would describe in *The Souls of Black Folk* as the psychic experience of being in it but not of it. Peeling back the layers of black Philadelphia, Du Bois entreats readers to trust his capacity to discern and convey the truth even as he confronts the limits of his own praxis.

Although Du Bois and Miller were equally invested in the social survey and hungry for an alternative to Hoffman, when *The Philadelphia Negro* was published, Miller was curiously silent; he neither issued a review nor acknowledged the book in any public forum.[120] But if Miller was ambivalent about *The Philadelphia Negro*, he was excited about the sociologics of a different project: *Imperium in Imperio* (1899), the first novel by preacher-turned-writer Sutton Griggs. Griggs was born in Texas in 1872 and began his life following the footsteps of his father, a Baptist minister. He attended seminary before establishing himself as an editor in Richmond, Virginia, later settling in Nashville, Tennessee, where he launched his writing and publishing career. In 1899, fresh off a heated dispute with the editor of the *Richmond Planet*, Griggs published *Imperium in Imperio* with the Cincinnati-based Editor Publishing Company. As he finalized the manuscript for release, Griggs sent Miller, whom he characterized as his close friend and mentor, a copy of the book manuscript along with a request for a review. Griggs hoped that positive feedback from "one of the greatest minds that nature has given to this age" would boost sales and galvanize the black reading public.[121] Griggs's commitment to literary practice as a form of political activism was driven by the belief that cultivating a collective of like-minded, well-informed, politically active readers was key to intervening in race discourse and securing black citizenship rights. Championing the formation of a black reading public as an alternative to physical resistance ("the resort to arms") or enfranchisement (the "ballot box"), his 1902 pamphlet *The New Plan of Battle and the Man on the Firing Line* called for a "new species of warfare" fueled by black readers. In what was perhaps a nod to Miller's review of Hoffman's *Race Traits*, Griggs positions black literary militancy as the latest articulation of the political work performed by *Uncle Tom's Cabin*, that "conscience shifting" book that "turned the contempt the world had for the Negro into pity." Acknowledging the political architecture of the domestic sphere and literary representation's capacity to transform public sentiment, if only toward "pity," Griggs advocated a revolution in writing and reading, one that would shift the "scene of battle" from the public sphere to "the family fireside, where the American people are to learn from books what to think and do with regard to the Negro."[122]

Publicity and circulation were crucial to Griggs's notion of politically transformative readership. In addition to establishing his own publishing company, Griggs regularly embarked on bookselling missions, including traveling throughout the American South to reach what he understood to be an untapped demographic of readers and instantiating impressive public relations campaigns by sending his books to notable African American intellectuals like Miller. As he describes in his autobiographical pamphlet *The Story of My Struggles*, obtaining Miller's public stamp of approval would create the recognition necessary to legitimate his authorial debut. "Having secured the strong endorsement of this great character, I felt the success was assured," he recalled.[123] Ultimately, Griggs's plan floundered. *Imperium in Imperio* was a "financial failure"—sales were low, and with the exception of a few reviews, the work did not receive critical attention.[124] The book's reception in the black community was similarly tepid; it received little notice in local or national black newspapers that regularly announced new publications. Although Griggs remained active as an author and publisher—he would go on to write five more novels and countless pamphlets—*Imperium in Imperio* was out of print until its reissue in the late 1960s.

Although the public did not embrace *Imperium in Imperio*, Miller did recognize its contribution to contemporary debates surrounding the "Negro Problem" in especially sociological terms. Miller reportedly gushed, "Your book deals in a comprehensive way with all the factors of the race problem, and from the standpoint of grasp upon essential features and analytic treatment, it has no superior of its class."[125] Miller's celebratory review is an unmistakable echo of his assessment of Hoffman's *Race Traits*, which he also admitted "presents by far the most thorough and comprehensive treatment of Negro problems, from a statistical standpoint, which has yet appeared." Whereas the success of Hoffman's statistical orientation came at the expense of an integrated sociological approach that could attend to the environmental and economic roots of racial inequity, Miller's phrasing suggests that Griggs seamlessly negotiated the division between empirical information and social analysis. Perhaps convinced that this new fictional enterprise could succeed where the statistical had failed, in the months after its publication Miller invested a great deal of time promoting *Imperium in Imperio*. According to Griggs, Miller "carefully selected twenty of the more prominent Negros in public life at that time and sent to each of them a copy of the book with a request for comment upon the same."[126]

Griggs's interest in securing a public notice from Miller registers the sociological intervention that he believed the book advanced and alerts us to Griggs's place among a long tradition of African American writers whose literary work bore the imprint of social-scientific paradigms and, conversely, whose social-scientific frameworks doubled as aesthetic praxis. As Finnie Coleman and Eric Curry have detailed, *Imperium in Imperio* is an early articulation of Griggs's theory of collective efficiency, an interdisciplinary framework that draws on "sociology, history, ethics, religion, chemistry, biology, zoology, entomology and other available sources" to argue for an African American political identity grounded in a collective enterprise rather than a smattering of individual representatives.[127] In *Imperium in Imperio*, Griggs's brand of what Curry calls "liberation sociology" contributes to and revises the debates staged by uplift sociologists like Miller and Du Bois, offering a model of social advancement that rejected the myth of individualism in favor of a mode of relationality whereby "being is always being in relation to others."[128]

Although he would formally express this paradigm in his 1923 text *Guide to Racial Greatness*, *Imperium in Imperio*'s formulation as a novel that would work doubly as a social-scientific text was not entirely uncommon at the turn of the century. Postbellum African American writers regularly pitched their texts as multidisciplinary productions that could augment historiographical and social-scientific frameworks that regularly excluded African Americans. For example, the subtitle of Pauline Hopkins's 1900 novel *Contending Forces* classifies the work as a "romance," but her preface designates the "homely tale" an archive. Against the long-standing charge that African Americans lacked history, Hopkins fashioned a historical compendium, wagering that "fiction is of great value to any people as a preserver of manners and customs—religious, political, social. It is a record of growth and development from generation to generation."[129] To take *Imperium in*

Imperio seriously as liberation sociology, as a methodology that simultaneously rivals and reworks Hoffman's *Race Traits*, and as a work that, like Hopkins's, is always exceeding its genre designations, is to understand the text as more of a social survey than a novel. But it is also to ask, What sociological labor can literature perform when the very subject of sociology is black sociality and the political horizon is the production of a transformative and enlivened body of racial knowledge?

Griggs's insistence that *Imperium in Imperio* does not only bear the imprint of sociology—it *is* sociology—also resonates with Du Bois's classification of his 1911 *Quest of the Silver Fleece* as less novel than "economic study." Undoubtedly, Du Bois's phrasing is an attempt to qualify, if not dismiss, a text about which he was decidedly ambivalent. But it was none other than Alain Locke, Du Bois's eventual collaborator and the self-professed progenitor of the New Negro Renaissance, who, in deploying the term "social document fiction" to make sense of the work's generic inscrutability, unwittingly positioned *Quest* as agent of sociological critique and site at which the very meaning of social science was reshaped from a field of classification and taxonomy to a diffuse terrain open to experimentation. Locke's assessment of *Quest* appeared in the *Annals of the American Academy of Political and Social Science*'s special issue "The American Negro." Published in 1928 as what amounts to its own survey of black cultural production, the issue printed a variety of contributions, including "The American Mulatto," "Legal Aspects of the Negro Problem," and "The Color Line in Europe." In "The Negro's Contribution to American Art and Literature," Locke traversed a familiar pathway that he had carved out three years earlier in his 1925 special issue of *Survey Graphic*: "Harlem: Mecca of the New Negro." Establishing cultural and social development as interlocking domains that doubled as a clearinghouse for black contributions to American cultural life in general and racial politics in particular, he sketched a teleology of black aesthetic production that moved seamlessly from what he described as the "second rate" literature of slavery to the post-Reconstruction moment of literary recovery to the New Negro Renaissance, a flashpoint marked by the "revival of first-class artistic production."[130]

Locke was aware of the fissures threatening his forward-looking genealogy. For instance, the literature of slavery, marked by a body of African American "imitators" of European styles and norms, is at times heralded as only historically important and at other times celebrated for its aesthetic sophistication. *Quest* similarly functions as an aberration in its own right, an anomaly that disrupts the literary momentum that Locke sees turn-of-the-century black writers like Paul Laurence Dunbar and Charles Chesnutt nourishing. Yet while Dunbar and Chesnutt were refining the black literary canon, "it was in this period," Locke explains, that Du Bois and Booker T. Washington's opposing political agendas ultimately triggered an aesthetic rupture. With "the peasant cause and the mind of the Negro intellectual," painfully "estranged," aesthetic development followed suit. While those who adhered to the "dialect" school and "peasant" cause gathered around Booker T. Washington, intellectuals invested their interests in Du Bois and turned away from writers like Dunbar, whom Locke unabashedly championed, and toward Du Bois himself. Interestingly, Locke does not identify *The Souls of Black Folk* (although he does briefly gloss it) as paradigmatic of Du Bois's turn-of-the-century thinking. Rather, he pinpoints *Quest*. With support from the "majority of the talented class," he explains, Du Bois undertook a "semi-propagandist school of social document fiction, of which 'The Quest of the Silver Fleece' (1911) is representative." Locke's assessment was not entirely pejorative. For even as he cloaks the critique within what was by 1928 the well-rehearsed division between art and propaganda, Locke ultimately concedes that "this literature of assertion and protest did perform a valuable service," for it "encouraged and vindicated cultural equality, and at the price of much melodramatic sentimentalism, did induce a recovery of morale for purely cultural pursuits and self-expression."[131]

Despite the seemingly straightforward classification, as a school of literature, social document fiction is strikingly vague. Belonging neither to the world of empiricism nor to the purely literary, and collapsing melodrama with the polemical, social document fiction follows the roving path of the social survey, cutting across and reassembling literary genres, aesthetic strategies, and scientific theories. On the level of plot alone, *Quest* is a formally hybrid novel that blends meticulous accounts of cotton production and analyses of global capitalism with fantastical descriptions of conjured cotton seeds and enchanted swamps. Emerging at the intersection of economic treatise and magical realism, in *Quest*, characters like Zora, the "wayward" female protagonist, exist in defiance of what Roderick Ferguson describes as sociology's regulatory functions. "Black, and lithe, and tall, and willowy," she is a tangle of "wildness and weirdness" whose "soul seems quivering and whirring in the poetry of her motion."[132] Initially refusing to comport with performances of uplift that are expected of her, for at least the first half of the text Zora "refutes the ideals of the epistemological subject of sociology and the citizen subject of the US nation-state."[133] In Du Bois's hands, and with Zora as its guide, *Quest* exceeds the terms of either domestic fiction or plantation romance that critics have affixed to it and instead emerges as a composite form to match its heroine. In this respect, social document fiction names a genre and a methodological horizon that is attuned to what evades its disciplinary boundaries while announcing new social-scientific paradigms; or to return to Du Bois's labor in *The Philadelphia Negro*, social document fiction houses the statistically extraordinary. Rather than taking the empirical intransigence of black social life as the exception, as that which can find expression only in margins, footnotes, or methodological caveat, social document fiction names the elusive nature of facts as its very horizon.

Although Locke's literary synopsis ignores Griggs altogether, *Imperium in Imperio* could easily join *Quest* as a member of the school of social document fiction. For its part, *Imperium in Imperio* explores the nuances of intra- and interracial power dynamics in ways that mirror the social survey's logics as its eccentric plot and structure continuously stretch sociology's protocols while refusing to arrest its subject: black social life. Constructed in sketch-like chapters that carefully track the coeval relationship between structural conditions and opportunity, the book follows the political ascendance (and decline) of protagonists Belton Piedmont and Bernard Belgrave, the former black and economically disfranchised, and the latter a white-passing biracial son of a white congressman. Mobilizing the mode of comparative analysis that Morris argues is at the heart of Du Bois's and the social survey's social-scientific methodology, *Imperium in Imperio* shows Bernard breezing through Harvard to emerge as a political force, while Belton flounders to achieve the social standing that he believes his education and embrace of middle-class norms should afford him, instead confronting a relentless series of setbacks. The comparative approach illuminates the structural underpinnings of the "Negro Problem": Belton does not end up a penniless patriarch because he lacks education or is incapable of assimilating into the folds of citizenship. Rather, white supremacy's haunting presence propels Belton's unavoidable economic and social descent.

Rejecting and reworking the conventions of realism, the genre that is most often taken as literary analogue to social science, *Imperium in Imperio* bears more in common with *Quest* than it first seems. Linked by an investment in what Mark Seltzer describes as the project of "accounting for persons," realism and social science's "insistence on a compulsory and compulsive visibility" finds expression in a suite of technologies that ultimately "provide models of individualization: models for the generic, typical or average man—what we might describe as the production of individuals as statistical persons."[134] Here, the realist novel's obsession with "type" literalizes what Maeve Adams describes as social science's "epistemological preoccupation with what might be termed aggregation: namely, the classification of individual people into homogeneous groups (or aggregate wholes) defined by geographical location, occupation, and other socio-demographic features."[135] With an almost exclusive focus on intraracial dynamics, *Imperium in Imperio* departs from realism's dependence on the aggregate and dissolves the notion of a racial type, consistently puncturing the racial arithmetic that would fuel an aggregative model of race.

Registering a resistance to realism's regulatory functions, in his autobiography Griggs describes *Imperium in Imperio* simply as a "book." In their struggle to classify the work, scholars similarly echo Griggs's ambivalence, an inconsistency that indicates the work's genre-bending design. While *Imperium in Imperio* flirts with elements of melodrama, naturalism, and realism, it also touches fantasy and mystery. Two-thirds of the way through the book, Belton and Bernard's coming-of-age narrative takes a series of unexpected detours, eventually leading to the discovery of an all-black secret government in Texas, the Imperium, and the emergence of a plot to violently overthrow the US military and establish Texas as an independent black state. Even as Belton and Bernard often surface as competing types whose fates reveal the impact of social forces on their respective destinies, the work also stages disaggregating acts at every turn. That is, if realism compels life to visibility, transforming subjects into

statistical persons and working overtime as a technique of racial classification and management, then *Imperium in Imperio* drives its two
protagonists further into its recesses toward a site of political formation, the Imperium, a terrain whose success is owing to its existence
beyond a (white) disciplinary gaze. As Griggs imagines it, visibility is
not the road to subjectivity, as realism would have it. Instead, when
understood as a technique of mastery and tool of categorization, it
leads to political disintegration and social abandonment. From this
stance, the "good" that *Imperium in Imperio* generates is the demon-
stration of the social survey's transformative capacity, its ability to figure black life as multitudinous and register the social landscape a site
of dynamic interaction, a site that houses a social elsewhere.

Faulty Surfaces, Unruly Eyes

Like *The Philadelphia Negro, Imperium in Imperio* registers skepticism
about a statistical orientation and its physical embodiment, the detached observer. Yet while Du Bois adopts the posture of the surveyor
only to run directly into its limitations, Griggs summons and reworks
the social survey's perambulating observer to craft a trenchant critique
of the disinterested social-scientific eye. Although it was pitched as a
transformative visual technology and embraced as a revolutionizing
methodology, when it was put into practice, the social survey almost
always codified a disciplinarian gaze, signaling its deep relationship to
nineteenth-century technologies of surveillance—from the census
to the criminal mug shot to statistics. As Eileen Janes Yeo discloses,
"whether the view [of the observer] was up-close or panoramic," in
the context of the social survey movement, "the gaze was usually that
of people in command or aiming to be in command and the investigation was often being made for the purpose of governance."[136] Unable to wrest free of its institutional ties to reform culture's managerial
agenda, the social survey always struggled to actualize its potential.

In *Imperium in Imperio*, decoupling the observer from surveillance's
power structures and disrupting the statistical gaze's capacity for violent subjection is achieved through a conceptual and epistemological
overhaul, one that reorders the observer's perceptual faculties by de-
centralizing the place of sight in a visual economy of race. Central to

the project are social surfaces, which are reframed as dynamic sites of interaction rather than fixed boundaries that harden binary systems of identification or inflexible limits that calcify classificatory containers, and a social surveyor who approaches them with a mix of curiosity and skepticism. Equipped with a suite of sensory faculties, through *Imperium in Imperio*'s newly reconstituted observer the social survey emerges as the democratic medium that Du Bois, Miller, and Locke briefly imagined it to be. While Griggs would ultimately advance sound as a medium that could reorder visuality and generate new perceptual possibilities, this section focuses on how *Imperium in Imperio* begins to frustrate the chain of association linking sight, power, and detached observation.[137] By imagining new techniques that might engender a new kind of observer, *Imperium in Imperio* invests in reconstituting visual terrains. For even as the social survey purported to issue forth an observer who was both ambulatory and attached, his ocular-centrism ultimately rendered him at best impotent and at worst a conduit of racial management. And it is here, when we consider the degree to which *Imperium in Imperio* strives to actualize the potential of the social survey to emerge as a revisionary methodology and technology, that we can begin to understand Miller's embrace of Griggs's idiosyncratic novel.

Imperium in Imperio's visual reordering is directed through Belton, whose attempts to distinguish himself as a "man of tact, intelligence, and superior education moving in the midst of a mass of ignorant people" are perpetually frustrated by the limits of a binary-driven visual logic.[138] Staged as a series of confrontations with faulty surfaces, themselves metaphorizations of a color line that is as precarious as it is pervasive, Belton's encounters critique a racial economy that takes the visible surface as index of inner truth and signpost of racial difference. Take, for instance, an early vignette. In the opening moments of the novel, Belton's mother orchestrates a Sunday dinner for the local parson, who she hopes will offer some sage parenting advice (Belton, we discover, is receiving unwarranted punishment from his teacher on account of his darker skin and class). When Belton and his brother get wind of the invitation, they devise a "preconcerted plan" to ensure that they receive the leftovers from the highly coveted meal, which amounts to carefully watching every morsel the parson consumes. Perched in a shoddy loft above the kitchen, Belton's brother "found a little hole in the loft directly over the table, and through this hole he did his spying." Meanwhile, Belton "took his position at the larger entrance hole," poking "his head down far enough to see the preacher, but held in readiness to be snatched back, if the preacher's eyes seemed about to wander his way."[139]

Literalized as a makeshift camera obscura, the loft and its safety temporarily allow Belton and his brother to perform the role of idealized observing subjects that early visual technologies produced. Within the dark confines of a loft punctured by two imperceptible openings, the camera obscura situates the boys as "isolated, enclosed, and autonomous" observers whose physical separation from their visual subject (the preacher) by the loft's flimsy floor "decorporealiz[es] vision" and "sunder[s] the act of seeing from the physical body."[140] This brief scene is in many ways a clumsy, almost comical repetition of Harriet Jacobs's garret in *Incidents in the Life of a Slave Girl.* Jacobs's forced enclosure in an attic that is dangerously close to her captors prompts what Michael Chaney has described as "a withdrawal from the observed external world" that becomes the "precondition for an ideal type of viewing." From her hiding place, Jacobs "surveys the landscape that grounds her social and juridical subjection," ultimately reengineering the very terms of gendered freedom and fugitivity.[141] In *Imperium in Imperio*, however, the value of watching from a remove does not instantiate a perceptual and epistemological overhaul but instead produces the exact opposite effect. As the parson's meal comes to a close, the loft's floor gives way and Belton is forced into an encounter with the "external" world. As Belton tumbles into the kitchen, "the startled preacher ar[is]e[s] from the table and gaze[s] on the little fellow in bewilderment."[142] Rather than engendering a radical enactment of freedom, sustained and detached observation is structured as an impossibility, and boundaries are fashioned as loosely constructed thresholds that always threaten to give way.

In Griggs's literary world, material surfaces are not the only staging grounds for deception. Skin and photography also figure as mutually constitutive and always contingent surfaces that reveal the limits of photography's status as an indexical medium that yokes race to corporeality. Refashioned as fleshy counterparts, photographs and/as body and skin are sites of mediation and confrontation rather than pathways to unimpeachable truths. The stakes of splintering photography from skin comes into sharpest relief toward the end of the novel when Belton's wife, Antoinette, gives birth to a visibly "white" baby. Faced with what he believes is a biological impossibility (both Belton and his wife are figured with dark skin), Belton accuses Antoinette of adultery, deserts his family, and temporarily enters a career as an investigative reporter on race relations, a decision that requires him to go undercover as a female domestic, a perceptual masquerade that also troubles the putative relationship between visual perception and truth. When he reunites with his wife a decade later, Belton finds that the baby he mistook as racially white has grown into a visibly black adolescent.

Nineteenth-century African American novels are replete with scenes of racial revelation, misidentification, deception, and transformation. As Carla Peterson has shown, in postbellum historical romances like Frances Harper's 1896 *Iola Leroy*, for the "white" characters who "become" black, whether by learning of hidden black parentage or through disclosed family secrets, "blackness signifies neither color nor blood but lived experiences."[143] And as Shawn Michelle Smith maintains, for writers like Pauline Hopkins, the construction of black characters who signify as white functions to "dismantle the scientific categorization of racial difference by highlighting the contradictions in an ontological system in which 'race' is defined according to a visual epistemology that literally, and ironically, 'fails to see' what it attempts to delineate."[144] For Belton's child, "becoming black" is not so much a process of acculturation; nor does it depend on the viewer undergoing an epistemological overhaul that would instantiate a racial reckoning with the notion that the alleged fact of blackness is in fact not always expressed as such. Instead, for Belton to claim kinship with his estranged child, he must adopt a sustained and durational viewing process that is attuned to slow and often imperceptible developments, a practice closer to that of the ideal surveyor.[145]

To convince Belton, for whom skin is an undeniable index of race and familial blood lines, Antoinette reaches for none other than a family photograph album. Banking on photography's veridical status, Antoinette "rushed to her album and showed him pictures of the child taken at various stages of its growth." Looking on, he experiences a gradual racial revelation: "Belton discerned the same features in each photograph, but a different shade of color of the skin."[146] That

Antoinette did not simply reach for photographs, but a complete family album, is significant. By the end of the nineteenth century, family albums emerged at the intersection of a eugenics movement that aimed to standardize racial data and a cultural moment that positioned white mothers as arbiters of an ideal American genealogy. In each instance, the family album functioned as an evidentiary document tasked with predicting important information about biological capacity and inherited character traits. What is evidenced in the Piedmont family album, however, is skin's instability as a racial index and the photographic object's precarity as a disciplining technology. Far from affirming genealogical inheritance or proving race as a measurable biological trait, the Piedmont family album analogizes racialization as a photographic process that gains its traction with the aid of technological intervention. As it gradually develops, in this case over years, the photograph unsettles the "epistemology of perception" that Robyn Wiegman has argued "equates the racial body with blackness" and that finds material validation in photography. If skin and photography are linked together as sites of affective mediation and as the locus where racial difference is articulated, then a photographic archive in perpetual development unsettles the "visible relation that collapses social subjectivity with skin" and reveals the process by which race is affixed to the body through visual technologies.[147] Here, photography proves that race is a flexible category while the body pushes against its assigned value as stable referent. And while kinship cannot be deduced through physical similarities alone, the album does call for a sustained viewing practice, a consistent return to the photographed subject's development. Reconstituted as an ensemble of perpetually evolving surfaces, Antoinette's album unhinges the direct relationship between inner states and outer appearance that photographs would promise to codify.

Having reconstructed skin and photography as sites of mediation that neither engender a detached and idealized observer nor confirm visual economies of race, *Imperium in Imperio* reconceives perception as multisensory and issues forth an observer who is capable of realizing the social survey's potentials: the reader. Nowhere is this more clearly dramatized than in the chapter "On the Dissecting Board," a harrowing description of Belton's interrupted attempt to teach at a black Southern school. As the chapter opens, Belton is a recent college graduate who leaves behind his rural Southern upbringing and commits to educating the black "masses." An embodiment of what race reformers like Miller and Du Bois would variously embrace as a "self-help component" of uplift politics, Belton is committed to "rehabilitat[ing] the race's image by embodying respectability enacted through an ethos of service to the masses, and projecting the style and comportment of the middle class."[148] As he commences his journey, Belton's efforts appear to pay off. Smartly dressed in a new suit, he purchases a first-class ticket to board a train for his teaching post in the town of Cadeville, Louisiana, where he will personally undertake what Kevin Gaines describes as uplift's work of "reform[ing] the character and manag[ing] the behavior of blacks" himself.[149]

If Belton performs uplift politics, then despite steadily progressing toward the black middle class, where he would ostensibly claim his place among Du Bois's talented tenth, he lacks the racial awareness that is at once a historical problematic and a condition of possibility for black America—or, he lacks "double consciousness." In Du Bois's famous formulation, double consciousness is the traumatic psychic disruption that emerges at the scene of violent racial misrecognition when one is forced to reconcile self-image with a distorted image of a racialized self reflected through the eyes of whites. Or, as Du Bois explains in no uncertain terms, "this sense of always looking at oneself through the eyes of others."[150] The scene of gross (mis)recognition instantiates an irreparable fracture that incubates racial consciousness. Importantly, for Du Bois, double consciousness is a birthright that, along with the "veil," is "gifted" to every black person in "this American world," engendering a heightened sense of self, a self that is always doubled, always split. Following this line of thinking into *Imperium in Imperio*, double consciousness would not only invest Belton with a nuanced racial sensibility (of how he is seen through the eyes of others). In its fullest expression, double consciousness would also cultivate new visual epistemologies altogether, that is, new frameworks through which race is perceived and valued. Despite moving toward the black middle class, which presumably requires a racial reckoning with the color line and activates double consciousness, Belton remains perceptually stilted. Even as he relentlessly encounters the color line—first as a student in the elementary school, a site that Du Bois marks as a natal scene of racialization—Belton fails to conceive of himself as both a seeing subject and a racial object. Instead, he falsely understands himself as a psychically sutured individual who can go toe-to-toe with other middle-class (white) subjects. Throughout his journey as a highly dramatized black middle-class subject who nevertheless lacks double consciousness, Belton cannot perceive how he is being seen, and he remains blind to the way that his own performances of middle-class respectability reproduce the dehumanizing workings of racism through the terms of class differentiation.

But Belton's train ride is not simply a critique of what Gaines describes as the philosophical and ideological constraints of uplift ideology, its inability to "disrupt the racial and economic status quo" or reimagine patriarchal driven values.[151] On the contrary, and still more complex, the series of visual encounters between Belton, the material world, and various technologies of mediation—namely, train and newspaper—on his trip articulates the deadly consequence of refusing to adopt an expansive notion of what it means both to see and to be seen. During the train ride he sits "quietly reading a newspaper," and "now and then he would look out of the window at the pine tree forest near the track" and the ditch of muddy water that ran next to the train.[152] Although he sees and reads, Belton's perspective is blunted so that his momentary glances fail to register for him the reality of his surroundings, and he never quite actualizes as a savvy seeing subject. He, for instance, fails to perceive his body as threatening to the whites on the train, and he ignores the ghostly violence haunting the "pine tree forest" and the newspaper, sites that carry the specter of lynching and racial violence. The stakes of Belton's narrow viewing practice, of refusing to comport with his assigned role in the theater of racial gazes, are immediately apparent. From the moment he boards the train, Belton confronts the realities of Jim Crow segregation, and in a familiar trope that repeats across postbellum African American literature, he is required to give up his ticketed seat and move to the train's "colored" section. When Belton refuses to relocate from the first-class car, he is violently removed by a group of white passenger-vigilantes who throw him from the train and into a ditch. Enveloped in mud, he is symbolically and physically reinstated to his place within a racial hierarchy. Importantly, his refusal to comply with social custom is not due to sheer ignorance; nor is his decision to sit in the first-class car explicit protest. Rather, Belton's social transgression registers the limits of his uncritical investment in performances of personhood that are organized around binary relationships—self and other, subject and object, interior and exterior—and their capacity to confer subjectivity and recognition by the state as citizen. That is, if double consciousness names a psychic and social fracture, an irresolvable and productive split between how one sees oneself and how one is perceived by others, then Belton overcommits to middle-class comportment's (education, suits, and a first-class seat) capacity to redress the negative image of blackness.

As a character whose psychological fragmentation comes to bear violently on his status as a failed seeing subject, Belton invites us to return to terms of black subjectivity and visuality that Du Bois first theorizes as double consciousness in his 1897 essay "Strivings of the Negro People." In 1903, the essay would reappear as the opening chapter to *The Souls of Black Folk*. The original publication date is important here because it draws a line of connection between the theory of double consciousness, *Imperium in Imperio*, and visuality that have thus far gone largely unnoticed. Although the relationship between double consciousness and *Imperium in Imperio* remains undertheorized, scholars *have* routed their discussion of double consciousness and visuality through visual paradigms, namely the veil. Shawn Michelle Smith, for instance, argues that the "veil functions as a cultural screen on which the collective weight of white misconceptions is fortified and made manifest," a scrim that, in enabling blacks to see how whites perceive them, produces a heightened self-awareness that is the bedrock of double consciousness.[153] Just as the veil mediates the pathway to double consciousness, it also "produces a vision that pierces the structures of racism construed as the natural order of things."[154] But if the veil shatters racial hierarchy and fortifies double consciousness, then we must also ask what it means to approach the veil as a supple interface that can yield new racial vistas.

Throughout "Strivings of the Negro People" and *The Souls of Black Folk*, the veil is multidimensional, tactile, and itinerant. In its preface and first chapter alone, it is alternately figured as a cavernous terrain ("I have stepped within the Veil, raising it that you may view faintly its deeper recesses"), a dividing line separating "two worlds" (those "within and without"), and a porous boundary that one could either "creep through," "tear down," or "rise above."[155] Black Americans alternately shroud themselves in the veil, move within and above the veil, and are enveloped by the veil, postures that collectively yield a birthright that engenders a particularly black viewing practice. By highlighting the flexibility of metaphor, I do not mean to diminish the power or utility of Du Bois's formulation. Nor am I interested in trying to concretize the veil, a concept that derives its power from its mercurial nature. Instead, by drawing out the multiple iterations of the veil, I highlight the full range of its metaphoric force. Like the surface politics that the social survey calls forth, the veil is a site of interface, a threshold of mediation like the photograph and/as skin. And although it refracts vision, it promises neither a concrete outline nor a secure boundary. Notwithstanding its protean nature, in the hands of the black middle class, actualizing double consciousness vis-à-vis the veil was posited as an avenue by which blacks could leave their status as observed objects and become observers themselves.[156] A kind of exit strategy, the veil is figured as a pathway to transcend the violent terrain of racialization. Indeed, it is from above the veil that in the opening moments of *The Souls of Black Folk*, Du Bois describes being able to achieve a semblance of peace: "I had thereafter no desire to tear down that veil, to creep through; I held all beyond it in common contempt, and lived above it in a region of blue sky and great wandering shadows. That sky was bluest when I could beat my mates at examination-time, or beat them at a foot-race, or even beat their stringy heads."[157] Staking out a similar position, in her reading of the middle-class photographic albums that Du Bois assembled for the 1900 Paris Exposition as counterarchives, Smith argues that insofar as they reverse the disciplining gaze of white supremacy, the photographs of men, women, and black institutional life collectively materialize the "gift of the veil." What concerns me here is how these readings reify the construction of a world that is authorized by the figure of the authoritative spectator and ultimately legitimates a binary logic whereby reversing the gaze or looking back secure black personhood.[158] And although Du Bois's photographic labor, especially the albums for the 1900 Paris Exposition, is positioned as the material manifestation of the veil's racial epistemology, the flexible and multidimensional aspects of the veil align more closely with a technology like the survey.

As it experiments with the possibilities for social (re)formation produced by a dynamic conceptualization of the veil, *Imperium in Im-*

perio directs us toward a view of the social that might come into focus when something like the survey's ideal observer manifests. And yet, as long as Belton subscribes to the myth of a visually legible liberal subject, envisioning clothes and comportment as a sheath that simultaneously protects him from the violent gaze of whites and separates him from the masses whom he plans to teach, he is also ripe for the violent and disciplining gaze; that is, he has bought into a visual economy that will always devalue him.

In this moment, Griggs metaphorizes the unavoidable epistemic violence wrought by the gaze as the physical dissection enacted by the mob of white vigilantes turned race scientists. After being thrown from the train and extracting himself from the ditch, Belton finally arrives in Cadeville to assume his teaching post. Belton's social transgression on the train, however, triggers a band of white vigilantes, the "N——r Rulers," who commit to recalibrating the racial logic that Belton temporarily disturbed. Led by the town's local physician, Dr. Zackland, members of the mob insist that Belton is "the finest looking darkey I ever put my eye on." In what is undoubtedly a nod to the violent and dehumanizing lineage of race science and the emergence of anatomy as a field—which itself negatively calibrated racial perception—Dr. Zackland offers "one of the finest kegs of whiskey in [his] cellar" to anyone who will help him "get his body to dissect."[159] With an obsessive desire to gain possession of Belton, the mob places him under strict surveillance so that any small transgression of Southern custom is grounds for lynching and dissection. Thus, when Belton attempts to help a white woman in church find a passage in a hymnbook, his actions are deemed an irredeemable repudiation of Southern custom and he is ordered to be hanged, shot once in the head, and then taken down for bodily dissection.

In *Imperium in Imperio*, the lynching is carried out but Belton survives. Nonetheless, he is taken for dead and they enthusiastically proceed with the plans to dissect him. While surgical operation would typically confirm the racialized power dynamic by compelling Belton's interior to visibility and inspection, the project is disrupted in a dramatic series of events:

Dr. Zackland came to the table and looked down on Belton with a happy smile. To have such a robust, well-formed, handsome nigger to dissect and examine he regarded as one of the greatest boons of his medical career. Belton had now returned to consciousness but kept his eyes closed, thinking it best to feign death. Dr. Zackland cut off the hair in the neighborhood of the wound in the rear of Belton's head and began cutting the skin, trying to trace the bullet. Belton did not wince. "The nigger is dead or else he would show some sign of life. But I will try pricking his palm." This was done, but while the pain was exceedingly excruciating, Belton showed no sign of feeling.[160]

Like the flimsy loft floor and the steadily developing photographs, Belton's skin is contextualized as a porous surface that fails to delimit life from death. Instead of functioning as the occasion for racial recognition, as in Frantz Fanon's theorization of epidermal schema, or confirming the boundary between interiority and exteriority, the skin refuses to yield to the eye's demands for bodily knowledge. Unable to produce scientific information or reconfirm a eugenicist's logic of racial inferiority, Belton's skin is an obfuscating surface that frustrates the doctor's objectifying operations (visual and physical). While Dr. Zackland misreads Belton's body, falling into the statistical trap that equates black life with social death, Belton reverses the scene of violence, jumping up from the table and murdering his assailant. Presaging and reworking Fanon's formulation of the visual sphere as site of evisceration and atomization—"the white gaze, the only valid one, is already dissecting me, I am fixed," he writes—Belton's near-deadly encounter stages the violence of the visual economy only to insist that black life is, to borrow from Hortense Spillers, entirely irreducible to flesh.[161]

One way of reading Belton's visual trials is as a mode of indoctrinating readers into the perceptual terrain of the social survey, one that Griggs, Miller, and Du Bois understood to be crucial to visualizing the vicissitudes of black life and to approaching a new social and political order. By staging Belton's persistent and erroneous encounters with surfaces, *Imperium in Imperio* generates a readerly practice that is akin to surveying. By the end of the novel, the stakes of this outlook are taken up quite explicitly. In the final chapters Griggs assembles Belton and Bernard in the Imperio, an all-black secret government that remains intransigent to the white gaze and imperceptible to the general public. If the social survey could direct the reader's perspective beyond the visible world, producing "wide revelations and vivid pictures of things previously unknown," to recall Carl Taylor's phrasing, without restoring a binary logic, then perhaps surveying would perceive an autonomous black nation-state. Impervious to the extractive procedures and processes, whether visual or economic, it is here that Belton is at least temporarily restored to wholeness. I discuss the social and political architecture of the Imperium in chapter 2, but for now I draw our attention to its status as a social world that is at once highly visible and entirely opaque to the trained observer. Located in Waco, Texas, the Imperium is "another government, complete in every detail, exercising the sovereign right of life and death over its subjects" that "has been organized and maintained within the United States for many years." Its longevity is matched by its size. "This government," Bernard explains, "has a population of seven million two hundred and fifty thousand."[162] The wonder is not so much that the Imperium exists, but that it has never been discovered. A kind of political horizon that comes into focus when the observer is reconfigured according the social survey's idealized logic, the Imperium emerges as a geographic otherwise, a version of black sociality that could emerge under a new visual regime.

Everywhere and Nowhere: The Social Survey's Nongeography

Figures like Kelly Miller, W. E. B. Du Bois, and Sutton Griggs confronted the social survey's capacity to document social life and, in the case of Griggs, tried to imagine the racial, political, and formal payoff that an actualized social survey could engender. The remainder of this chapter takes up two seemingly "traditional" social surveys to show how even as they express moralizing outlooks, both "The Negro in the Cities of the North" and *Survey Graphic*'s 1925 special issue "Harlem: Mecca of the New Negro" articulate a black geographic and social elsewhere. Moving in this direction means attending to the institutional fractures and the ideological flexibility undergirding progressive reform agendas in general and the social survey in particular. If the social survey was form and method, technology and outlook, then it was also, to return to Taylor's assessment, a "spirit" whose power is most forcefully felt when the survey's constitutive elements break down and reassert themselves. This was certainly the case with *Imperium in Imperio*. But perhaps counterintuitively, the sites that appear to be formalized expressions of the social survey are where its status as a bureaucratic tool of social management is, in the face of black life, unsettled and remade. When read with the survey spirit in mind, "The

Negro in the Cities of the North" and "Harlem: Mecca of the New Negro" register an unmappable racial imaginary and an intractable modern black subject, one whom Locke would christen the "New Negro."
What is "traditional" about these works' status as social surveys is not
their institutional backing, as we will see, but their capacity to unsettle
the putative relationship of race, visuality, and data.

On June 17, 1905, Paul Kellogg wrote to Du Bois outlining his plan
for "The Negro in the Cities of the North." After negotiating deadlines
and fees for weeks on end, Du Bois finally agreed to submit an essay on "the subject of citizenship in Philadelphia" for payment of fifty
dollars.[163] Four months and countless deadline extensions later, the
special issue was set to appear in October. As the publication deadline
loomed, Kellogg was justifiably nervous. Just two years earlier Kellogg had joined *Charities'* staff as assistant editor. Within months of
his appointment, the magazine transformed from a practical resource
for social workers and progressive reformers to a visually appealing
publication committed to exposing and investigating social issues.
Pitched to a broadened reading public, *Charities* incorporated photographs, drawings, a reader-friendly font, and features like letter to
the editor, which led to a spike in sales and circulation. As a part of its
rebranding, in 1904 *Charities* introduced a series of "special numbers"
focused on "ethnic" life in America. The series began with "The Italian
in America" and "The Slav in America." But it was "The Negro in the
Cities of the North" that set new publication records, with ninety-six
pages and a print run of three thousand.[164]

"The Negro in the Cities of the North" reflects a discursive shift
characterizing early twentieth-century debates about the "Negro
Problem." Increasingly dissatisfied with Darwinist arguments about
black inferiority, race theorists began to replace their biologically
driven claims with cultural ones. With its focus on the environment's
impact on racial degeneracy (and by extension, morality) from the al-
leys of Washington, DC, to the experimental settlements of the South,
the special number boldly entered the debate, marking what Muhammad describes as "the moment when the North officially became
the universally accepted proving ground of African American fitness
for citizenship in modern America."[165] While the turn to culture registered a disciplinary reorientation (as the century wore on, Franz
Boas would emerge as the leading proponent of what would become

known as the culture concept), it also indexed the reality that by 1905 the "Negro Problem" remained as opaque as ever. Kellogg's answer was, at least on the surface, to collate an impressive roster of theorists and activists, including Boas, Booker T. Washington, Fannie Barrier Williams, and James Weldon Johnson, who together would offer a well-rounded view of the "problem." Progressives' inability to reach consensus on how to approach and "solve" the problem of free black life was mirrored in *Charities'* own amorphous outlook. The editors of the issue explained, "In this special number of Charities devoted from cover to cover to the social interests of the Negroes in the northern cities, it has not been attempted to study exhaustively any one locality, or to cover the whole country in even a restricted statistical inquiry." Eschewing an extensive investigation and sustained research, the issue favored sweeping outlooks and broad outlines. "It has been sought rather to afford a suggestive survey of the common situation," the editors concluded.[166]

Yet before its editors would stitch together an ensemble of black intellectuals, reformers, and social workers to attest to the promises and perils of black life in the North, Kellogg drafted an outline that reveals an understudied ambition of the special issue. As he explained in his pitch to Du Bois, the demand for an updated analysis on the "Negro Problem" went beyond a responsibility to account for the shift from biology to culture: there was simply a dearth of thorough, nuanced research about black life outside of the South. With the exception of Du Bois's own *The Philadelphia Negro*, which would go unrivaled for decades, and Lillian Brant's study of black St. Louis, Kellogg admitted that "the suggestion has been made that in the various discussions of the Southern situation, the needs and advance of the Negro in the Northern cities has been overlooked." By "publish[ing] several brief articles taking up special phases of the situation in given cities, and also special lines of work; these largely by representative Negros," the issue, he maintained, would provide a "survey of the ground to see what changes have followed since your more elaborate study."[167] Expanding its geographic focus and zeroing in on patterns of migration from North to South, but also from South to North, Kellogg sketched an aspirational table of contents with essays tackling topics like "industrial opportunities, from Boston," "the women and the home, from New York," and "social organizations from Chicago."[168]

When Kellogg wrote to Du Bois, he was on the brink of directing a large-scale social survey in Pittsburgh that would ultimately publish its findings as *The Pittsburgh Survey*. In terms of technique and form, Kellogg's work in Pittsburgh would become emblematic of the social survey movement and the social survey. The culmination of three years of research, investigation, and community organizing, the findings and recommendations were collated in six illustrated volumes. Yet "The Negro in the Cities of the North" was quite different from the Pittsburgh project; it also dramatically diverged from the works by Du Bois and Brandt that Kellogg identified as its antecedents. Most notably, rather than focusing on a single location, the 1905 issue offered an in-depth look at a single demographic—black Americans. And while the title suggests that the social problem under study would be black life in the North, the issue ultimately addressed a swath of progressive hot-button issues, including urbanization, rural education, and new theories of cultural anthropology. If the eclecticism of the *Charities* number is out of step with the issue's professed goals, then a closer look at Kellogg's vision sheds light on the publication's curious contours. For as he shared with Du Bois, Kellogg's model for the issue was not Booth, Addams, or even Du Bois's social surveys. Instead, Kellogg sought inspiration from the African American poet Paul Laurence Dunbar.

Just after outlining the publication timeline, Kellogg offered Du Bois insight into the creative inspiration behind the issue: "I was reading some sketches by Paul Lawrence [*sic*] Dunbar, which have been brought out under the title 'Happy Hollow,' and in its preface the poet defines Happy Hollow as any community north and south in which Negros are neighbors one to the other, and in which the characteristics of their community life find play." "As this is the subject of our number," he continued, "it occurred to me that possibly Mr. Dunbar would be interested in the issue—perhaps to the extent of contributing a stanza or two, bringing out the same idea of his preface, in verse? Do you think he would?"[169] Du Bois responded enthusiastically and encouraged Kellogg to reach out to Dunbar: "I think Mr. Dunbar would be glad to cooperate with you." Evidently, Dunbar did not end up contributing to the issue. Yet Kellogg's decision to seek a rubric in a series of fictional black sketches deserves further pause.

In his synopsis of *The Heart of Happy Hollow*, Kellogg gets Dunbar's phrasing slightly wrong. Published just one year earlier, Dunbar prefaces his collection with a query that anticipates readers' desire to geographically locate black life while also refusing to fulfill that very desire: "Happy Hollow; are you wondering where it is? Wherever Negros colonies in the cities or the villages, north or south, wherever the hod carrier, the porter, and the waiter are the society men of the town . . . there—there—is Happy Hollow."[170] As Dunbar imagines it, Happy Hollow is less a real place than an unmappable cartography. Neither urban nor rural, Happy Hollow "announces its intent to destabilize symbolic geographies that polarize North and South," explains Andrea Williams.[171] In locating Happy Hollow everywhere and nowhere—or wherever black folks are—Dunbar relies on the strategy "of orienting and disorienting readers to black Americans and their lived experiences in order to move beyond fanciful characterization that his stories appear to offer."[172] Mobilizing an outlook that he perfected in his well-known poem "We Wear the Mask," Dunbar exploits readers' willingness to approach blackness as a knowable entity only to reveal that, at best, blackness is a practice rooted in the persistent evasion of expectations, in the process of perpetual unmasking. What Kellogg describes, then, as Dunbar's capacity to capture the site at which "black community life finds play" is an apt description of his uncanny ability to render black sociality as a network of relations that are always in dynamic relation to each other and always exceeding a social-scientific gaze.

When he suggested Dunbar's sketches as a model for the special issue, Kellogg was likely hoping to emulate the notes of authenticity for which Dunbar is most often read. Yet his phrasing has the unintended consequence of structuring an issue in which a motley masthead and conflicting reformist visions cohered into disorienting perspectives that opened avenues for perceiving alternative (non)statistical realities while affirming literature's capacity to do some social work. And yet the social labor that the 1905 issue performed was not in the name of advancing the ethos of "cross-class affiliation and repair," which Laura Fisher spotlights as fundamental to the Progressive Era's literary agenda. Rather, what emerged was an elsewhere that surfaced at the intersection of the Happy Hollow's world of imaginary play and the Imperium's radical opacity, a location that strained the systems of order and measurement demanded by traditional geography. The issue's editorial, for instance, railed against what it termed the trend toward "statistical generalization," or statistics' tendency to reduce individual cases into an undifferentiated mass. In an explicit nod to Hoffman, statistical generalization was charged with fueling the "more bitter elements of the race," which tended to reduce the "Negro Problem" to a sectional issue that neither North nor South wanted to claim.[173] In its place, the issue offered an idiosyncratic tapestry of case studies, sociological sketches, photographs, and economic reportage.

To be sure, from the Happy Hollow's elsewhere, "The Negro in the Cities of the North" paints a generally bleak portrait of black life in Northern cities. Drafted by social workers and reformers, contributions like "Mission Sketches" offered admittedly narrow sketches of New York tenements. Working within literary conventions of the case study, the sketches depict a broad cast of characters that, though "interesting," nevertheless "squander" their potential in "nests of disorder" and immorality.[174] Striking a similar chord, the essay "Social Settlement in Washington" links the prevalence of "adult delinquency" to the "bouts of meager, stinted, childhood existence" among the nation's highest concentrations of African Americans.[175] Such hopeless condemnations, however, are juxtaposed to celebrations of African American cultural and institutional contributions, such as James Weldon Johnson's "The Negro of To-Day in Music" and L. M. Hershaw's "The Negro Press in America."

The issue's ideological whiplash coheres in the final contribution, Thomas Jesse Jones's "In the Country at Large." In contrast to the issue's opener, a polemic against statistics, Jones's punctuating essay is patently statistical. As it reprints charts and graphics by Du Bois and the statistician W. F. Wilcox, the essay seems to offer an empirical justification for and visual display of the issue's claims. However, instead of legitimating warnings about moral decay, Jones undercuts the project's argumentative force. Cautioning against the impulse to read the preceding character sketches and institutional analyses as typical, Jones offers a corrective statistical reading, suggesting that "a statement of some of the more important facts discovered by the twelfth census may serve to correct any tendency to generalize from the urban conditions presented in this series of articles."[176] As it turns out, Jones concludes that *Charities* has trained its focus in the wrong direction. After all, the census data show a large concentration of "Negros in the

South over the North." Moreover, if conditions in the South were any indication, Jones continues, black life was thriving. Although Jones concedes that his data visualizations are not comprehensive—"the chart does not show the quality or efficiency of colored labor"—he does afford a positive conclusion: in the main, "a commendable percentage of the race is engaged in gainful occupations."[177]

On the one hand, Jones's statistical denouement makes the entire issue an unreliable experiment in social surveying. On the other hand, we might read the issue as instruction in how to responsibly read (or in this case, not read) racial data. In other words, the graphics and analysis emerge as accurate only in the context of the reading practice that the issue has habituated, one that requires moving across genres, geographies, and political views, or what Dunbar describes as the site of play. The social survey's composite nature thus encourages a nimble reading strategy, also not unlike the one espoused by Griggs. The presumed focus on breadth over granular details of black life encompasses the "plexus" of problems that Du Bois argued were obscured by normative sociological methods. In its capacity to hold competing positions, at least in theory, the social survey could desediment "the Negro" as a knowable subject while promoting a habit of sight that privileged a surface view over deep penetration. In turn, the designations of the city and the rural South, like Dunbar's Happy Hollow, are also geographically bankrupt fictions.

That the social survey would always, even despite its best editorial efforts, render a vague and fuzzy outline, a picture that was "wide and deep" and a social landscape that was fundamentally a site of dynamic play, invites us to return to what is perhaps the best-known survey, *Survey Graphic*'s wildly popular March 1925 special issue "Harlem: Mecca of the New Negro," also known as the "Harlem number." In its well-known origin story, the 1925 special issue was the fortuitous outcome of the 1924 *Opportunity* magazine dinner party, a gathering that merged black literary elite and white publishing powerhouses. At the dinner, Kellogg, then editor of *Survey Graphic*, invited both Locke and Charles Johnson, editor of *Opportunity* magazine, to edit a special issue, perhaps in an attempt to course correct the 1905 issue. In the end, Locke was the sole editorial voice. The final issue was *Survey Graphic*'s most popular one, and the publication that would cement Locke's self-professed standing as the midwife of the New Negro Renaissance.

From its opening notes, Alain Locke leveled an attack against statistics. In a resounding echo of Kelly Miller's rebuke of Hoffman and Sutton Griggs's implicit call for a "new" kind of observer, Locke's denigration of statistics as a regressive analytical technique confirms the social survey's unwritten history as a tool of sociological dissent and the incubator of aesthetic experimentation. Harlem, he explained in the issue's introductory essay of the same name, was far more than geographic location or cultural destination for Manhattan's white pleasure seekers. As a site energized at once by "fighting advocates, inner spokesmen, poets, artists, and social prophets"; "the fluid and ambitious youth"; and the "migrant masses" steadily arriving from the South, Harlem symbolized a crisis in knowledge production.[178] For even as "professional observers," who Locke insisted simply could not perceive black social life, remained curious about the "physics and movement" defining the "new generation," they were "largely unaware of the psychology of it, of the galvanizing shocks and reactions, which mark the social awakening and internal reorganization which are making a race out of its own disunited elements."[179]

If Locke somewhat passively celebrated psychology and physics as two branches of the sciences that were better equipped to theorize modern black living, then just pages later he refined his charge and shored up his targets. If "professional observers" were missing the dynamism of modern black life, then statistics were the culprit. In the now-famous first lines of "Enter the New Negro," Locke extolled:

> In the last decade something beyond the watch and guard of statistics has happened in the life of the American Negro and the three norns who have traditionally presided over the Negro Problem have a changeling in their laps. The Sociologist, The Philanthropist, and The Race Leader are not unaware of the Negro Problem but they are at a loss to account for him. He simply cannot be swathed in their formula. For the younger generation is vibrant with a new psychology; the new spirit is awake in the masses, and under the very eyes of the professional observers is transforming what has been a perennial problem into the progressive phases of contemporary Negro life.[180]

Locke's opening salvo returns us to the very actors with whom I began the chapter, like Du Bois and Miller, who endured through the late nineteenth and early twentieth centuries and dominated debates on racial futures. Armed with a toolkit that Locke dismissed as equivalent to a technology of discipline and surveillance that both watched and kept guard, social scientists, reformers, and activists were simply ill equipped to perceive the watershed transpiring among the "younger generation." Identifying the very limit that *The Philadelphia Negro* staged and that the 1905 special issue encountered, Locke submits that a statistical orientation could not apprehend the spirit, artistry, or political inclinations of the "New Negro." Extending the critique of professional observers and their targets that he announced in "Harlem," in "Enter the New Negro" Locke clarifies statistical operations' status as a visual technology that obfuscates the burgeoning race consciousness. Shifting his focus to that which remained opaque to statistics, on the forms of life and art taking form beyond the statistician's narrow gaze, Locke called for a perceptual overhaul and a renovated relationship between data regimes and black life. Equipped with a perspective akin to a pair of "dusty spectacles," the professional observers who had tirelessly labored to distill the "Negro Problem," he argued, were missing the contemporary phase of progressive modern black life.

Locke's prefatory essays were certainly intended to distinguish the Harlem issue from a previous generation of social-scientific and reform journals. In the early 1920s, *Opportunity*, the official organ of the National Urban League, was leading this charge. Helmed by Locke's sometimes collaborator Charles Johnson, *Opportunity*, writes Anne Elizabeth Carroll, mobilized "strategies of representation common in sociology and social work to provide persuasive information about African Americans."[181] Building on the deep lines of affiliation linking reform, race relations, and sociological methodology, *Opportunity* began from the premise that "facts and information can challenge assumptions and change actions."[182] In contrast, Locke's editorial experiment privileged the nebulous terrain of psychology and spirit, fields and abstract areas that signaled a new modern black subject and promised to celebrate both material and nonmaterial gifts. While his critique of the sociologist, race leader, and reformer was in part targeted at their single-minded commitment to empiricism, he also renders these figures inefficient observers "embedded within a system of [disciplinary] conventions and [methodological] limitations" that would always produce a stilted portrait of black life.[183] But if Locke was both seeking and announcing a radical break from a previous mode of doing social work, how can we understand his decision to stage this charge in the pages of a social survey? After all, even as the social survey purported to offer insights into untrammeled social terrains while preserving the vitality of the social landscape, far too often its aspirations collapsed under the weighty desire of progressives' demand for social regulation through detached observation and a relentless appetite for objective racial data, the very aims that Locke derided.

While the role of the survey has been sidestepped, critics have long celebrated the Harlem issue as a transformative moment in black literary arts. Focusing largely on its status as the precursor to Locke's 1925 anthology *The New Negro*, Barbara Foley, George Hutchinson, and Jeremy Braddock, among others, have tracked the lines of continuity and divergence between the two texts.[184] In what remains one of the most incisive scholarly treatments of the Harlem issue, Foley's *Spectres of 1919* meticulously uncovers the changes between "Harlem of the New Negro" and *The New Negro*, arguing that Locke's own shifting politics are reflected in the editorial decisions and directions that set the two works apart. Yet within these literary and cultural histories, while *Survey Graphic*'s institutional history is glossed, its conceptual and experimental roots remain uninterrogated.[185] As a result, the publication emerges in the history of the black literary arts as little more than a necessary stepping-stone toward the publication of *The New Negro*. When its institutional affiliations do get unfurled, both *Survey Graphic* and Kellogg are characterized as burdensome constraints that required nonstop negotiation. In his recent biography of Locke, Jeffrey Stewart draws out a protracted publication timeline that owed as much to Locke's fickle relationship with would-be contributors and missed deadlines as it did to the difficulty of using a white publication to announce a black social and artistic moment. He asks, "How was Locke going to represent the bubbling racial self-assertiveness of young, Black writers in a magazine whose editorial staff did not want to be known afterward as the voice of militancy or social equality?"[186] To offset Kellogg's commitment to a racially palatable issue that celebrated assimilation over separatism and that privileged sociologically inflected contributions over either aesthetic or anthropologically oriented ones, Locke had to constantly perform editorial interventions. Spotlighting the slippery deployment of the racial type throughout the issue, a standard tool in *Survey Graphic*'s reporting repertoire, Martha Jane Nadell asserts that Locke "seemed to find the patterns of the magazine constricting. Perhaps he found its bias toward the documentary and its claims of accuracy limited, not 'new' enough to get at the core of the New Negro."[187] Where contributors like Charles Johnson, she suggests, refused to collapse African Americans into single racial type, insisting that black Harlemites "defy classification," the issue's inclusion of a series of racial "types" sketched by the German artist Winold Riess threatened to undercut that very supposition. Against such contradictions, Locke used the introductory essays to push "against the pre-established form of the social survey."[188] But what would it mean to approach the survey as a condition of possibility rather than a mere constraint?

The Harlem number's institutional ties to the social survey are impossible to overlook. *Survey Graphic* was, after all, a direct descendant of the American social survey movement and a favored tool of Progressive Era social scientists, the very class of race theorists whom Locke dismissed. When it hit stands in 1921, it was billed as an illustrated "experiment in social interpretation."[189] With its high-gloss color photographs, the monthly publication was designed to augment *Survey*'s weekly publication and appeal to a broader, nonspecialized public. By 1925 *Survey Graphic* emerged as a successful magazine that "provide[d] educated, upper-middle-class urban readers" with "graphic" portraits of issues faced by the public.[190] Before the Harlem issue's release, for instance, *Survey Graphic* published special issues on "Gypsies" and Mexicans, topics that resonate with the early twentieth-century social survey movement's belief that illuminating the "facts" was a pathway to mutual understanding and reform. The Harlem number's overlap with the social survey movement was more than simply thematic. Even as *Survey Graphic* was promoted as a departure from the kind of Progressive Era social-scientific rigor characterizing its sister publication *Survey*, its link to the social survey movement is undeniable. *Survey Graphic* was a descendant of *New York Charities Review*, a philanthropically driven publication that reported on the activities of the New York Charities Organization, one of the city's largest reform agencies and the meeting point for leading reformers like Mary White Ovington, Fannie Barrier Williams, and Jane Addams. In 1901 *New York Charities Review* merged with *Lend a Hand*, Edward E. Hales's monthly "journal of organized charity" before absorbing two more publications, *Commons* and *Jewish Charity*. In 1904 the publication was rebranded once again, this time as *Charities*. In this instantiation the journal's longtime editor Edward Devine hired Paul Kellogg and Arthur Kellogg as assistant editors. Finally, in 1909 and under the editorial leadership of the Kellogg brothers, *Charities and the Commons* was rechristened as *Survey*. During this time Paul Kellogg solidified his personal relationship to the social survey movement, culminating in the published series *The Pittsburgh Survey*.

It is easy to read this genealogy as evidence of a deeply codified sociological terrain that Locke had to navigate and negotiate in order to forward a "new" and modern black subject. But might it also be that Locke's argument could manifest only on the pages of a social survey? What if Locke did not need to push against the form of the social survey but harnessed it as the rubric for the New Negro and his or her aesthetic? To think of the survey and the New Negro's consonance is to consider the overlaps between the survey spirit and what Locke describes as the spirt of modern black life. In both "Harlem" and "Enter the New Negro," the "younger generation" is defined by movement that is psychological and spiritual. Shifting attention away from the material toward the immaterial, Locke's theory revises the outdated views of students of the "Negro Problem" who understand black migration solely as a reaction to outward manifestations of white supremacy or economic factors. "The tide of Negro migration, northward or city-ward, is not to be fully explained as a blind flood started by the demands of war industry coupled with the shutting off of foreign migration, or by the pressure of poor crops coupled with increased social terrorism in certain sections of the South and Southwest," he explained. Likewise, Locke continues, "neither labor demand, the bollweevil nor the Ku Klux Klan is a basic factor, however contributory any or all of them may have been." Replacing the visual iconography of black migrants arriving in the North with blackness's incalculable, amorphous deluge, Locke offers the "new spirit" as the impetus for the "wash and rush of this human tide on the beach line of the northern city centers."[191] Drawn together from across the globe and attracted to Harlem and to one another by "common consciousness," and not "common condition," the "Negro Community," Locke argues, is compelled by a newly awakened sense of "self-determination." Importantly, the scene of racial awakening and the northward trajectory eschews the progressive teleology that publications like the 1905 *Charities* special issue unsuccessfully tried to impose on migration. Instead, the patterns of physical and emotional arrival figured are an invisible and unmappable force. Notwithstanding what Locke describes as the "cruder and more obvious facts of a ferment and a migration," those that can be perceived and assessed, he also characterizes an "internal reorganization" brewing beneath the surface, a kind of "seed-bed" that eschews legibility.[192] If together "Harlem" and "Enter the New Negro" celebrate and imagine a New Negro who is intransigent to statistical representation and elusive in the face of progressive techniques of observation, then the essays also call for an expressive form that matches the physical momentum and the psychological movement of modern black life.

In Locke's work from the mid-1920s, scholars have recognized the innovation and invention of a new aesthetic form that has epistemological, racial, and artistic implications. In his reading of *The New Negro* anthology, Jeremy Braddock locates the emergence of a collecting aesthetic, one that emerges from Locke's relationship with institutions like the Barnes Foundation, as well as his own deep investment in assembling black archival objects—art, books, and printed ephemera. Here, what Braddock describes as the "compelling heterogeneity of the texts and images that compose Locke's anthology ... bears a meaningful resemblance to the idiosyncratic and suggestive association of objects at the Barnes foundation," ultimately revealing the "necessarily 'composite' nature of contemporary African American subjectivity."[193] Yet if we take seriously the Harlem number as more than an exercise or an unfulfilling first draft of *The New Negro*, then Locke's theory of black subjectivity bears an even more meaningful resemblance to the social survey. As we have seen, the survey's expressive and imaginative force lies in its asymmetry, in the dissonance between the deployment of a term like "racial type" and the juxtaposition of essays that stake out radically different views on assimilation and cultural particularity, as is the case with Melville Herskovits and Konrad Bercovici's contributions. Looking back from the Harlem issue, these exposed seams are precisely what structured *The Philadelphia Negro* and served as the imaginative launchpad for *Imperium in Imperio*. The racial epistemology that emerges not only is opaque to the white gaze but also takes movement as its organizing principle. Here we might recall the closing lines of "Harlem," the issue's inaugural essay. As he gives a brief sketch of the contributors' charge, namely "to voice these new aspirations of a people," Locke summons the language of dramatic performance and pageantry that theorists of the social survey also deployed: "But more significant than either of these, we shall also view it as the stage of the pageant of contemporary Negro life. In the drama of its new and progressive aspects, we may be witnessing the resurgence of a race; with our eyes focused on the Harlem scene we may dramatically glimpse the New Negro."[194]

That Locke offers a glimpse rather than a complete picture or stable object of study returns us to the very intractability to data regimes that this book argues is at the heart of black expressive practice. Even more concretely, Locke's terms are an undeniable nod to the social survey's spirit that this chapter opened with, a spirit that also finds its formal expression in the pageant, the theatrical, and the roving gaze that can do more glimpsing than gazing. It is as if Locke could articulate the New Negro as such only in the pages of a social survey, a form that manifests blackness as an object of knowledge that always exceeds the very containers that would seek to delimit it. Here, the social survey will always produce a subject who strains against and explodes the categories that realism and social science would seem to produce. Seeping through the statistical chart and evading the social scientist's gaze, blackness is everywhere and nowhere or, to return to Dunbar, wherever blackness is. Hidden in plain sight and refusing the atomizing gaze of social scientists and sociologists, modern black life comes into focus in the survey's very enactment of the failure to capture it.

2
Photography

LOOKING OUT

Seeing Survival

In the penultimate scene of Sutton Griggs's 1899 novel *Imperium in Imperio*, the all-black secret government, the Imperium, assembles to witness its protagonists Belton Piedmont and Bernard Belgrave debate "the whole question of the relationship of the Negro race to the Anglo-Saxons," or, the "Negro Problem."[1] Under the watchful gaze of their delegates, Belton and Bernard engage in a dramatic oratorical standoff to determine the Imperium's political trajectory. While Belton proposes a conciliatory model of interracial cooperation premised on the "abandon[ment] of the idea of becoming anything noteworthy as a separate and distinct race," Bernard resolves to violently annex Texas and establish it as a separate black nation-state, ultimately inviting his delegates to "at all hazards, strike a blow for freedom."[2] *Imperium in Imperio*'s oratorical theatrics have been widely theorized as a pivotal moment in postbellum African American literature.[3] Bernard's impassioned plea for violent secession in particular has secured both Griggs's and the novel's position in a progressive genealogy of "literary black nationalism," one that looks back to Martin Delany's 1859 serial novel *Blake; or, The Huts of America* and forward to the 1960s Black Arts Movement, the very moment when the novel was "recovered" and returned to print.[4] Though certainly important for mining Griggs's contribution to a distinct brand of black literary politics, these readings have largely overlooked that the novel's climactic episode pivots on the highly publicized 1898 lynching in Lake City, South Carolina, that killed Frazier Baker and his nearly two-year-old daughter Julia, and wounded his wife and five children, all of whom survived.[5] In *Imperium in Imperio* the surviving Bakers are recast as the "Cooks" and their presence in the Imperium provides the occasion for envisioning a political horizon whose contours are determined by the corporeal presence of lynching survivors. Refusing the designation of lynching as a spectacular expression of white supremacy that always ends with death, the Bakers wager a difficult question: when it comes to racial violence, how to document the living? Taking this question as its point of departure, this chapter uncovers the multimedia performance archive—one that spans photography, performance, and legal testimony—that was choreographed around and by the Bakers. In tracing the ways that black survival unsettles the intimacy between photography and blackness that both lynching and anti-lynching discourse relied on, this chapter reframes lynching photography as an encounter that, above all else, challenges the self-evidentiary status of racial data.

Visual scholars and historians have uncovered lynching and photography as co-constitutive enterprises, with lynching's relentless violence finding its technical analogue in photography's reproducibility. Likewise, that lynching rituals "objectified bodies and rendered them permanently still" resounds with what John Tagg has described as the instrumental routes through which photography emerges as a disciplinary regime in which the "body [is] made object."[6] As a temporal position that shatters the progressive teleology that lynching and lynching photography depend on, survival reorders the turn of the twentieth century's photographic logic by insisting that any visual account of lynching must record, not just capture, the duration of anti-black violence. As I unspool an account of photography and lynching's asymmetries, the courtroom and the reform stage emerge as disciplinary sites where the interplay of embodiment, race, and vision are sharpened and also upended. Moving away from the focus on the data regimes deployed in academic disciplines like sociology, this chapter situates photography as a technology that was conscripted in a racial data regime as "a means of record and a source of evidence," and conversely the very ways that blackness disrupts those disciplinary processes that aimed to, recalling the words of Harvey Young, still blackness.[7]

In July 1897, Frazier Baker arrived in Lake City, South Carolina, a self-described "white man's town," to assume his appointment as the local postmaster. By the end of the year, his wife, Lavinia, and their six children—Rosa, Cora, Lincoln, William, Sarah, and Julia—joined him. In the late nineteenth century, when social custom was akin to law, Baker's extensive experience—he had served as treasurer and postmaster in nearby Florence County before moving to Lake City—and his appointment to a government position in a town with "not more than a dozen negroes living in the place and not one owning a foot of land within the corporate city limits," were deemed actionable offenses best legislated through rogue intimidation tactics.[8] Within weeks of his arrival, Lake City's aggrieved white residents set fire to the post office and orchestrated a series of violent ambushes on Baker and his friends with the sole intention of forcing him to resign. Refusing to acquiesce to their threats, Baker quickly pivoted and resumed postal operations from his family's home, nearly a mile from the center of town. When in early 1898 they realized they were facing off with a target who displayed an unexpected degree of stamina, two hundred of the town's self-described "better citizens" appealed for federal support and sent a signed petition to Washington, DC, calling for Baker's immediate removal. In their outline of grievances Baker was portrayed as unqualified, "uncivil, ignorant and lazy." Drawing on a well-rehearsed rhetorical tactic that also foreshadowed his lynching, the letter concluded by claiming that he was deemed "impolite to the ladies," phrasing redolent with the specter of rape.[9] After a team of investigators dismissed the complaints, Lake City decided to assuage the "long suffering" people and "determined to do their work efficiently this time."[10]

On February 12, the *Lake City Times* and the *Charleston News and Courier* called for Baker's lynching. Adhering to the requisite components of large-scale lynchings that were "prepared for and often publicized in advance," both newspapers reprinted the original petition along with an account of Baker's so-called transgressions and the directive to "surround the little shanty and set fire to it."[11] Just before midnight on February 21, 1898, a mob of between "300 or 400 vigilantes gathered around the Lake City post office, which doubled as the Baker's home."[12] Arriving on horseback and armed with torches and firearms, the mob riddled the home with bullets before setting it on fire. As flames engulfed the building, Frazier and Julia Baker were shot and killed in the house, their bodies reportedly "burnt to a crisp" with "some parts . . . found among the charred remains of the cabin."[13] Miraculously, Lavinia, along with Rosa (age 18), Cora (age 14), Sarah (age 8), Lincoln (age 15), and William (age 5), managed to escape, albeit with bullet wounds and severe burns.[14]

Although the Baker lynching attracted the attention of anti-lynching activists, most notably Ida B. Wells, who traveled to Washington to agitate on their behalf for a relief package, in Griggs's rendition the Lake City lynching is the catalyst for the Imperium's fateful meeting. Mounted as the shadowy counterpart to the bombing of the USS *Maine* and the onset of the Spanish-American War, in Griggs's hands the lynching "naturally aroused as much indignation among the members of the Imperium as did the destruction of the war ship in the bosoms of the Anglo-Saxons of the United States." An act of terrorism that threated democracy and demanded a national response, the Baker lynching also required an urgent "reconsideration of questions of vital import to civilization."[15] That *Imperium in Imperio* makes recourse to lynching at this key narrative moment is certainly not surprising. Whether working to cement a national discourse of white supremacy and black bestiality or attempting to parse what Jacqueline Goldsby has described as a "cultural logic" that allowed lynching to flourish as an engine of modernity, rather than an exception to it, time and again African and American writers mobilized the trope of lynching in their racial imaginaries of the late nineteenth and early twentieth centuries.[16] Indeed, among the countless novels published in the aftermath of Reconstruction, it is difficult to find one that does not include a lynching. Haunted by the specter of rape and the threat of miscegenation, the figuration of lynching in turn-of-the-century literature is most often theorized as a multilayered metaphor used to articulate and dissemble anxieties about sexuality, citizenship, and social change—or, simply, modernity.[17]

Literature's trope of the malevolent black male body found its visual counterpart in statistical graphics and the now-canonical photographic image of the hanging, usually male black corpse surrounded by a crowd of eager white onlookers. By the turn of the twentieth century as the number of lynchings peaked, the public's interminable appetite for spectacular displays of black suffering was sated by an onslaught of lynching photographs. Reproduced as postcards and albumen prints, photographs played a critical role in the lynching spectacle, consolidating it as a highly visual affair and securing the crucial place of lynching photography in a racial field of vision that would determine how blackness was seen and, in turn, how African Americans imagined themselves as distinctly seeing subjects. That lynching's apex corresponds with technological advances like photography is certainly not coincidental. As Goldsby has detailed, photography and lynching were co-constituted in a visual milieu that "encouraged looking for its own sake, and that sanctioned the threat of mass injury to be fun."[18] Beyond their ideological overlaps, advances in photographic technology—shorter exposure times, the emergence of the amateur snapshot, and new flash equipment—authorized and amplified lynching's logic, enabling the production and circulation of images of mob violence that at once threatened blacks into silence and submission while emboldening white supremacist sentiments. Together, their shared frenetic logic, one that approximates what Lindsay Reckson has recently described as a shuttling between widespread movement and violent stilling, supplied the conditions for yoking the forms together as twinned forces that disciplined bodies according to race and class while confirming the fungibility of the black body and its seamless transmutation to, on the one hand, evidence of racial degeneracy and, on the other hand, lifeless data that could be easily assimilated into paradigms of objectivity and empiricism.[19]

Refusing to let the force of lynching photography go uncontested, anti-lynching activists harnessed photography's deleterious dynamics and produced a diverse, data-driven visual and discursive repertoire—including pro-lynching photographic imagery, crime statistics, and journalism—to discredit the popular myth of the dangerous black male body and replace it with a narrative of black endangerment, innocence, and embodied citizenship. Capitalizing on photography's presumed status as an evidentiary technology and working in a long tradition that understood the presentation of truth as the pathway to justice, lynching photographs were repurposed to expose the cracks in the logic of white supremacy. In what remains one of the most sophisticated, well-known mobilizations of documentary evidence and social-scientific discourse in the name of anti-lynching reform, Ida B. Wells fused press reports, lynching statistics, and photographs, to form what Leigh Raiford describes as an "arsenal of evidence . . . to offer testimony to lynching's antidemocratic barbarism" and to "categorically challenge each one of lynching's underlying assumptions."[20] Refracted through new frames, the facts of lynching were "re-cast as a call to arms against a seemingly never-ending tied of violent coercion."[21] Treading carefully through a photographic and data inflected terrain that always threatened to reduce the facts of lynching into an anti-black rhetoric, one that risked reifying the very kind of passive voyeurism that allowed lynching to thrive, postbellum anti-lynching campaigns worked to challenge the very racial principles from which lynching photography was born and to reconceptualize modes of spectatorship and blackness that lynching photographs sought to delimit. Yet the assumption that lynching's data—whether expressed visually or numerically—was always equivalent with a record of death risks a violent erasure of lynching survivors and consolidating the temporal and spatial boundaries of lynching as a geographically coherent event that unfolds in a linear fashion.

By replacing the visual and literary iconography of abject black (male) victimhood with a textual panorama of women and children that pivots on the Bakers, *Imperium in Imperio* clears a space through which lynching and its representational forms, especially photography, confront one another on new terms. In the Imperium, the gendered scene of survival is restaged as the authorizing impetus for black political expression and recast with women and children. By reterritorializing lynching's visual grammar, the women and children quite literally coordinate new black political futures. As Griggs describes, on one side of the speaker's podium where Belton and Bernard would proffer their respective manifestos, "there was a group of women in widow's weeds, sitting on an elevated platform. . . . their husbands having been made the victims of mob violence since the first day of January just gone"; on the other "were huddled one hundred children whose garments were in tatters and whose looks bespoke lives of hardship. These were the offspring robbed of their parents by the brutish cruelty of unthinking mobs."[22] To be sure, this staging of splintered domesticity articulates what Raiford, Deborah McDowell, Claudia Rankine, and Koritha Mitchell have identified as the political purchase of mourning.[23] Whether in photographic iconography, as in the case of the photograph of Ida B. Wells and the widow and children of Thomas Moss who was lynched in Memphis, or drama, such as the one-act lynching plays that Mitchell has recovered, the "black mother/wife . . . bears witness to what it means to live with lynching" and embodies the "terror with which too many women lived" while "acknowledging emotional and physical pain" beyond that of the black male victims who dominated lynching's visual domain.[24] Yet in its decision to suspend the trope of black male suffering as an index of democracy's failures and replace it with a scene of wounded kinship, *Imperium in Imperio* maps a pathway to racial justice that moves through endurance, survival, and gendered performative practices.

Put another way, if lynching's dual logic of white supremacy and black degeneracy hinges on the sight of the violated black corpse, then the Bakers' status as lynching survivors are the site around which the very workings of race and racial violence could be (re)scripted, (re)staged, and (re)imagined. Here racial violence is reconceptualized as endurance and the "stage of sufferance," to borrow a phrase from Saidiya Hartman, expands beyond the gendered scene of murder that lynching photography circumscribes and toward the stage, the photography, the studio, and the courtroom, but also toward the street, and the quotidian locales where black life comes into being.[25] Rather than signaling a celebratory narrative of escape or a progressive account of resistance and perseverance, in *Imperium in Imperio* the Bakers invite us to see survival as that which lives on or exceeds injury (physical or otherwise) and yet is irreducible to the act of violence itself. Survival structures what Tina Campt usefully calls a "visual grammar of futurity," one that emerges against the conceptualization of lynching as death, abjection, and foreclosure, and which is concerned with neither naive hope nor aspiration but with engendering a methodology for engaging with racial violence that might illuminate the full range of its expressions and instantiations.[26]

Telescoped through the presence of the Bakers, this scene in *Imperium in Imperio* registers an understudied node of nineteenth-century political, aesthetic, and visual anti-lynching agitation, one that is not so much organized around communicating the "facts" about lynching (that it really happened), representing black humanity (reclaiming the victim from the terrain of social death), or communicating lynching data (the sheer number of victims). Instead, the women and children of the Imperium point us to an iteration of anti-lynching activism that takes documenting and accounting for the configuration of survival and survivors as its primary charge. The task at hand, it turned out, would require wrestling with photography and lynching's indelible bond and rescripting lynching not as something that one is victim to but as an encounter that moves and moves through the body, creating a deferral that is as temporal as it is corporeal. Writing of his own narrow escape from a lynch mob, James Weldon Johnson equates this temporal impasse with permanently existing inside the space of death. Caught between the traumatic memory of his near demise and the fear of imminent annihilation, Johnson's "horror complex" names a psychic in-between, an inescapable suspension between past and future.[27] But even before Johnson shared his own near lynching, the titular narrator of his *Autobiography of an Ex-Colored Man* realized that to be black in America is perhaps to always be narrowly avoiding a lynching, a revelation that leads to confinement in his own kind of permanent racial purgatory. The temporal and critical tangle wrought by survival, Rebecca Schneider reminds us, signals a crisis that is as metaphysical as it is corporeal. Troubling the seemingly impermeable boundary between life and death, survival is, Schneider elaborates, a "constant (re)turn of, to, from, and between states in animation," a critical relationship to the past that refuses to let the past pass.[28]

But if survival shatters linear conceptions of time and unnerves bodily states, then it also upends documentary strategies that rely on the immutability of evidence, proof, and data. Here we might think beyond Johnson and the Bakers toward the interwoven terrains of photography, lynching, and performance that survival cuts through. Lynching has long been understood as a kind of theater, a performance ritual that indoctrinated white Americans into a racial field where black life was always under siege and to a visual economy where, as we saw in chapter 1, race was an incontestable and highly visual fact borne out on the body. In addition to lynchings being highly public and well-attended "events," press reports, advertisements, photographs, and literature, as well as the dissemination of lynching souvenirs, accustomed Americans to the specific components of lynching's ritualized violence and authorized what theater scholar Kirk Fuoss describes as lynching's "performance complex," the "entire web of performance woven in and around lynching."[29] Yet the Bakers' status as survivors disrupted lynching's customary dramaturgy in ways that were at once curiosity inducing and cognitively dissociating. For unlike the widely circulated photographic record of the hanging black body or the lynching souvenirs collected as "real" evidence of the crime (pieces of burned flesh, hair, rope) that both confirmed the black body's commodity status and attempted to fix it in historical time, even as it pushed against those very containers, the Bakers belonged to a different category: living, breathing remains.

As I argued in chapter 1, by reworking realist modalities in favor of an experimental aesthetic that veers toward the fantastical and the utopic, *Imperium in Imperio* begins to offer formal answers to the temporal and epistemological web wrought by survival. Recall that Belton himself survives a lynching that is carried out by none other than a white postmaster before finding temporary refuge in the Imperium. Moreover, as the survivors' presence in the Imperium makes plain, the subterranean black capital in Waco is a geographic "elsewhere" that can hold social configurations, like survival, that are incompatible with progressive historical narratives and binary models of personhood. But while *Imperium in Imperio* attempts to work out this entanglement through formal experimentation and speculative plotlines, this chapter is concerned with the various aesthetic strategies—performative, visual, creative, and editorial—that were taken up in the interest of registering lynching as an ongoing state of crisis, one that pushes against the spatial and temporal boundaries of an "event" to emerge as what Ariella Azoulay describes as a "threshold catastrophe." Distinct from a catastrophe, a spectacular site of violence that coalesces as an event with a clear beginning and end, "threshold catastrophe" names a "chronic and prolonged situation that does not interrupt routine."[30] To think of lynching as a threshold catastrophe is to suspend its status as a temporally and geographically delimited "event not to be missed" that necessarily ends in death.[31] Attending to such temporal and spatial boundlessness of violence unsettles photography's status as a referential medium that is congruent with racial violence. This perspective also demands that we interrogate not only how one begins to document a threshold catastrophe, as Azoulay does, but also whether that can even be done.

This is not to suggest that postbellum black life was a never-ending lynching. Rather, what interests me here is how without recourse to legal or state protection, black life, and especially black women's lives, remained vulnerable to various iterations of violence. To think of lynching as a threshold catastrophe, then, is both to be alert to how racial violence endures long after the perpetrators have dispersed and to occupy a state in which violence not only is regular but also fails to instantiate a state of emergency. This was certainly the case in Lake City. Just days after the attack, the *News and Courier* reported: "There is no excitement whatever in Lake City. Everything seems to be going on in the even tenor of its way. Stores all open and businesses going on just as if nothing has happened, except that all are now perplexed as to how they will get their mail."[32]

When theorized as a threshold catastrophe, the political horizon of anti-lynching necessarily shifts from the public recognition of humanity to the production of a visual praxis that would envision the breadth of lynching, that is, an embrace of both the slain and the living. In this regard it is especially important to recall that the "Imperium" is an exclusively black space that has thrived for centuries without public recognition or validation. Protected from the violating white gaze, within the walls of the Imperium Griggs can imagine the emergence of black politics outside of an oppositional framework. *Imperium in Imperio* thus articulates the political futures and appeals that can be staged when racial violence is figured as an ongoing state of emergency and the political possibilities that cohere outside of the inherited patterns of knowledge production and its attendant visual schemas. Rather than rehearsing a project that assimilates into familiar politics of recognition, whereby the symbol of the violated black body anticipates embodied black citizenship, *Imperium in Imperio*'s turn to lynching survivors stages a problematic between what counts as evidence of racial violence and the contours of survival.

Griggs was not the only postbellum cultural producer to mobilize the Bakers in the hopes of otherwise constituting the narrative of lynching and engendering a visual epistemology through which racial violence emerged as an ongoing crisis. In the aftermath of the Lake City lynching, Lavinia and her five surviving children materialized at nothing short of a cultural phenomenon. While press coverage of what was quickly dubbed the "Famous Lake City Lynching" initially orbited around the details of the crime and President McKinley's controversial decision to open a federal criminal investigation into the mob, the public's attention ultimately shifted to the Bakers themselves. In April 1899, the family was thrust into the spotlight when they were called as key witnesses in the criminal trial of the eleven men charged with murdering Frazier and Julia Baker, destroying government property (the mail), and endangering Lavinia and her children. Shortly after, the Bakers were featured in a traveling multimedia anti-lynching spectacular produced by Lillian Clayton Jewett, a young white reformer who promised an "object lesson" in "living evidence." During the weeks leading up to and surrounding their stage debut as stars of the Baker Exhibit, the family was the subject of more than one hundred newspaper articles, a motion picture directed by B. W. Bitzer (who eventually signed on to produce and finance much of *The Birth of a Nation*), countless press illustrations, and a series of photographic portraits that were printed as cabinet cards and eight-inch-by-ten-inch albumen prints. Press reports also describe Baker-inspired posters, although such artifacts have not been recovered. Although what we might think of as Baker mania lasted for just over five months (from July through December 1899), the Bakers retained some symbolic purchase through the early years of the twentieth century. In 1904 the *Colored American National Newspaper* printed a full-page photograph of the Bakers on its cover, and in 1905 Biograph Pictures rereleased the film under a new title, *Miss Jewett and the Negroes*.

In what follows I recount the bizarre rise of the Bakers to cultural prominence and argue that the task of rendering racial violence as an enduring violation underpinned the efforts of anti-lynching activists as much as drawing attention to the spectacle of death. In so doing, I counter the popular view of lynching as a theatrical event amenable to photographic documentation and instead maintain that anti-black racial violence presented a conceptual and representational conundrum for turn-of-the-century anti-lynching activists even as it activated new political imaginaries, aesthetic strategies, and insurgent performances. My reading of the Baker archive moves through three key sites—the courtroom where the family testified against their assailants, the multimedia performance spectacle produced by Lillian Jewett, and the photography studio where the Bakers posed for a series of portraits—knitting together performance studies, theories of photography, and deep archival readings. By inviting us to accompany a family who survived a lynching, this chapter argues that any study of lynching and photography must adopt a theoretical structure that matches the way that turn-of-the-century cultural practitioners interrogated the utility of visual evidence as a tool that might document black living. To do this, I read the survivors of the Lake City lynching as theorists of photography whose formulations concerning photography's role as an arbiter of truth and a data regime capable of effecting political change was systematically explored and exploited. The final part of the chapter considers W. E. B. Du Bois's decision to publish lynching photographs in *The Crisis* magazine. Here I argue that far from holding a resolute position, Du Bois grappled to locate an editorial strategy for printing lynching photographs without reducing racial violence to a historical event that could be conscripted to the past. To circumvent this, he also used a multimedia approach and drew on conventions of speculative romance, a genre that he turned to throughout his long literary career. Du Bois's turn to the terrain of experimental literary aesthetics acknowledges and disrupts the process whereby photographs of lynching get reduced to little more than data. Where Du Bois experimented with framing the still photograph as a means to get the image to announce an emergency claim, Jewett worked to reshape the experience of seeing racial violence by crafting a generically hybrid visual display that continually pushed against the status quo of reform practices. But before either Jewett or Du Bois set to work, the Bakers themselves intervened into the terrain of lynching and photography.

Deep Black Mourning: Lynching's (Anti)Photographic Logic

On the morning of April 10, 1899, "white and colored crowds" lined the corridors of the US Circuit Court at Charleston, South Carolina, to witness the latest development in the "celebrated trial" of the eleven men charged with conspiracy to murder Frazier and Julia Baker.[33] For two weeks, spectators followed the daily developments in the unprecedented legal affair that was ultimately deemed a "deplorable spectacle." By the turn of the century, lynching was embedding itself into the national fabric at an alarming speed. Yet rarely were the accused made to stand trial, and even then they were almost never found guilty. As Arthur Raper explained in one of the earliest studies of lynching, when it came to identifying the guilty, "leading citizens are compromised into letting the matter alone, affording lynchers virtual immunity."[34] Whether coerced to nonaction by a sense of indifference or manipulated by members of the mob, potential witnesses were "maneuvered by prolynchers into a position of silent acquiescence."[35] In this regard, what made the Baker trial both spectacular and deplorable was that it even occurred. In spite of its predictable outcome (writing in 1933, at the height of anti-lynching agitation, Raper notes that of the thousands of lynching perpetrators and onlookers, fewer than fifty were charged and only four were sentenced), the case boasted an impressive roster of white and black witnesses, all of whom promised to publicly identify the attackers or confirm their own participation in the violent act. Among those who appeared on the witness stand were Dr. Alonzo McClennan (the surgeon who treated the Bakers' injuries), the civil engineer who oversaw the construction of much of Lake City, two members of the mob who became state witnesses in exchange for immunity, and the Bakers themselves.

Even as the sight of eleven white men being indicted for conspiring to kill a black family was certainly enough to draw a courtroom crowd, in its capacity to disrupt and redirect the legal status quo, the trial's "celebrated" status and its emergence as a landmark legal affair follows the trajectory that Shoshana Felman draws out in her influential analysis of trauma and courtroom spectacle. Identifying three primary factors that contribute to a trial's historical significance—its "complex traumatic structure," its "cross legal nature" (or how it reenacts familiar legal events), and its "attempt to define something legally that is not reducible to legal concepts"—Felman maintains that in a "landmark" case "something other than the law is addressed in legal terms."[36] Felman trains her attention on two twentieth-century trials, the 1995 O. J. Simpson trial and the 1961 trial of Adolph Eichmann. In the former, the "something" extralegal is the intersection of racism and domestic violence; the latter seeks to distill collective trauma within the limiting boundaries of a legal apparatus. Insofar as the witnesses at the Baker trial recounted the lynching and the Bakers' embodied presence in the courtroom conjures a lengthy and familiar repertoire of African American legal disappointment in which black people were transmuted into evidence, the Baker trial certainly qualifies as a "cross legal" performance. Adding to its repetitious nature, the trial also "attempts to define something legally that is not reducible to legal terms," namely, lynching.[37] By definition, lynching operates outside the law—

there are neither juridical frameworks nor discursive terms to account for acts of extralegal violence or for the perpetrators who purport to act when the law fails. Thus, to bring a lynching to trial and force it into a legal container of murder and endangerment triggers an explosive encounter between law and juridical surplus. Lynching was, after all, an excessive spectacle that pushed at the limits of the knowable and seeable.[38] Thus, to adjudicate an act that defines itself against legal frameworks is an impossible endeavor that requires nothing short of legal alchemy.[39]

Just as the terms of the case strained against the law's grammar, so too did the Bakers' fleshly courtroom presence manifest as something "extra." As victim and survivor, evidence and eyewitness, the Bakers trouble the categorical distinctions that racial violence depends upon, transforming the case from legal aberration to pure spectacle. For twelve days, from April 10 to April 22, 1899, the courtroom was "crowded by white and colored people every day," all of whom were eager to get a glimpse of the Baker family and hear the details of the crime that, as one reporter put it, "smacks of the time of Indians."[40] Reframed as a frontier fantasy evacuated of Native genocide and anti-black violence, the Baker lynching was situated alongside those popular turn-of-the-century disaster spectacles that resolved fears about modernity's promises by ensuring viewers that in the end, society would endure the moment's technological, political, and social upheavals. But if in witnessing a disaster spectacle part of the pleasure was that the "emergency dramatized . . . was invariably sutured shut," then the Bakers' presence in the courtroom simultaneously punctures the fantasy of control and provides the opportunity to recalibrate the racial order.[41] Thus, when on the second day of the trial Lavinia Baker approached the witness stand and "drew every eye in the courtroom," the stakes were a radical disruption to a visual field that was supported by a photographic logic that understood racial violence in general and black life in particular as markedly visible.

But while racial spectacles promised to body forth an acutely perceptible subject, Lavinia nearly evaded perception. She was, offered the journalist for the News and Courier, "a small woman, very black, and wore deep mourning." Almost entirely absorbed by her grief, here Lavinia's corporeality and her mourning dissolve into each other and at least momentarily tease the possibility of evading the entire legal

scenario. Yet Lavinia did appear on the stand and, if the trial's "spectators were looking for something thrilling and bloody" in her eyewitness account, then they were at least partially satisfied. In a somewhat brief testimony, she recounted being "aroused by the roaring of
fire," her husband's desperate, and ultimately futile, attempts to throw
buckets of water on the flames, and the frantic and cacophonous cries
of her family who alternated between "sounding the alarm" and "crying out," "I'm shot."[42] Lavinia also described how "[Frazier] Baker
walked up and down, and prayed," all before approaching the details
of the murder of her daughter and husband: "At the door the baby was
shot, the baby was shot out of my arms. I said, 'See baby's dead.'" At
this point in her testimony, Lavinia reconstructed the night's events in
graphic detail:

> Baker stepped back and saw his dead child; then he opened the door
> and was shot. . . . Baker fell over and died, leaning against my lap. . . .
> I looked to see if the baby was breathing. It did not, and there was a
> wound on its right side; the wound looked like a bloody bruise. It was
> large, as if made by a slug. There was a large hole in the side, and blood
> was flowing. . . . The blood was gushing from Bakers back when he fell.
> I held my head down to hear if he was breathing. He said nothing. I
> held up my left hand, and was shot above the wrist.[43]

In the absence of the bodies of her husband and daughter, Lavinia
punctuates her account by offering her own limb as surrogate
evidence, "show[ing] the jury the scarred mark on both sides of
her arm."[44]

Teeming with blood-curdling screams, flying bullets, and wounded
bodies, Lavinia's testimony renders the lynching a scene of sensory
overload, what the anonymous narrator of *Autobiography of an Ex-
Colored Man* would describe as a frenetic performance scored by "rebel
yells" that move with the force of "an electric current."[45] But if Lavinia's
sensational account of the night's events satiated the audience's desire
for a "bloody" story, then as legal testimony, her statement falls short
at a crucial juncture: the description of her encounter with the mob.
In contrast to the explicit, highly detailed account of the violence that
occurred behind closed doors, when it came to identifying the mob
and describing her escape, Lavinia submitted a highly abridged expla-
nation, simply noting, "I got the children . . . and we ran as fast as

we could." Thus, where she satisfies the audience with an account of bruises, gushing blood, and relentless flames, Lavinia abstains from describing her assailants, a strategy that her daughters Rosa and Cora would replicate in their own testimony. Lavinia does not, for example, "remember" if the attackers were white or black or if they arrived on horseback. Nor did she "notice what they had" (likely referring to weapons). According to the *News and Courier*, which provided daily dispatches from the trial, Lavinia "said that when she rushed out of the house after her husband and baby were dead, she saw men dodging about, though in the darkness she could not tell whether they were white men or negroes." And in a not entirely surprising move that anticipated the likelihood of violent retaliation from the accused, under cross-examination Lavinia firmly maintained a posture of ocular impairment, simply explaining, "When we left the building, in the light of the fire, I saw men on the north side, a few steps from the building. Could not see whether they were white or colored."[46]

Lavinia's carefully tutored description of the violence wrought inside her home leaves little to the imagination, but her artful account of escape is what Daphne Brooks might describe as "spectacularly opaque." Emerging "at various times as a product of the performer's will, at other times as a visual obstacle erupting as a result of the hostile spectator's epistemological resistance to reading alternative racial and gender representations," performances of spectacular opacity circumvent the transparency that is "systematically" imposed on black bodies.[47] Offering her body as visual evidence of the crime only to thwart the gesture's argumentative force by refusing to visualize her encounter with the mob, Lavinia's spectacular opacity interrupts lynching's performance cycle. Thus, while her exposed wounds fulfill the trials quotient for spectacle, her purposeful withholding constructs an ocular barrier that prevents the courtroom from fully witnessing either the miraculous escape or the site of annihilation. In so doing, the violent climax is refigured as a tragically intimate encounter between husband and wife, leaving spectators and jurors alike to grapple with lynching's "recalcitrant invisibility."[48] Reconstituted as a black domestic nightmare rather than a public display of white supremacy, Lavinia's testimony at once impedes the process of firsthand identification that would allow white courtroom spectators to identify with the mob and frustrates the pathway to empathetic identification that might encourage anti-lynching sentiment.

In the end reporters concluded that although Lavinia's testimony "did nothing more than prove the fact of the shooting and burning," it was still "considered of value."[49] That her assertion was considered valuable even though the accused were not charged suggests that the significance of her presence on the witness stand was less a matter of proving the identity of the attackers or the details of the crime than it was an attempt at (re)staging the spectacular scene of violence, verbally, by recounting the crime, and physically, by exposing her wounds. An extension of what Fuoss describes as lynching's performance complex, the courtroom registers an obsession with deviant bodies, excess, corporeality, and physical endurance. And like lynching, the courtroom is a site at which subjectivity is both unraveled and secured. Yet what, if not the facts of the crime, was the "more" that Lavinia's testimony failed to produce? Far from merely accounting for the events, the "more" that she was expected to deliver but failed to was a particular role in the lynching drama: the mourning mother.

Even as Lavinia Baker offers both her own and her husband's body as evidence of the crime, her testimony disrupts and redirects lynching's script by refusing a public performance of gendered grief. Indeed, if Lavinia's highly anticipated appearance speaks to the desire for proximity to racial violence and the spectacle of violated black flesh while witnessing what might have been a legal windfall, it also registers the value of the public-facing nature of black female mourning that would ultimately become a key symbol in the anti-lynching movement and that was reworked in Griggs's political imaginary. Largely marginalized from narratives of racial violence, women entered the lynching narrative as grieving mothers whose relationship to maternity was interrupted by anti-black violence. Within this framework, black grief is gendered and public, it becomes the pathway that facilitates the spectator's intimacy with black life and lubricates a national catharsis. This was, after all, the task that Mamie Till-Mobley took on when she encouraged all the world to "look" upon the ravaged body of Emmett Till and her own grievous encounter with his corpse. It is also the labor that Ida B. Wells undertook when she posed for a portrait with the widow and children of Thomas Moss, her friend and collaborator who was murdered in the 1892 Memphis lynching that would fuel

Wells's anti-lynching agitation. Such public displays of gendered grief galvanize a brand of politics premised on claims to black sentience, humanity, feeling, and the (denied) right to black maternity. In other words, the figure of the mourning mother bespeaks a kind of subject position that was denied black people, that of a fully embodied life. At the same time, such performances of grief sediment the expectation that for a death to matter, black families must openly mourn. This presumed "right" to bear witness to black mourning mirrors the public demand to "see" the bodies of the victims of lynching, or in the case of the Bakers' trial, to "hear" the ghastly crime in gross detail.

Lavinia Baker's testimony, however, is uncannily measured and perfectly rehearsed; on the witness stand she does not divert from her task—producing evidence of the crime. As one reporter noted, her responses were nearly identical during cross-examination. In offering the facts, by way of displaying her injuries and describing her husband's, Lavinia refuses to either make her mourning legible or give access to the affective workings of her interior life. Insofar as she denies spectators access to her private grief, the testimony circumvents the process of subjection that animates white supremacy and emboldened a mode of anti-lynching politics whose political horizon is subjectivity by way of recognition of humanity by the state. Deep and dark, private and quiet, her mourning forecasts a visual and political practice that wrests lynching from its status as highly visual spectacle and firmly resituates it within a landscape of opacity, intransigence, and impenetrability

Lavinia's strategy of withholding her attackers' identity and keeping her mourning deep and dark is amplified in her daughter Rosa's testimony. While the courtroom spectators likely dismissed Lavinia's refusal to identify her assailants as a curious lapse in memory—they had, after all, already received their "bloody" story—both the prosecutors and the defense were understandably frustrated. Thus, when nineteen-year-old Rosa, the eldest of the Baker children, took the stand, the defense attorney once again asked for an account of the night's events. Picking up where her mother's story trailed off, Rosa explained: "When I got out [of the burning house] I saw three men near the side of the door, but in the smoke could not recognize them. They had guns, for I saw them. As I ran I heard more shooting; they were shooting at the house and at me, for the bullets came whistling by. *I saw the light* from the guns pointing towards me; the *flash* was towards me" (my emphasis).[50] Evidently unsatisfied with Rosa's vague account, during cross-examination the defense attorney, George Legare, asked her to clarify what she meant by "the light." However, even as she carefully addressed Legare's line of inquiry, Rosa maintained her original account of impaired visibility, explaining: "I saw only one shot fired at me. I saw only one bullet coming toward me; I saw the bullet come flying by me; the bullet was moving rapidly. . . . I did not see any horses that night. . . . I call the bullet the light, and I saw the light coming at me; the blaze from the gun was very close."[51] By beginning each sentence with "I saw" Rosa insists on her value to a courtroom drama that, without photographs of the crime scene, relied on her eyewitness testimony as key evidence. Yet what Rosa ends up crafting is far more powerful than a virtual mapping of the crime scene, a task that was ultimately outsourced to Lake City's engineer. By clarifying that "light" refers to the bullet, Rosa figures the gun as an electrical source that produces the current of anti-black violence and supplies the energy to a paradoxical racial logic whereby racial violence is simultaneously the mechanism that makes blackness legible (as abject, disposable, and object) and the organizing engine of white social life. Throwing a wrench in a legal mechanism that relies on evidence to evaluate and produce "truth," Rosa's pointed phrasing renders the racial violence its own kind of deep black event that cannot be rationalized or recognized by the law.

Although not as substantial as Rosa's admission, when her siblings took the stand, they recounted their experience with the mob in equally enigmatic terms. Fifteen-year-old Cora, for example, testified that, although she did not see the mob, she heard them approaching on horseback: "I was in the house when I heard the horses; that was after the fire started. . . . I did not see any horses, but I thought I heard them before I came out."[52] For his part Lincoln Baker echoed the account of visual impairment. While he saw "two men . . . going across the street," he could not tell if "they had anything, and could not tell if they were black or white."[53] Cora and Lincoln's account resists being ordered into what Nicholas Mirzoeff has described as the process by which the legal system uses evidence (photographs, maps, testimony) to "divide up an event into a series of measurements and objects to create a legal scenario" that grounds the crime in "space and time" and prepares it for adjudication.[54] Cora's account, for instance, defies spatial or visual logic; she hears the horses after the fire but does not see them when she comes outside, even though she heard them. Likewise, in Lincoln's description, two possible members of the mob are rendered less material as his account unfolds. I do not mean to suggest that Rosa, Cora, or Lincoln is an unreliable witness. Rather, their testimony fractures the legal proceedings by suggesting that the scene of racial violence is neither as visual nor as visible as we might expect.

Certainly, the Bakers' oblique phrasing on the witness stand is a survival technique; after all, to publicly name one's attackers was to make oneself vulnerable to another attack. At the same time, the Bakers' refusal to provide closure to the otherwise dramatic narrative also reframes lynching as an ongoing catastrophe that does not end in death and that certainly exceeds the scene of murder. In this respect, the Bakers' prosecutorial silence announces the absence of a visual grammar capable of holding lynching survivor narratives and insists that the spatial and temporal boundaries of the crime scenario are unmappable, incalculable, and—perhaps most important—hostile to visual arrest. What gets evidenced in their strategic reticence, then, is the necessity of a visual vocabulary and a critical praxis that can apprehend and register a protracted scene of racial terror. Moreover, the level of opacity that underpins Lavinia's and Rosa's testimony in particular coordinates a critique of photography and its relationship to racial violence. That is, might we read Rosa's and Lavinia's courtroom performance as a reassessment of photography's presumed role in the theater of lynching? Approaching their testimony from this angle means taking seriously what it would mean to treat Rosa and Lavinia as theorists of lynching photography.

Realizing the stakes of this line of questioning requires tuning into the photographic frequencies of Rosa's testimony. For not only does she provide the most detailed account of what she did not see; when we return to her phrasing, its technological idioms come into sharp relief, manifesting its status as photographic theory. Over the course of her testimony, Rosa repeatedly analogizes the flying bullet to blinding light—"I call the bullet the light, and I saw the light coming at me."[55] Simultaneously heralding and unraveling the well-rehearsed connection between photographic technology and racial violence, Rosa intervenes into a well-documented and expansive body of scholarship that takes for granted the mutual constituting terms of racial violence and photography while also cutting across photography's legal standing as evidence. Such connections are certainly well founded. Over a decade before the Baker lynching, Kodak released a handheld automatic camera with the popular slogan "point and shoot."[56] Weighing just two pounds, the camera transformed the picture-making process and shored up lynching as a particularly visual affair. Upon hitting the market in 1888, the new Kodak became a mainstay at public lynchings. In a well-known 1915 NAACP field report from a lynching in Fayette County, Tennessee, describes how shutterbugs set up a "portable printing plant . . . and reaped the harvest in selling postcards showing a photograph of the lynched Negro."[57] Alongside the cheers of crowds and the victim's cries, the incessant clicking of "hundreds of kodaks" supplied the soundtrack to the lynching landscape.

With its rapid speed and easy portability, new photographic technology was especially conducive to the structure of the lynching, itself defined by its visuality and ephemerality. Lynchings, writes Harvey Young, were constructed as "flash occurrences in which little advance notice of the event was given" and "wherein little, if anything, remained after the crime."[58] Likewise, "lynching spectacles were conducted within locales that were selected for their preexisting features, such as the presence of a tree or streetlight, or the ability of the site to accommodate a large crowd. . . . In fact, lynchings occurred with such rapidity that the site, even when not dismantled for souvenirs, bore few, if any, visible signs or markings of the events that occurred there," he continues.[59] Free of cumbersome equipment and long exposure times, the new Kodak could keep pace with lynching by producing highly coveted photographic souvenirs. Reprinted as postcards and usually with the image of a dead black body surrounded by a crowd of white perpetrators and eager spectators, the new technology's rapid-fire speed mirrored what scholars like Young describe as the "flash" temporality of the lynching event itself. As Ken Gonzales-Day has outlined, violence and photographic technology's overlapping logic was evoked even more explicitly in the Scovill and Adams' manufactured Solograph Flash Pistol's marketing slogan: "shoots sunshine all over." Crafted like a handheld gun, the technology replaced makeshift lighting sources like automobile headlights and magnesium powder. For lynch mobs who often performed their work under the cover of night, the Solograph Flash Pistol illuminated a new visual landscape and solidified photography's intimate role perpetuating violence, solidifying what Gonzales-Day describes as the "curious parallel between photography and firearms."[60] Photography's networks of circulation and its technical properties buttressed its promise to capture its subjects, rendering them eternally available for future spectators. Emerging largely from its status as a referential medium through which a viewer can always encounter the past, the photograph is not only indelibly linked to death; its logic also proceeds according to a linear plotting that, like lynching, should always already culminate in death.[61] More simply put, photography's technical, ideological, and material properties seamlessly "fit" with the structures of racial violence, allowing lynching to flourish while directly affecting modern ways of seeing.[62]

Yet in Rosa's lexicon, lynching's force and photography's logic do not "fit." Instead, the monotonous droll of the camera shutter gives way to the whiz of flying bullets, and the relay of light onto film is refigured as the blinding glare produced at the intersection of firearms and flames. Here, the flash obscures more than it can reveal, and technologies of light render a chaotic scene of blindness. Rosa's testimony does more than simply puncture photography's logic of violent arrest, however. In mapping a terrain of sensory overload that disorders the temporality of both lynching and the photographic event, Rosa asserts that photography's utility to lynching is owing to neither its referentiality nor its capacity to materially demonstrate the aims of white supremacy. Likewise, lynching photography does not accrue value by bolstering what Amy Wood has described as the "assumptions about spectatorship" that encouraged pro-lynching and anti-lynching thought: "that to see an event was to understand its truth."[63] Instead, in Rosa's photographic lexicon, the field of lynching is antagonistic to photographic documentation; but so too is the victim, the photograph's presumed target. As Rosa asserts, in the theater of lynching, photography alerts us to the action that is still occurring off the stage, to what takes shape beyond our field of vision and in excess of available discursive terms for thinking either blackness or racial violence. If lynching photographs endeavored to secure a racial hierarchy, confirming the myth of black criminality and the black body's status as inanimate and exchangeable, then in Rosa's newly conceived logic, photography can only attest to what black life is not: invariably available to photographic capture.

As a nonevent that cannot be rendered photographically, lynching resists and reorganizes photography's rational teleology, what Peggy Phelan has described as a "linear notion of temporal intervals." Routing her discussion through Roland Barthes's theorization of photography as a medium whose meaning is tethered to the past tense, Phelan draws out the progressive temporality that she identifies as "implicit" to his formulation: "the photograph was taken in the past, seen in the future, and projected into the futurity of the subject's death."[64] Photographic viewing, of course, rarely proceeds according to this neat schema. And as scholars of photography have detailed with great clarity and precision, bringing the past into the present produces profoundly disorienting possibilities. Yet Rosa's photographic principle figures the moment of picture taking as a disruptive encounter that can neither be seen in the present nor projected into the future. As photographic aporia, lynching retains its status as an irresolvable encounter that refuses to be ordered according to the logic of visual recognition or legal rationality. That is, if photography belongs to a philosophical tradition that privileges sight and deploys visual operations to affix subjectivity and racial value to the body, then as an encounter that produces a "deep dark" lacuna, Rosa's testimony repudiates the operation that would fix black life as a visual object.

And yet, Rosa's phrasing does not discount photography altogether. Indeed, if photography cannot bear witness to lynching as a temporally coherent event that always ends in the death of its victim, then what it does evidence is an aesthetic encounter. To think of photography as an aesthetic encounter is to deprioritize its materiality, its evidentiary purchase, and to reposition it as site of dynamic interplay between sights and senses, disrupting the very work that photography is compelled to perform in the theater of lynching: imaging its victim. We might think here of the discordant sensory landscape of Rosa's testimony in which the sound of flying bullets cuts across the flash of the bullets and the glaring flames flood her field of vision. In Rosa's photographic landscape, sounds, smells, and tastes interrupt the process that would transform the photographed subject into an object.

Lynching was of course a highly documented affair; a quick glance at the hundreds of photographs and postcards of lynching assembled by James Allen for his 2000 exhibit *Without Sanctuary* makes this point. Still, Lavinia and Rosa's visual glossary encourages us to regard the historical interplay of lynching and photography in light of their temporal and representative incongruities, inconsistencies, and contradictions rather than their seamless correspondence. Reframed as a cultural phenomenon that exceeds the purview of turn-of-the-century documentary practices and extends far beyond the click of the shutter or the flash of a pistol, lynching reemerges as a crime replete with a new set of questions: If photography's logic can break down in the face of racial violence, then what alternate analytics, practices, and archives might begin to make lynching visible as an ongoing catastrophe? If photography contributes to a cultural logic that nurtures lynching, then what creative practices, cultural contexts, and photographic strategies did reformers mobilize to disrupt the visual economy enabling lynching to endure as a cultural norm? Finally, could photography and racial violence ever exist in productive tension, or would the lynching imagery only ever register lynching as an event confined to the past, a redoubling of violence, and ultimately, death? Which is to ask, what does a photography of survival look like?

"Let Them See": Photography, Performance, and Reform

On the night of July 16, 1899, more than a year after the Lake City lynching and in the wake of the trial's conclusion, Lillian Clayton Jewett stood before an at-capacity crowd, including Boston's leading black activists, at St. Paul's Baptist Church and announced her plan to construct a traveling anti-lynching lecture performance featuring the Bakers (see fig. 2.1). At just twenty-four years old, Jewett seemed to materialize out of thin air. The daughter of a wealthy businessman, Jewett surfaced as an unknown white activist with no prior connection to Boston's well-established reform circle. A fledging novelist, Jewett was inspired to enter the anti-lynching fold when "her [African American] maid suggested the idea of making an address" to her congregation, St. Paul's.[65] As a July 29 press feature dedicated to uncovering the emergence of the white anti-lynching ingenue explained, after stumbling upon the topic of lynching and expressing a desire to find a location to "talk very plainly about it," her maid,

FIGURE 2.1 "Miss Lillian C. Jewett Makes an Address," *Boston Herald*, July 17, 1899

who remained unnamed throughout the article, suggested that "any of our colored churches" would be "glad" to give Jewett an audience. Fortuitously, Jewett's political awakening dovetailed with Benjamin Farris's developing "interest in the lynching question." The reverend of St. Paul's Baptist Church, Farris believed that Jewett was the answer to his prayer that "somebody might come forward who could help the colored race out of their difficulties." "Enthusiastic over the possibility of getting a young white woman to appear in his church," Farris busied himself creating posters advertising the July 16 appearance of "Miss L. C. Jewett," a "white woman with strong ties to the South."[66]

For her part, Jewett worked diligently to supply Farris and his congregation with a platform proportional to their demands. In preparation for her debut, she "read with more interest than ever the accounts of the lynchings." When she encountered the story of the Bakers, whose relocation to the North was also a subject of the Colored National League's recent meeting, Jewett made the last-minute decision to redesign her platform, replacing her prepared remarks with a renegade plan to "do all in her power to stop lynching by showing the Baker family as a great object lesson."[67] Wagering that an innovative design would trump inexperience, Jewett's pitch propelled the Bakers into the public sphere, where their bodies were charged with activating the public to take social and moral responsibility in the name of protecting black domestic life. In the following months, Jewett was dragged through the press as an opportunistic woman in search of fame and with a predilection for mental illness. But for at least eight weeks, Jewett emerged as a long-awaited anti-lynching liberator, even as her newfangled plan would have to confront what Rosa and Lavinia Baker understood to be racial violence's visual obstinance.

As she approached the podium, clutching her address to her chest, Jewett asserted that when observed in the flesh the Bakers would offer the North the kind of politically transformative evidence of racial violence that she believed the anti-lynching movement craved but hadn't quite found. Public lectures on lynching like the one staged at St. Paul's were popular in the postbellum North, the most famous example being Ida B. Wells's 1892 speech at New York City's Lyric Hall, which set off an international wave of anti-lynching speeches and rallies. Building on the success of antebellum anti-slavery lectures, Afri-

can American activists and reformers used the highly visible platform
to express strategies for political action and collective organization.
Activists couched their agenda in a kind of public relations campaign
designed to re-form the image of the black body in the public sphere
through the strategic re-presentation of ostensibly objective facts,
data, and images. What qualified as "proof" shifted according to location and audience demographic. When, in the aftermath of her ex-
ile from the South, Wells broke down in tears during her Lyric Hall
"testimonial" about the Memphis lynching that claimed the life of her
close friends and catalyzed her anti-lynching agitation, her "streaming
face" was received as evidence of her sentience and proof of lynching's enduring impact.[68] Yet when she agitated throughout Europe,
Wells armed herself with an authenticating letter from Frederick
Douglass, who "vouched for both her facts and her virtue," and with
a catalog of lynching photographs.[69] The documents functioned as
defensive weapons, assuring audiences that Wells was a credible witness and that, as difficult as it was to imagine, lynching thrived in the
United States.

Jewett moved within and through this tradition while innovat-
ing a new body of anti-lynching evidence. Even as she capitalized on
the political value of embodied grief and the efficacy of a multimedia show—Wells's 1892 appearance, for instance, featured her name
emblazoned across the stage and printed on silk pins—the novelty
of Jewett's project was the proposed source material: living remains.[70]
Yoking the Progressive Era's investment in objectivity to a sentimental
ethos rooted in the politicization of empathetic identification, Jewett
outlined a plan that centered on "get[ting] the Baker family up here
[North]" and presenting them as "living evidence" of lynching. Weaving together as many affective registers as she would performance
genres, Jewett explained:

> There can be no more powerful appeal than the object lesson to be
> found in the three poor, maimed children and their mother, scarred
> and crippled by shot wounds.... The movement to end lynching must
> begin right here. Something must be done to bring our people a true
> picture of the conditions south of us.... Let them see the people who
> are being persecuted and shot down. Bring the Baker family here to
> Boston. Let them see the helpless children, the maimed and destitute

mother, whose husband and little one were killed because the former
was a servant of our government.[71]

In Jewett's reform imaginary, an intimate encounter with live lynching survivors would activate a visual and political transformation,
and Lavinia and her children would correct spurious descriptions of
Southern race relations. Thus, while the press cast white women and
black men as the leading actors in a lynching drama that expanded on
antebellum notions of white female fragility and black male criminality, the Baker family was proof that black women and children were
victims as well.

Although the project was pitched as a revolution in anti-lynching
reform, Jewett's vision banked on the tried-and-true tactics of antebellum reformers who understood spectacle as a central methodology that could, as Amy Hughes has shown, get spectators to simply
look differently. Put forward for a Northern audience, the Bakers'
"scarred" and "crippled" bodies would operate as postbellum iterations of "enfreaked" individuals whose "extraordinary bodies violate
rules, disrupt conventions, and defy expectations."[72] And just as her
predecessors harnessed bodily vulnerability and endurance to facili-
tate the pathway to feeling and sentiment, on the stage, the Bakers
were submitted as symbols of physical precarity while the home was
offered as a primary setting in what would turn out to be a wildly popular sensation scene. Faced with the taxonomic and affective excess
that visitors to sites like P. T. Barnum's museums or anti-slavery lectures would have experienced, Jewett reasoned that audiences would
experience a perceptual overhaul.

But if the rhetorical force of Jewett's appeal was a call for a return
to antebellum political strategies, then the repeated appeal to visual
transformation, "let them see," registers an implicit critique of reform
practices that invested in the power of lynching's death toll and focused on the spectacular sight of the brutalized corpse. Instead of
visual revelation, Jewett reasoned, the onslaught of lynching data created a curious blindness. In this regard, her proposal challenged extant reform tactics that she saw as enforcing passive voyeurism and
the uncritical consumption of the black body through grossly insufficient representational strategies. As she wrapped up her speech,
Jewett brought this point into sharp relief by drawing on none other

than the April 23, 1899, lynching of Sam Hose. Hose's lynching was the sort of highly publicized mass spectacle that was increasingly popular at the century's end. According to reports, more than six thousand Georgians came to witness the torture, mutilation, and burning of Hose, which ended in a mad dash for his charred remains and, ultimately, their sale as souvenirs. Du Bois would later identify his own visual encounter with Hose's dismembered body as the signal event that punctured his faith in empirical methods. When, in the midst of conducting research at Atlanta University's sociology lab Du Bois learned that Hose had been accused of murdering his landlord's wife, he traveled to Atlanta with a "reasoned statement concerning the evidence" and the hope that the facts might stave off the bloodthirsty mob. But when his pointed plan was interrupted by the sale of Hose's remains, Du Bois experienced a professional and political awakening. "Two considerations thereafter broke upon my work and eventually disrupted it," Du Bois recalled. "First, one could not be a calm, cool, and detached scientist while Negroes were lynched, murdered, and starved; and secondly there was no such definite demand for the scientific work of the sort that I was doing."[73]

As it had for Du Bois, for Jewett, Hose's lynching and the public response to its ghastly details also occasioned a reassessment of prevailing anti-lynching strategies. Yet for Jewett, the significance of Hose's spectacular and barbaric murder was not so much the ability to awaken the nation's consciousness but the opposite: its capacity to encourage the commodification of anti-black violence and impede reform. "What is the use of the people in New England harping on the story of Sam Hose?" Jewett asked. After all, she reasoned, the horrendous facts of Hose's murder had not actually led to any political or social change: "The North knows that the ears of this unfortunate man were cut off, that he was skinned alive, yet the North, with all the power, offers a feeble protest and does nothing."[74] For Jewett, the persistent mobilization of Hose by anti-lynching activists unwittingly enforced the cultural logic that was intimately bound up in modernity's claims to progress and that allowed racial violence to flourish alongside developments in mass consumption, voyeurism, and visual technology. In other words, Jewett implied that recounting the details of Hose's murder and the Southern public's enthusiasm around it repeated the violence

wrought by the circulation of lynching images, effectively abstracting his life to exchangeable data.

To be sure, Jewett's rhetoric is as troubling as her directorial debut
would be. But rather than dismissing her work as a case of a white liberal reformer gone wrong, seeing Jewett's attention to the tension between visual evidence and racial violence, between lynching data and
political action and their capacity to erase as much as they reveal, is
crucial to understanding the exhibit's curious design. For unlike either
photographic or statistical evidence, both of which risked reducing
racial violence to mere data points, at least in theory, a performance
of "live" evidence, a term that in and of itself is ambiguous, if not paradoxical, could hold and indeed visualize lynching survivors.

In the days following her St. Paul address, Jewett emerged as a
promising new face of the anti-lynching movement. In response to her
July appeal, "the colored people in the audience, and most of them
were colored, were frantic with enthusiasm" for Jewett, reported the
New York Journal.[75] The press dubbed her a "New Champion," an unexpected "savior," and, in what was undoubtedly a direct response to
her use of antebellum tropes, Jewett was heralded as "the new Harriet Beecher Stowe," a moniker she proudly embraced.[76] Members of
Boston's black community vowed their allegiance by establishing the
Lillian Jewett Anti-Lynching Council to raise funds for the Bakers'
resettlement in the North. And in an odd case of transracial iconography, one press report likened Jewett to Harriet Tubman, dubbing her
journey south the new "underground railroad."[77]

Even before the Baker "spectacle and sensation" reached Boston,
Jewett's plan was already generating an impassioned series of responses. Early on, the proposal was challenged by members of the
black community, likely because just days before announcing her platform, the Colored National League was debating whether to organize
its own relief effort for the Bakers. On Tuesday, August 1, the *Boston
Herald* reported on a "Red Hot Meeting" at which Jewett's detractors, who labeled her an opportunist and worried that removing the
Bakers from their homes was shortsighted, faced off with her ardent
supporters who resolved to "assist Miss Jewett in every conceivable
way in arousing the sleeping conscience of the nation to the terrible
system of lynching."[78] According to one reporter, the meeting came to
an abrupt end when Josephine St. Pierre Ruffin, the longtime editor of
the *Women's Era*, nearly came to blows with Jewett.

As press reports swirled, Jewett was making good on her promise to curate the anti-lynching showcase and immediately began setting in motion a plan to bring the Baker family north for all to "see." Having raised close to $1,000, on August 2 Jewett boarded a train to Charleston, South Carolina, where she planned to meet Lavinia Baker and convince her to return to Boston; she was joined by her mother and R. G. Larsen, a staff correspondent for the *Boston Herald* who was exclusively hired to document the story. By August 7, just five days after Jewett left Boston for South Carolina, the Bakers were headed north, where they were scheduled to headline the Baker Exhibit. The first stop would be in Providence, Rhode Island; from there they would head to Boston before launching a national tour across "lecture rooms and lyceums."[79]

The Bakers' anticipated arrival was a carefully curated visual affair designed to secure their role as the new face of the anti-lynching movement. Having already established Jewett's celebrity with a series of illustrated press reports, the Baker-Jewett publicity machine set to work orchestrating a performance complex, including signature costumes and a well-rehearsed gestural repertoire. As early as July 19, just three days after the St. Paul meeting, the *Boston Herald* printed a full-line drawing accompanied by the headline, "All Acting Together: White and Colored People Aroused by the Efforts for the Baker Family" (fig. 2.2). Rendered in crisp blouses and neat skirts and ties, the image stands in stark contrast to the article's textual description of the Bakers' impoverished living conditions. In a lengthy quote taken from Reverend John Dart, who attended to the family in South Carolina and would soon emerge as one of Jewett's biggest critics, when Jewett announced her plan, the Bakers were living in "almost destitute circumstances." Lavinia, he explained, "has no money and no means of getting any, and at present is being supported by the colored ministers of the community."[80]

The incongruence between the visual depiction of exemplary domesticity and the textual narrative of familial crisis is important here. Absent the specter of poverty and lynching, the image recalls a pre-lynching iteration of intact domesticity while looking forward to the reconstituted kinship that Jewett's efforts promised to deliver. Together, Jewett's plan for domestic rehabilitation and the line drawing recall the work of nineteenth-century educational reformers who, as Laura Wexler has argued, capitalized on the appeal of the "before

ALL ACTING TOGETHER.

White and Colored People Aroused by the Efforts for the Baker Family.

MRS. FRAZIER B. BAKER AND HER FIVE CHILDREN.

These are the surviving members of the family of the late postmaster of Lake City, S. C., whom Miss Lillian Clayton Jewett proposes to bring North as an object lesson against lynching. Mrs. Baker and three of the surviving children were shot, and at least two are maimed for life.

The colored people of Boston have become enthusiastic over the offer of Miss Lillian Clayton Jewett to bring the family of Postmaster Frazier B. Baker North as an object lesson on lynching, and active measures are now being taken to send the young white woman on her mission. It is proposed to call a meeting of white people interested in the cause of the negro, and some of the most prominent representatives of the negro race in Boston, so that action can be taken at once.

The presence in this city of the Rev. Dr. J. L. Dart, president of the Charleston Normal and Industrial Institute, has added to the interest in the matter. Several members of the Baker family are now being educated in Dr. Dart's school, and he has come North for the purpose of raising funds for their support.

Dr. Dart is a large man, and an effective speaker. He addressed the anti-imperialistic meeting in St. Paul's Church Monday evening, and was one of the speakers who broke away from imperialism to take up the matter of lynching.

When seen yesterday by a Herald reporter in reference to the Baker family, and the probable success of Miss Jewett's effort to bring them North, Dr. Dart said:

"I have been trying for some time to induce Mrs. Baker to come North, but she has steadfastly refused to agree to any proposition of the kind. She is now living a short distance from my school, where the children are receiving instruction, and she is in almost destitute circumstances. She has no money, and no means of getting any, and at present is being supported by the colored ministers of the community, who take up collections in her behalf. All the money she has received from other sources has been about $70, which was allowed her as witness fees from the court when she gave evidence against the lynchers.

"Mrs. Baker is a small woman, and very timid. She is intelligent, and has lived in the country all her life, and does not like the city. I have tried to induce her to come North, and my wife has also brought every argument to bear, but so far we have been unsuccessful. I have just written a letter, however, to my assistant pastor, asking him to again see Mrs. Baker and tell her about the movement that is on foot here in Boston, and I have no doubt that something will be done.

"Since Miss Jewell made her remark-able address, affairs have taken a different turn. I met her yesterday, and there is no doubt about her determination to do all she has agreed to do. This young white woman is thoroughly aroused over the condition of affairs in the South, and I fully believe that she will be able to accomplish a great deal.

"I have told her about the difficulty I had in trying to persuade Mrs. Baker to come North with me, but, after talking with Miss Jewett, and hearing the arguments she brings to bear, I feel that she must be successful in what she undertakes. This is the first time that a white woman has offered to take action, and I cannot help feeling that Mrs. Baker will realize the fact that in coming North she will be doing a great service to her race.

"Mrs. Baker has been under a terrible strain since the lynching. She has been in the hospital part of the time, and has had to appear before the courts, so that she is thoroughly tired of all the notoriety she has been receiving, and would rather live quietly if she had any means of support.

"Her friends in the South petitioned the government in her behalf, but nothing has been done, and it now looks as if nothing would be done. She has, however, been very hopeful of receiving some redress from the government, and before I came away spoke about it. This may be one of the reasons why she has been averse to coming North. If Miss Jewett goes down there, I hardly see how she can withstand the arguments which this young woman brings to bear, and I for one will do everything in my power to assist her."

The Baker family now consists of the mother and five children. When the little building in which they lived, and which was the postoffice of Lake City, S. C., was burned Feb. 22 of last year, Baker, after trying unsuccessfully to quench the flames, found that he and his family were surrounded by an armed mob, the members of which began to pour a volley of bullets into the building. Baker and his youngest child were killed, and four others were shot, including Mrs. Baker. The boy was shot in the arm and stomach, and all were so badly injured that they had to spend some months in a hospital.

The lynchers were tried in April of this year, two of the number turning state's evidence, but one of these was not allowed to testify, it being shown that, on account of having served a term in prison, he was not competent. This man, it was shown in court, had been arrested three weeks after it was learned that he had turned state's evidence, on a charge of failing to return a cross-cut saw which he had borrowed some time before, and he was sentenced and put in a chain gang. The evidence on this point was of the most sensational character. The jury in the case disagreed, and it will come up for trial again in November.

and after" model to advertise the efficacy of reformers' intervention and Indigenous peoples' capacity to be civilized.[81] Rather than marshaling the visual pairing to course correct a path that was believed to be incapable of ever reaching industrialized civilization, Jewett evoked the paradigm to index a not-too-distant past that she could help retrieve. Within this new temporal economy, the "after" image registers a time before the before. A special dispatch from her personal journalist Mr. Larsen added additional fuel to the temporal crosshatch. In his account of the Bakers' presence at the train station where they would commence their journey to Boston, Larsen simultaneously conveyed the transformative work that Jewett had already begun while suggesting that the Bakers' current condition was a welcome return to prior domestic bliss: "They were all very black and of slight build, and as they sat there were very different from what they were when Miss Jewett visited the little ramshackle cottage on the outskirts of the city the day before. At that time the trousers of the boys were out at the knees and were supported by one suspender." In contrast to the scene of domestic havoc that Jewett supposedly encountered, after embracing Jewett's offer, the Bakers, Larsen reported, are "rigged out in new clothing, furnished though the generosity of Miss Jewett and the Bakers are all well and happy."[82]

The dissonance between image and the text—that is, between the visual register of domestic idealism and the narrative description of familial precarity—begins the temporal deferral that would ultimately recalibrate the binarism separating living and dead, evidentiary and live, and past and present, all of which the exhibit would come to both exploit and manage. And just as the sketch heralds a past moment while calling forth an unrealized future, it would also turn out to be a preenactment of the exhibit itself and ultimately the photographic portraits. But even before the Bakers emerged on stage, the line drawing was picked up by press outlets as the exhibit's official iconography, creating an additional temporal rerouting. On July 23, the *Boston Post* printed a sketch nearly identical to the image that had appeared in the *Boston Herald* a week earlier (fig. 2.3). What interests me here is the way in which a temporal crisscrossing gets sewn into the Baker Exhibit's fabric, which ultimately provides the occasion for both performative irruptions and political reordering.

On August 8, and in the midst of an onslaught of visual media, the Baker Exhibit premiered in Providence as an interactive show-and-tell

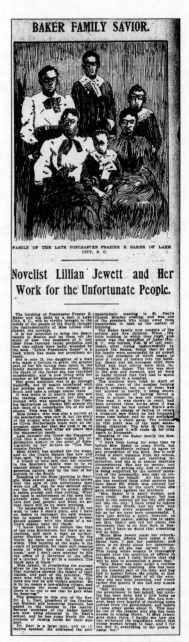

FIGURE 2.3 Sketch of the Baker family, based on the July 19 drawing in the *Boston Herald*, published July 23, 1899, in the *Boston Post*

and reenactment of the *Herald*'s line drawing. Billing it as a display of "living evidence of lynch law and mob violence," the city prepared for the Bakers' Providence Music Hall debut by plastering the city with posters. Featuring a large "picture of Miss Jewett" and emblazoned with the slogan "Lynching must be stopped," the poster praised Jewett as "the champion of justice and humanity" and urged viewers to come see what lynching "looked like."[83] Costumed in the clothing Jewett had recently purchased, and that would quickly become their signature attire, the Bakers entered the hall to a reported three thousand mostly black spectators "cheering, whistling, and stamping [their] feet."[84] As the show began, Jewett led the Bakers on stage and directed them to a sofa where they assumed what was quickly becoming their signature configuration that was also an animation of the press drawings: the Baker children surrounding Lavinia, seated in the center. For at least an hour, various lecturers took the stand, alternating between praising Jewett and denouncing racial violence. Reverend Farris, Jewett's consistent champion, declared that just as God had sent "the great abolitionists" Harriet Beecher Stowe and *Uncle Tom's Cabin*, so too did God respond to this equally pressing "time of need" with "Lillian Jewett who delivered the thunderbolt from St. Paul's Church." Isaac B. Allen, a city councilman, urged the audience to continue supporting the exhibit: "Miss Jewett can do more for Mrs. Baker's cause than all the negroes in New England. We know what has got to be done. You have got to do it our way."[85] For their part, the Bakers metabolized their newfound status as object lessons and living evidence by remaining completely silent and utterly still. As one reporter for the *Boston Post* described it: "The Bakers sat there dumfounded, wondering what it was all about. There was not a movement made by any of them, but around and about them were many who spoke for them."[86]

In the midst of speeches "made by nearly all the representatives of the race," Jewett offered cursory remarks, choosing to focus most of her stage time on the Bakers' bodily presence. In lieu of delivering the "address [she] had in mind," Jewett simply offered the assessment, "I think I have in Mrs. Baker and her family one of the greatest object lessons that has ever been brought North." Redolent of both the objectifying enterprise of human exhibitions that populated world's fairs and the display of the formerly enslaved on the antebellum lecture circuit, Jewett concluded by offering fourteen-year-old Lincoln as living proof of lynching's relentless reach. "I wish to show you little Lincoln," she exclaimed, before "leading him to front" and pointing out how he "was mutilated for life." Toward the end of the show Jewett further disaggregated the mise-en-scène and invited the entire family to the front of the stage, where they were compelled to reveal their injuries and scars to the audience. "Here is the evidence of the barbarism which prevails in the South," Jewett exclaimed as she coaxed Lincoln Baker "to the front showing the audience where he was shot in the eye."[87] That Jewett's directorial decisions repeated the very act of corporeal atomization that motivated lynching was evidently lost on her audience. For rather than spurning Jewett's decision to reexpose the violated body, when the exhibit concluded, dozens of spectators jockeyed for a place in line to attend a reception during which the audience was invited to move "forward to see Mrs. Baker's wounds and also her injured son." In this bizarre corporeal show-and-tell, Jewett induced her audience to experience empathetic identification through an intimate and fleshy encounter, proffering the living body as an index of black physical endurance and of lynching's barbarity. According to the *Pawtucket Times*' coverage, "All the sympathy of the audience was aroused, and it took tangible shape later in the contribution given and the feelings expressed as the audience shook the hands of even the baby boy."[88]

Following a highly successful opening in Providence, the Baker Exhibit traveled to Boston, where it premiered, albeit with substantive changes (see fig. 2.4). Where the Providence show had embraced a restrained aesthetic, leading one reporter to proudly announce that the performance was "no monkey cage show," in Boston the production morphed into a generic hybrid of nineteenth-century theatrical forms, namely, the reform lecture, musical theater, and minstrelsy.[89] The inclusion of musical selections by the famous white abolitionist singer J. W. Hutchinson, who was also involved in the stage adaptation of *Uncle Tom's Cabin*, fortified the show's antebellum character, and the appearance of the popular black vocalist "Miss Nannie Varrs," a ten-cent admission fee, and garish costumes pushed the performance into the terrain of the modern variety show. In the midst of the performance chaos, the Bakers sat with a host of guests on a platform that "was banked with flowers."[90] Reprising her then-standard speech, Jewett began by proclaiming, "I think that the bringing of the Baker

FIGURE 2.4 "Lillian Jewett Brings the Bakers to Boston," *Boston Post*, August 6, 1899

family to Boston contains the greatest moral lesson humanity could be taught," before bringing "Lincoln Baker to the front of the platform" where she "stood with her arm around him."[91]

Somewhere between their stage duties the Bakers posed for a series of portraits in J. E. Purdy's studio, a white Boston-based photographer who also produced photographs and engravings of Jewett. Whereas the Boston show capitalized on the entertainment value of violated bodies, the portraits register a politics of respectability that suggests a desire to correct the exaggerated and racist trappings of the popular stage. Printed as eight-inch-by-ten-inch albumen prints and three-inch-by-five-inch cabinet cards, the photographs restage their performance postures and reenact the drawing printed in the *Post* and the *Herald*: Lavinia Baker sits surrounded by Rosa, Cora, Sarah, William, and Lincoln. In keeping with the conventions of Victorian-era studio photography, the prints reveal an ornate studio outfitted with curtains, wallpaper, gilded picture frames, and a large velvet pillow strategically placed in the outermost corner, gently grazing Sarah's foot (see plate 1). In a second series the backdrop has been removed and the Bakers are joined by six men, including Reverend Farris. A final configuration offers a closely cropped image of the Baker family, absent the race leaders and studio props. By August 18, the images were deposited for copyright at the Library of Congress, suggesting that Jewett expected to sell the cabinet cards at the show. Commissioning photographs, it seems, was always part of Jewett's plan. When the group arrived in Boston on August 9, Jewett "refused to allow the Bakers to be taken to a photographers" right away, suggesting that a session had already been scheduled, or that Jewett imagined that seeing the Bakers around Boston would intensify the public's appetite for photographic Baker paraphernalia.[92] On the pages of the press and in the hands of spectacle attendees, themselves eager to possess a piece of the Bakers, the photographs and cabinet cards would cement the family's celebrity status and role as object lessons.

There is an additional and perhaps unintended consequence of the studio session. It might be, as Rebecca Schneider argues, that the photographs do not so much capture the Bakers, arresting them in time and preparing them for circulation and reproduction as photographic souvenirs. Instead, the photographs operate as a reenactment of the exhibit that was itself a reenactment of the line drawing, which reenacted a pre-lynching family configuration. Trapped in this maze, between the preenactment of the sketch and the reenactment of the photograph, the constituent parts of the Baker Exhibit trouble the "habitual line of binary opposition between 'the live' and the 'archival remain,'" between the photographic object and the performing subject that Schneider reminds us are the circumstances for disruptive and irruptive performance.[93] Less a condition of confusion than an opening for seeing and performing otherwise, the intermedial leakage provides the conditions of possibility for improvisation and dissent.

Such promises quickly came to fruition. On the second night of the show's Boston run, spectators received "something of a shock" when Lavinia Baker performed an impromptu dance that was "not down on the program."[94] According to reports, just as "the white haired abolitionist singer" J. W. Hutchison took the stage, Lavinia lost all emotional and bodily control. She "dropped her little son, Willis [sic], who had been sleeping in her arms and strode around the platform, rolling her eyes and waving her arms."[95] Corroborating and extending this account, another review describes her performance as an amalgam of choreographed dance and religious exhilaration: "On the first night, under the graphic recital of Southern outrages on Negroes by Miss Jewett, the Baker woman got religion, dropped her baby and pranced around the stage in a true corn shucking style" of the kind that was the "peculiar manner of her race."[96] In a somewhat restrained description, the *Boston Post*, which was incredibly generous to Jewett, dismissed the performance as the culmination of "nerves" and "exhaustion." While Jewett recounted the details of Frazier's and Julia's murders, "Mrs. Baker was overcome by her emotions, but after being assisted by her friends, regained her composure" (see fig. 2.5).[97] Echoing this position, the *Boston Herald* reported that Lavinia was inadvertently lulled into unconsciousness by the show's musical selections: "When Mr. Hutchison was singing after Miss Jewett had concluded, the audience was startled by Mrs. Bakers sudden fainting. She sat on the left of the platform near the singer, and the strain under which she had been all the evening proved too much for her when the relaxation, afforded by Mr. Hutchison's soothing southern melody came. It took several minutes to revive her."[98]

It is impossible to know exactly what transpired on stage, but I want to speculate a bit about Lavinia's surprising solo. The curious collapse

FIGURE 2.5
"Mrs. Baker Yields
to Her Emotions,"
Boston Post,
August 8, 1899

of a "corn shucking" style and "getting religion" is especially instructive. For it is highly unlikely that Lavinia performed the corn shuck, a choreographed dance that usually requires a partner. What is more likely is that the journalist perceived, and ultimately dismissed, her movement—perhaps she made percussive use of her body or perhaps she was moved to religious ecstasy in the tradition of Jarena Lee—as mere "darky antics" and ill-timed celebration.[99] In this regard, Lavinia Baker's "peculiarly" black "religious exhilaration" recalls a different kind of embodied movement, the shout. Relinquishing the tight choreography of something like the corn shuck, a "shouter," Ashon Crawley has explained, would spontaneously and without warning "jump up and down . . . hold arms up, bent at the elbow moving to the rhythm of a repetitious song or chant" or of their own heart.[100] The repeated attention to Lavinia's religious "exhilaration" along with the visual imagery of her arms flung and body falling back that accompanies the articles, not to mention the undeniable disruption she caused, situates Lavinia's dance in a long tradition of black eccentric performance, one that not only encompasses the religious shout but also points toward the varied forms of black embodied movement that eluded legibility and yet captured audiences curiosity. Constructed as a frenzied and frenetic body, like her testimony, Lavinia's dancing refused legibility and fractured the representational frames put in place by anti-lynching and pro-lynching advocates alike.[101] In fact, so disorienting was Lavinia's dance to the exhibit's imagined impact that one reporter remarked, "It was with the utmost difficulty that the woman was induced to become quiet, and hereafter Miss Jewett will probably find it necessary to avoid the introduction of religious songs and talks as a feature of the Baker show."[102]

Lavinia's corporeal reaction interrupts and redirects the performance of passive mourning that Jewett crafted. Rather than publicly revealing her own injuries and remaining still, Lavinia Baker's dance is an embodied ritual that calls attention to the ways that racial violence quite literally moves, and moves through, the body. Here, mourning and lament take shape in improvisatory gestures, unscripted solos, and ephemeral movements so that the "event" or "object" of the rituals, the violence wrought on the Bakers, is unmoored from space, geography, and physical referent. The interruption confronts viewers with the question, How do you mourn that which is still happening? In its capacity to disturb the program and confound spectators, in its refusal to be temporally bound, Lavinia's ecstatic performance challenges the political claims that, much like the trial, rely on quantifying injury and abstracting violence. And by denying the performance ritual the visual iconography that would convert her into a spectacular site, she also denied the violent process of objectification and quantification that would allow her life to matter so little.

As it turned out, Lavinia's reminder that she was "still living" was too much for Boston's black attendees to manage. Faced with a categorical crisis—what kind of "lesson" in racial violence could survivors offer? What did it mean to consume living evidence? Could a family photograph ever be conscripted into the anti-lynching storehouse of data?—the Baker Exhibit's attendees quickly lost interest; within a week of its opening, the show permanently closed, and shortly thereafter the Jewett Anti-Lynching Council dissolved. Lillian Jewett eventually left Boston and made her way to the South, where she continued to agitate against lynching and even attempted to locate additional lynching survivors. The Bakers were given over to the care of Boston's leading reformers. Yet the challenge to lynching's visual logic embedded in the Bakers' performance repertoire and archived in its visual ephemera would continue to endure, taking hold in unlikely places and haunting visual strategies, editorial practices, and photographic archives.

Looking Out: Toward a New Visual Epistemology of Survival

On November 11, just months after Lavinia Baker's ecstatic performance brought the Baker Exhibit to a screeching halt, the *Richmond Planet* published "Appeal to the Colored People of the United States." An unmistakable riff on David Walker's 1829 *Appeal to the Colored Citizens of the World*, the *Planet*'s plea was far less ambitious. Where Walker endeavored to legitimate African Americans' claims to national identity by crafting a text whose networks of circulation doubled as a rubric for free black mobility, the *Planet*'s "Appeal" turned to a particularly domestic setting: the Bakers' new home. Despite their ostensibly divergent political goals, both appeals imagine community building to be a matter of circulation above all.[103] Where Walker banked on secreted networks of black readers to disseminate his incendiary pamphlet, the *Planet* invested in circulation patterns of a family photograph.

Printed toward the bottom of the front page between articles defending the "virtues of the Negro woman of the south" and an update on "Negro Progress in Jamaica," the *Planet*'s editors entreated readers to "aid in furnishing the Baker home." According to the article, when the Jewett Anti-Lynching Council dissolved, "the white friends of humanity and justice" committed to rehabilitating the Bakers' domestic lives by "furnish[ing] the necessary means to purchase a home for the family of the late Frazier B. Baker in the hopes of raising a lump sum of 400 dollars." The "Appeal" invited "persons who desire to aid in the furnishing of a room in the Baker Homestead" to send in ".25 in cash and .01 in a stamp." As a token of gratitude, they would receive a photographic portrait "taken recently by Purdy, the celebrated photographic artist." According to the *Planet*'s calculations, it would take sales from "200 pictures," to furnish one room of the Baker home. Once the goal was met, "a photograph of it [the completed home] will also be mailed to each contributor who makes an application for them."[104] It is impossible to know which of the seven extant photographs made their way up and down the East Coast, or if a different image altogether did. But in the image nineteen-year-old Rosa Baker is almost certainly smirking.

Judging from her expression, when Rosa arrived in J. E. Purdy's studio to pose for a series of family portraits, she was flattered, amused, or simply disenchanted. Having already performed for at least two nights in the exhibit, Rosa could imagine how popular the photograph would be. After all, at least three thousand people attended the Providence and Boston premieres, and on opening night hundreds clamored for an in-person encounter with her mother. Thus, she was certainly not surprised when just days after the portrait session the photograph was reprinted on dozens of cabinet cards and showcased in the exhibition's lobby. Neither would she have been shocked when her image was emblazoned on the front page of the *Colored American National Newspaper*'s December 2 issue or in the August 13 *Boston Post*. So, when Rosa smirked, she was perhaps embracing her newfound celebrity, relishing the reality that, regardless of their intentions, dozens of people lined up to see her arrive at a train depot. Or perhaps given what she knew about the fragility of domesticity, she found it comical, if not ironic, to pose before the ornate backdrop with its simulated wallpaper and overstuffed cushions. Smirking might have been all she could do to keep quiet when Purdy recited his photographic ethos, "I believe the real or true function of photography to be to record and publish the truth."[105] For as she had heard her mother and sister recount on the witness stand just a few months earlier, it was nearly impossible to photographically record the "truth" about lynching. And so Rosa smirked.

In the large albumen print, which was also published as a cabinet card before being printed on the cover of the *Colored American National Newspaper*, Rosa is seated to her mother's left side. Dressed in a striped blouse and belted black skirt, most likely the clothing that Jewett purchased and compelled her to wear (first on the train ride from Charleston to New York and then during the exhibit), Rosa confidently rests her gloved hands on her thighs. Unlike fifteen-year-old Cora, who stands behind her, or her youngest brother William, wedged between herself and Lavinia, Rosa refuses to match their emotionless gazes. Nor does she let her shoulders cave in, like Sarah, who was perhaps recoiling from either Purdy's or Jewett's directive to sit up straight. Instead, Rosa resolutely pushes back her shoulders, tilts her head to the left, and smirks. Over the course of the series, her expression changes slightly from a smirk to a smile and then back to a smirk. When the family moves to a plain backdrop for the closely cropped cabinet cards, she retains her expression. Sometimes her family joins her, holding in smiles that threaten to burst through the script of black survival that the photograph is tasked with recording. Only when five leading "race men" enter the frame, their towering bodies endeavoring to contain the disruptive possibility threating to burst through the tightly curated arrangement, does Rosa restrain her expression. Tightening her lips and stiffening her shoulders, for at least an instant, she is disciplined within the terms of uplift and respectability that the photographic portrait purported to deliver and that the *Planet* promised to its readers.

But for most of what we see from the session, Rosa smirks. Rosa's expression invites us to read the photographs within the terms of citationality and theatricality, one that zigzags from the stage to the photography studio to the hands of the *Planet*'s subscribers, who, like their New England counterparts, were fascinated by the sight of living remains. Tracking the photograph's course requires reckoning with what Schneider reminds us is photography's theatrical history. Refusing the "long-standing assumption that photography offers thanatical 'evidence' of a time considered, in linear temporal logic, irretrievable," Schneider argues that like live performance, photographic time is not the time of disappearance.[106] For even as the photograph records an event, it is also always looking forward to "a live moment when the image will be re-encountered."[107] Thus, photography and live theater

MRS. FRAZER BAKER AND CHILDREN.

Family of the Murdered Postmaster at Lake City, So. Carolina.

MRS. FRAZER BAKER AND CHILDREN,

Family of the Murdered Postmaster at Lake City, So. Carolina.

MRS. FRAZER BAKER AND CHILDREN,

Family of the Murdered Postmaster at Lake City, So. Carolina.

MRS. FRAZER BAKER AND CHILDREN,
Family of the Murdered Postmaster at Lake City, So. Carolina.

Copyright 1899
by J. E. Purdy & Co.
Boston.

MRS. FRAZER BAKER AND CHILDREN,

Family of the Murdered Postmaster at Lake City, So. Carolina.

Copyright 1899
by J. E. Purdy & Co.
Boston.

MRS. FRAZER BAKER AND CHILDREN,
Family of the Murdered Postmaster at Lake City, So. Carolina.

MRS. FRAZER BAKER AND CHILDREN,

Family of the Murdered Postmaster at Lake City, So. Carolina.

Purdy   SUCCESSOR
To Hastings   146 TREMONT ST.
BOSTON.

Plates

Plate 1 "Mrs. Frazer Baker and Children: Family of the Murdered Postmaster at Lake City, So. Carolina." Photographic print by J. E. Purdy, Boston, ca. August 1899, gelatin silver print, 30.3 × 25.7 cm (Library of Congress, Prints and Photographs Division)

Plates 2–5 "Mrs. Frazer Baker and Children: Family of the Murdered Postmaster at Lake City, So. Carolina." Photographic cabinet cards by J. E. Purdy, Boston, ca. August 1899 (Library of Congress, Prints and Photographs Division)

Plates 6–7 Lavinia Baker and her children with prominent African American male leaders, ca. 1899. Photographic cabinet cards by J. E. Purdy, Boston, ca. August 1899 (Library of Congress, Prints and Photographs Division) are linked by a shared duration in which meanings steadily accrue. As she mines photography's theatrical ligaments, Schneider locates her argument in the *tableau vivant*, that particular genre of still performances in which still and living confront each other to produce a peculiar "temporal cross fashioning" that unravels the distinction between before and after, what remains and what disappears, original and reenactment.[108] Of all of the visual genres that structure the Baker Exhibit, the *tableau vivant* is perhaps the most evident. At the peak of its popularity, the trend of simulating scenarios and scenes was arguably the most widespread form of American entertainment.[109] During the Providence show, for instance, the Bakers assembled on a sofa that simulated a living room, itself a restaging of the sketches that had appeared in Boston's *Herald* and *Post*. Having likely already encountered the Baker iconography in the press, the performance would have certainly registered as reform-oriented *tableau vivant*. And in this moment of citational static, the boundaries between photograph, still pose, and line drawing decompose, as does the boundary between performance and photography.

Just as the Baker Exhibit traffics in the conventions of the *tableau vivant*, so too does Rosa's distinct pose resonate as a performative gesture, one that casts "a kind of hail cast into the future moment of its invited recognition."[110] The future moment is both the next iteration of the performance and the moment when her family's photograph will arrive in the hands of the *Richmond Planet*'s African American subscribers. At the very same time, the smirk gestures to a prior visual performance and medium, in this case the sketch that served as the photograph's blueprint and the embodied and emotional labor that the stage performance demands. Like her mother's eccentric and irruptive dance, Rosa's smirk exposes photography's performative contours, its irruptive place within a multimedia network of citation that strains against the terms of truth, evidence, or personhood that it is meant to denote. And just as Lavinia's dance and courtroom performance fracture the pathway to passive consumption of blackness or black embodied performance, in its capacity to unravel the temporality that both photography and lynching rely on, Rosa's smirk instantiates a gestic hail, one that I call "looking out."

Looking out instantiates a temporal slowdown that structures photography's future networks of circulation. A refusal to turn away, looking out is a durational practice during which the past continues to intrude on the present. But to look out is not simply about looking past the event at hand and toward the next, a gesture that would veer too close to dismissal. On the contrary, looking out identifies an ethical posture that is not about recognition or elaborating the "truth," but about sounding an alarm. For unlike looking back or reversing the gaze, analytics that have been especially useful for theorizing nineteenth-century black photographic practices, looking out does not depend on mutual recognition or make recourse to the authority of a dominant gaze. Looking out calls to a future where domesticity is always imperiled, where the best line of defense is to arm oneself with a "Winchester Rifle," as Ida B. Wells so cogently put it in *Southern Horrors*.[111] And although it evokes a spoken warning—as in "look out!"—looking out is less verbal command than a low frequency that animates black living. Here, looking out is a warning, but it is also a visual tactic that can perceive the still living and the survivor. It is perhaps what Maritcha Lyons and Victoria Earle Matthews had in mind when, upon delivering her speech at New York's Lyric Hall seven years earlier, they gifted Ida B. Wells with a gold broach, shaped like a pen and engraved with "Mizpah," the Hebrew word for "lookout." Described by Patricia Schechter as a "symbol of the power of words to create conditions for survival," looking out also names a kind of embodied posture.[112] Whether tucked into an album alongside *cartes des visites* of friends and families or hung on the wall of a Richmond home, Rosa invites us to look out at the black home as a threshold catastrophe and to think of the family photograph as lynching photograph. To look out, then, is to train one's attention on black living as the catalyst for political transformation, on the everyday practices and small gestures that make living in what Christina Sharpe might call the "wake" of white supremacy not only bearable, but also beautifully disruptive (see plates 2–7).[113]

Photographically Hesitant: The Visual Politics of
W. E. B. Du Bois's "Jesus Christ in Georgia"

Perhaps it was photography's capacity to cast a hail, to sound an alarm, to circulate at a frequency that disrupted any effort to relegate lynching to a past tense that W. E. B. Du Bois had in mind when he entered Purdy's studio five years later and sat for what would become one of his most famous portraits (fig. 2.6). In the photograph Du Bois sits slightly off kilter, his shoulders turning toward the camera while his head is firmly in profile. With eyes slightly cast down, Du Bois looks into the distance. One year earlier *The Souls of Black Folk* had appeared in print. Writing with what David Levering Lewis describes as the hope of "enlivening the inert and despairing," *Souls* was for Du Bois what the Baker Exhibit was for Jewett, an aesthetic response to Sam Hose's lynching and an effort to trace "the grain of hidden truth."[114] *Souls* was an immediate success, going through multiple editions within its first year and achieving record sales. Yet when he posed for Purdy, the "deeper recesses" of black social and spiritual life that Du Bois wagered might, when brought into focus, disturb the color line, remained mostly opaque. For his part, Purdy promised a photographic outcome that was nothing short of transcendent. In a 1908 interview for *The Arena*, Purdy described his work in terms that echo Du Bois's lexicon. "The legitimate sphere of photography," he explained, "is to publish the truth, not only as it appears realistically, but to get at the souls and express it all—the whole truth."[115] Du Bois may have been banking on Purdy's promise to "get at the souls" as a means to, as Du Bois put it, unearth the "grain of truth hidden there." And yet as he sat for Purdy, Du Bois was also looking out for a literary strategy that might approximate the "unique angle of vision" that *Souls* had promised and that the portrait could never entirely confer.[116]

Eight years later Du Bois was still embroiled with photography's "enlivening" potentiality, or the lack thereof. In the February 1912 issue of *The Crisis*, Du Bois found himself defending his decision to begin publishing lynching photographs in the magazine and wondering whether an editorial stance could also sound an alarm and direct attention to lynching's status as a threshold catastrophe. In the coming decades, the NAACP and *The Crisis* would rely on the strategic redeployment of lynching photographs as a primary tool in their line of defense against lynching. From its founding in 1909, racial violence was what Megan Ming Francis describes as the "gateway issue" around which the NAACP organized.[117] "The NAACP started with a lynching," Du Bois wrote in his posthumously published *Autobiography*.[118] Building on the strategies that Ida B. Wells pioneered in the 1890s, the NAACP reprinted graphic photographs of lynching in *The Crisis* and in their pamphlets that began circulating after 1915. When viewed

FIGURE 2.6
W. E. B. Du Bois,
photograph by J. E.
Purdy, ca. 1904,
Boston (Library of
Congress, Prints
and Photographs
Division)

alongside poetry, biography, articles on voting trends, and of course, lynching statistics, photographic evidence of anti-black violence was intended to foster an "alternate form of lynching spectatorship."[119] Here the image and text produce what Leigh Raiford describes as a "disjuncture in our visual epistemology" whereby anti-black violence is framed as particularly anti-democratic practice and white supremacy is made a spectacle.[120] The NAACP's reappropriation of lynching photography is in keeping with what Francis describes as its signature "opinion shaping strategy": transforming public perception to achieve civil rights. "The NAACP's initial exposure-focused strategy was predicated on the belief that white Americans would become so enraged that they would feel compelled to do something to end the tragedy of racial violence," she explains.[121] In 1916, and on the heels of the release of D. W. Griffith's *The Birth of a Nation* and the highly spectacular lynching in Waco, Texas, of Jesse Washington, a mentally challenged black man, the NAACP formalized its anti-lynching strategy. In addition to the editorial decision to strategically dovetail photographs and news reporting in *The Crisis* (before this they often appeared in a haphazard and unrelated fashion), it also extended the reach of its publicity campaign by increasing pamphlet circulation. But whereas *Crisis* readers would ultimately come to associate the genre of the illustrated lynching exposé with the NAACP, in 1912 they were suspicious of Du Bois's decision to reprint the symbols of white supremacy in a magazine geared toward an African American public.

Du Bois began experimenting with the place of lynching photographs in the 1911 Christmas issue.[122] Significantly, the photograph did not receive a full-page spread or even an identifying caption. Instead, Du Bois chose to artfully embed the photograph within a line drawing that served as the title illustration to his own short story, "Jesus Christ in Georgia" (fig. 2.7). Framed by a drawing of a wooden cross, the lynching photograph is nestled in the lower-right quadrant. In the center of the cross a thorn-crowned Christ gazes down on the hanged man surrounded by a crowd of white men who proudly frame the body. If the December design was an attempt to habituate readers to the sight of a hanging black corpse, by the next month, Du Bois had done away with all the protective scaffolding. The January 1912 issue features two lynching photographs. The first is the front and back of a postcard from a lynching in Andalusia, Alabama, addressed to the anti-lynching advocate John Haynes Holmes with the message: "This is the way we do them down here. The last lynching has not yet been put on card yet. Will put you on our regular mailing list. Expect one a month on the average."[123] Toward the end of the issue a second set of images appeared. Printed alongside the anonymously authored poem "The Vision of a Lyncher," the first photograph was taken at John Lee's lynching in Durant, Oklahoma, and the second is an enlarged image of the photograph featured alongside "Jesus Christ in Georgia," suggesting that having already seen a cropped image of the crime, readers would be prepared to receive the entire frame.[124]

While subscribers were unaccustomed to seeing lynching photographs in *The Crisis*, they were certainly familiar with the magazine's coverage of lynching. Each issue printed tabulated statistics

JESUS CHRIST IN GEORGIA

THE convict guard laughed.
"I don't know," he said, "I hadn't thought of that——"

He hesitated and looked at the stranger curiously. In the solemn twilight he got an impression of unusual height and soft dark eyes.

"Curious sort of acquaintance for the Colonel," he thought; then he continued aloud: "But that nigger there is bad; a born thief and ought to be sent up for life; is practically; got ten years last time——"

Here the voice of the promoter talking within interrupted; he was bending over his figures, sitting by the Colonel. He was slight, with a sharp nose.

"The convicts," he said, "would cost us $96 a year and board. Well, we can squeeze that so that it won't be over $125 apiece. Now, if these fellows are driven, they can build this line within twelve months. It will be running next April. Freights will fall fifty per cent. Why, man, you will be a millionaire in less than ten years."

The Colonel started. He was a thick, short man, with clean-shaven face, and a certain air of breeding about the lines of his countenance; the word millionaire sounded well in his ears. He thought—he thought a great deal; he almost heard the puff of the fearfully costly automobile that was coming up the road, and he said:

"I suppose we might as well hire them."

"Of course," answered the promoter.

The voice of the tall stranger in the corner broke in here:

"It will be a good thing for them?" he said, half in question.

The Colonel moved. "The guard makes strange friends," he thought to himself. "What's this man doing here, anyway?" He looked at him, or rather, looked at his eyes, and then somehow felt a warming toward him. He said:

"Well, at least it can't harm them—they're beyond that."

"It will do them good, then," said the stranger again. The promoter shrugged his shoulders.

"It will do us good," he said.

But the Colonel shook his head impatiently. He felt a desire to justify him-

FIGURE 2.7 First page of W. E. B Du Bois's "Jesus Christ in Georgia," *The Crisis*, December 1911

and reports of press coverage of recent lynchings. Alongside news of black achievement, the lynching coverage contributed to what Russ Castronovo has described as the magazine's "confrontational aesthetics."[125] Adopting what Jacqueline Goldsby has described as Wells's masterful strategy of repurposing lynching figures to "parody the patriarchal voice of rational objectivity to examine its limitations," each month *Crisis* subscribers were presented with a rapidly unfurling catalog of victim names.[126] Assuming journalism's detached voice, the column "Crime" offered cursory details of lynching—location, name, and abridged description of the offense—as it shifted the subject of criminality from blackness to white supremacy: "At Washington, Ga., a Negro charged with murder was lynched on October 28. At Caruthersville, M., two Negroes were lynched. . . . In Manchester, Ga., a Negro was lynched. . . . At Marshall, Tex., a colored man choked a white woman and demanded matches of her daughter-in-law. He was lynched."[127] Just two months earlier, Du Bois's editorial "Triumph" showed little restraint in his account of the lynching in Coatesville, Pennsylvania, which drew thousands of spectators from the neighboring cities of Philadelphia and Chester. Rendering in graphic detail the lynching's performance, including the requisite hunt for bodily souvenirs, the editorial recounted: "People walked and drove to the scene of the burning. Men and women poked the ashes and a shout of glee would signalize the finding of blackened tooth or mere portions of unrecognizable bones. By noon the black heap had been leveled and only the scorched ground was left to tell what had happened there."[128] But if readers were comfortable digesting facts, figures, and even graphic textual recitals of the barbarism of white mobs replete with descriptions of charred bodily souvenirs, lynching photographs were evidently too much to bear.

In the March 1912 issue, and in response to letters begging him to cease publishing the imagery, Du Bois addressed his position head on in the editorial "The Gall of Bitterness." Sketching a line of defense that anticipates his 1926 essay "Art and Propaganda," Du Bois explained that his determination to print "bitter" material, of which lynching photography is just one example, was designed to counteract the damaging pervasiveness of "sweet facts" that feed the color line. "True it is that this country has had its appetite for facts on the Negro problem spoiled by sweets," he explains. Sweet facts, he continues, are the popular fictions of black life that steer an easy course away from historically grounded politics and toward the exploitative and pernicious: "In earlier days the Negro minstrel who 'jumped Jim Crow' was the typical black man served up to the national taste. It was the balmy day when slaves were 'happy' and 'preferred' slavery to all other possible states. . . . In the last fifteen years there has come another campaign of Joy and Laughter to degrade black folk. We have had audiences entertained with 'nigger' stories, tales of pianos and cabins, and of the general shiftlessness of the freedman. This is the lie which *The Crisis* is here to refute."[129] Challenging the "lie," Du Bois reminds his readers, means confronting the "dark" side of things. And it is here, in his defense of truth as both an avenue to justice and an aesthetic category that will double as propaganda, that Du Bois proffers a defense of lynching photography:

> In so trying [to narrate the truth] we realize that the mere statement of the facts does not always carry its message. Often the lighter touch, the insinuation and the passing reference are much more effective. We know this, and yet, so often the grim awfulness of the bare truth is so insistent we feel it our duty to state it. Take those stark and awful corpses, men murdered by lynch law, in last month's issue: it was a gruesome thing to publish, and yet—could the tale have been told otherwise? Can the nation otherwise awaken to the enormity of this beastly crime of crimes, this rape of law and decency? Could a neat joke or a light allusion make this nation realize what 2,500 murders such as these look like?[130]

It is easy to dismiss Du Bois's stance as an uncritical celebration of photography's veridical power, its capacity to represent the unvarnished "facts" about racial violence and "awaken" the nation to knowledge-based action. Indeed, this was the stated goal of *The Crisis*: "[the] whole reason for being is the revelation of the facts of racial antagonism now in the world, and these facts are not humorous," concluded Du Bois.[131] Yet one such reading fails to take into account both Du Bois's long and deeply ambivalent relationship to photography and the first lynching photograph's intimacy with "Jesus Christ in Georgia."

To be sure, Du Bois frequently embraced photography as a powerful strategy in the fight for black citizenship, most notably in the hundreds of photographs he assembled for display at the 1900 Paris Exposition. Constituting what Shawn Michele Smith describes as a counterarchive, Du Bois's photographic practice "intervenes in dominant ways of knowing and representing race, envisioning a culturally authorized visual record's codification of racial information."[132] Yet if he marshaled photography to disaggregate the "racialized cultural prerogatives of the gaze," then just as often Du Bois withheld photographic evidence at the very moment we might have expected it to surface. Most notable here is the sweeping sociological study *The Philadelphia Negro*. Although that was certainly an exercise in visualization and visuality, Du Bois departed from the social survey's conventions discussed in chapter 1 when he decided against publishing photographs of Philadelphia's Seventh Ward.[133]

In the context of what is best described as a photographic hesitancy, the concluding query of "The Gall of Bitterness"—"could the tale be told otherwise"—flags an understudied reading of lynching photographs in the magazine.[134] That is, what happens when we take Du Bois's question seriously, as a question regarding the formal and aesthetic workings that might make lynching known not just as a "fact" but also as an ongoing crisis? Moving in this direction, the "otherwise" calls for a visual practice that invests the photograph with duration and time, but it also means tracking the range of narratives that a lynching photograph can announce. If, as the Bakers instruct us, a family photograph can be a lynching photograph, then might a photograph of mob violence index something other than either criminality or vulnerability? From this vantage point, the photograph is dislodged from the burden of proof and instead tasked with organizing a visual praxis for re-viewing lynching.

This strategy emerges at the intersection of the Oklahoma lynching photograph and "Jesus Christ in Georgia." Printed without any identifying information, the short story frames the image, directing us how to read it and adding a caption to the otherwise orphan image. In his influential account of photographs and captions, Roland Barthes maintains that a text quickens the photographic message, affixing floating signifiers and directing the viewers' gaze. "The text," Barthes explains, "constitutes a parasitic message designed to connote the image, to 'quicken' it with one or more second-order signifieds." For Barthes, this marks a significant "historical reversal." Where images once illustrated the text, in this new order, "text comes to sublimate, patheticize or rationalize the image."[135] When read as a caption to the unidentified image of the murdered victim, "Jesus Christ in Georgia" does not so much quicken the photographic meaning, as Barthes would have it, but slows it down, mirroring the temporal deferral that looking out instantiates. Here, the story's narrative incoherence and circuitous plot creates a productive disjuncture between image and text such that the photograph refuses to assimilate into a progressive historical narrative and instead continues to irrupt with an emergency claim.

"Jesus Christ in Georgia" narrates the spectral appearance of a "stranger" who appears in an unnamed Georgia town and is equal part social investigator and would-be savior. The story opens as the stranger bears witness to three white speculators—a convict guard, a promoter, and a colonel—espousing the profitability of convict leasing. Mistaken for a white man, he is invited to a dinner at the colonel's home. But when his racial identity is discovered, he quickly departs, only to reencounter a man who recently escaped the chain gang. Redirecting his fugitive path, the stranger implores the escapee to value work and property over theft and a life on the run. However, even as he adopts the principles of thrift and work, when the convict runs into his employer's white wife, toppling to the ground with her, he is charged with sexual impropriety and hanged while the stranger gazes on.

Like most of Du Bois's fiction, "Jesus Christ in Georgia" has received little scholarly attention and is almost never read in relationship to photography.[136] In his capacious two-volume biography of Du Bois, David Levering Lewis dedicates a passing clause to the fictional enterprise and simply explains it away as a short story "whose ethical and social messages the reader could readily interpret."[137] Likewise, Arnold Rampersad conflates the story with its descendant, "Jesus Christ in Texas," which was republished in the 1920 collection *Dark Water*. For Rampersad, the nearly identical versions demonstrate Du Bois's fascination with "the potential value of using religious forms for propagandistic ends."[138] Although the short story is mentioned in passing in Wilson J. Moses's *Black Messiahs and Uncle Toms*, his attention to Du Bois's messianic imagination offers the most useful framework for beginning to make sense of "Jesus Christ in Georgia." In works ranging from *The Souls of Black Folk* to his 1928 novel *Dark Princess*, Moses notes Du Bois's sustained investment in messianism. But where Du Bois's curiosity in the figure of a black savior "seldom emphasized retribution," in his messianic imaginary, "the ordeals of his black protagonists, whether real or mythical, were consciously identifiable with the redemptive suffering of Jesus Christ."[139] Although Du Bois was critical of American Christianity, Moses argues that he was nevertheless deeply committed to the possibilities that inhered in "sacrifice and self-denial."[140] Along these lines, in "Jesus Christ in Georgia" the stranger appears as a "messianic figure," a Christ reincarnate whose presence in the small town holds out the possibility of destabilizing the convict-leasing economy's racial logics and activating a fugitive's lapsed work ethic. Thus, when the stranger repeatedly questions whether the lease system "will be a good thing for them," the promoter reasons, "Well at least it can't harm them—they're beyond that," before admitting, "It will do us good."[141] Similarly, when the stranger commands, "Thou shalt not steal," the escapee rationalizes, "Seems like when I sees things I just must—but, yes, I'll try."[142]

But rather than signaling the pending arrival of a long-awaited emancipation earned through patience and sacrifice, Du Bois's messianic construction suggests that the future is best defined by an enduring proximity to more violence. What we might think of as failed messianism finds formal expression in the narrative boomeranging between moments of presumed revelation and concealment and between recognition and utter disidentification. Indeed, when the stranger abruptly appears, characters lose their self-possession. "In some way, they did not exactly know how" the colonel and his family get the "impression that the man was a teacher." Likewise, after a "curious conversation" in their home, "they did not remember exactly what was said and yet they all remembered a certain strange satisfaction in that long, low talk."[143] Unfinished thoughts, countless dashes, and vague pronouns fill each sentence so that everything and everyone emerges in a state of conceptual, visual, and narrative confusion. The "stranger" himself is "olive" but also "even yellow," a racial amalgam that anticipates Du Bois's claim in "The Church and the Negro" that, were Jesus still alive, "he would associate with Negroes and Italians and working people."[144] The moral compass in "Jesus Christ in Georgia" is equally vague. In the face of the stranger's "Thou shalt not steal" command, the escaped convict, for example, provides a convincing counterargument: "But what about them? Can they steal? Didn't they steal a whole year's work[?]"[145]

When read as a textual frame for the photograph, the uncertainty that abounds in "Jesus Christ in Georgia" invests the photograph with a temporality that pries apart the link between photography, evidence, and data. The ambiguous ending of the story draws this point into sharp relief. As the woman watches the convict's lynching from the safe distance of her window, the iconography of the hanging body fuses with a crucified Christ:[146] "He stretched his arms out like a cross, looking upward. Behind the swaying body, and down where the little, half ruined cabin lay, a single flame flashed up amid the far-off shout and cry of the mob. . . . Suddenly whirling into one great crimson column it shot to the top of the sky and threw great arms athwart the gloom above the world and behind the roped and swaying form below hung quivering and burning a great burning cross. There, heaven-tall, earth-wide, hung the stranger on the crimson cross, riven and blood-stained with thorn-crowned head and pierced hands."[147] Here, murky coordinates—athwart, above, next to—construct a chaotic visual field that refuses the reader's mastery over a scene of alleged and certain death. Indeed, even after combing through this passage and its syntax, it is unclear whether the victim is the stranger, the convict, or both. If "Jesus Christ in Georgia" assures readers that Jesus walks among us, and more specifically in rural Georgia, then the final textual moments invite a moment of self-recognition as the stranger gazes upon a murder that might be his own. And while this moment of identification is restaged in the photographic drawing—the thorn-crowned Jesus gazes down at the photographed victim—the nebulous conclusion opens more questions than it answers. Are we made to believe that he is viewing himself or sympathetically gazing on the victim? Rather than affixing death to the image or claiming photography as a referential medium that always registers a truly existing thing, in this moment of possible recognition between the victim and the stranger viewers confront what awaits them while the photographic meaning slackens. What I want to isolate here is a strategy for approaching and viewing vis-à-vis "Jesus Christ in Georgia" whereby readers see lynching photography as part of an ongoing scene that can likely never be captured in its entirety.

Du Bois's editorial experiment interrogates the structure of a photographic project that aims to tell a story of racial violence as an ongoing crisis, a state of emergency, and a crime whose impact resounds far beyond the "event" of lynching. In so doing, he confronts whether his editorial practice cannot just tell the story otherwise but produce a mode of seeing otherwise, a mode of looking out. Investing the photograph with duration, imbuing it with what Peggy Phelan would describe as the photograph's "performative force," Du Bois's textual artistry anticipates the turn toward film that would characterize black aesthetic and epistemological experimentation in the coming decades.[148]

3

Film

OVEREXPOSURE

Beyond the Frame: Overexposure and Zora Hurston's Filmic Practice

Sometime in the spring of 1932, Faustin Wirkus, a US marine turned amateur ethnographer, completed production on *Voodoo*, a thirty-six-minute highly sensationalized film of religious life in Haiti.[1] *Voodoo* was recorded on a 35 mm camera on La Gonâve, an island just off the coast of Haiti where Wirkus had been stationed since 1925 as part of the long-standing US military occupation of Haiti. Wirkus's entrance into the world of filmmaking followed the widespread success of his 1931 memoir, *The White King of La Gonave*, an updated account of William Seabrook's equally popular illustrated travelogue *The Magic Island* (1929). In both texts' colonial fantasies, La Gonâve's ten-thousand-person population becomes enthralled with Wirkus (the island's alleged sole white resident), ultimately formalizing their adoration by crowning him their "white" king. Capitalizing on the popularity of *The White King of La Gonave*'s romanticized version of an authentic cultural sphere untouched by modernity, Wirkus commenced a highly popular international lecture tour to accompany the book.[2] Encouraged by the public's appetite for his sensational tale, in 1932 Wirkus suspended his performance circuit and returned to La Gonâve to begin production on *Voodoo*. In April 1933, *Voodoo* premiered at New York City's Cameo Theater. According to a *New York Times* review, the film was an "authentic, if technically unskilled, travelogue" that "records a weird reality."[3] The weird reality of *Voodoo* owed as much to its hybrid motifs—"primitives" adopting a white marine and "the forbidden ritual of Voodoo"—as to the generically

confused final product, one that emerged at the intersection of sensation and scientific expertise.[4] It is just as likely that the strangeness
of *Voodoo* was an unavoidable side effect of filming a spontaneous,
private cultural practice. As Kate Ramsey explains, *Voodoo* included
a series of "decontextualized ritual performances" in which participants were tasked with repeatedly reenacting sacred performances,
a role that pressured them to take part as actors and as "consultants,
choreographers, or even directors."[5] Staged, rehearsed, and reenacted,
the "forbidden ritual" is reproduced and restaged as ethnographic evidence of racial difference. As a practiced and edited version of cultural
difference, the film codified the ethnographer's disciplinary mastery
while producing a colonial fantasy for popular consumption.[6]

To date, no copies of *Voodoo* survive. What does remain is a photograph of Wirkus and a collaborator in the midst of filming (fig. 3.1).
In the image Wirkus peers intently into a camera that is held steady
by a tripod while his collaborator gazes over his shoulder, perhaps
at a ritual under way, perhaps surveying the grounds for an upcom-
ing scene. Where *Voodoo*'s reviews suggest that La Gonâve is a site of
sensory overload whose "weirdness" surpasses viewer's expectations,
according to the photograph, the landscape is remarkably restrained:
the camera is stationed on a manicured lawn, framed by a series of
neatly arranged cottages. And with the exception of the two white
filmmakers, the image is devoid of activity. Although the photograph
purports to capture the world of active "filming," the camera's subject
is beyond the photograph's frame. At the same time, the ordered social landscape reinforces the film's construction of Haiti as an imperial
holding made better by what Eve Dunbar has described as the "social, political, and structural intervention by white, male agents of the
United States."[7] Here, the filmmakers' physical presence mirrors the
camera's disciplinary function: both entities seek to order an otherwise unruly terrain and assert themselves as technologies of control.
But if La Gonâve's residents, whose customs and culture were the subject of Wirkus's gaze and his desire, are absent from the image, then
someone else haunts the photograph: Zora Neale Hurston.

According to the photograph's caption, the image is as much a
behind-the-scenes look at the making of *Voodoo* as it is trace evidence
of Hurston. The catalog entry to the photograph reads "Photograph
of Kroll and Faustin Wirkus: taking 'movies' for 'Voodoo': at left, a

FIGURE 3.1
"Photograph of Kroll
and Faustin Wirkus:
taking 'Movies' for
'Voodoo': at left,
house occupied by
Zora Neale Hurston
at La Gonave, Haiti"
(Zora Neale Hurs-
ton Papers, Special
and Area Studies
Collections, George
A. Smathers Libraries,
University of Florida,
Gainesville)

house occupied by Zora Neale Hurston at La Gonave, Haiti." In its
efforts to script Hurston into the film, the photograph's owner takes
some chronological liberties. Hurston arrived in Haiti in 1936, four
years after production on *Voodoo* completed. After winning a Guggenheim Fellowship, she traveled throughout the Caribbean, arriving
in La Gonâve in mid-December.[8] During that time, she conducted the
preliminary research for what would become *Tell My Horse* (1938).
With minimal French and just enough Creole to get by, Hurston
relied on her friend Frank Crumbie to act as her translator; he also
likely identified Hurston's future home in the photograph (the image

is housed in his archive at the University of Florida, Gainesville and bears his signature handwriting in red). Crumbie's nod to Hurston draws a line of connection between her own fieldwork in Haiti and Wirkus's, a figure that scholars have argued represents the very kind of pseudoethnography that Hurston's methodology and writing revises.[9] However, Hurston's relationship to *Voodoo* and Wirkus is not simply an example of her role as a pioneering anthropologist who remains relegated to the discipline's shadowy margins. Nor does the caption photographically secure her place within a "rhetorical triangulation of Seabrook, Crumbie, and herself" where "Hurston is able to situate herself as a trained ethnographer against Crumbie's role as 'translator' and Seabrook's role as cultural voyeur and sensationalist," as Dunbar has argued.[10] Rather, Hurston's photographic specter simultaneously recalls and anticipates the central place of film to her aesthetic imaginary and racial logic.

Like her haunting presence in the photograph, Hurston's relationship to film is both speculative and enduring. Focusing particularly on the mid-1920s, when she began to publish in earnest and to record films of Southern black life, this chapter examines Hurston's efforts to reconcile film's promise of fidelity with her own developing theories of African American cultural life in particular and blackness more broadly. Perpetually curious about its representational capacity and epistemological potentials (and limits), Hurston turned to film as an idea and a technology as she labored to negotiate the cultural and disciplinary forces that sought to calcify black culture in space and time. Mirroring film and anthropology's status as emergent sites of knowledge production, Hurston's filmic engagement crisscrossed the boundary between the popular and the scientific, with black folk culture proving particularly valuable to both domains. For anthropologists, film, like the phonograph and the photograph, was thought to perfectly execute salvage ethnography's twinned value system of preservation and collection.[11] At the very same time, the popular appeal of African American songs, stories, and dance were treated as proof of blacks' potential to contribute to American cultural life and marketed to white and black consumers as an entry point to the "real," the authentic, and the especially valuable arena of a primitive culture untainted by modernity. It is certainly possible to read in Hurston's films an adherence to ethnographic scripts that prioritized romantic imaginations of a racial elsewhere and cultural myths of authenticity. It is just as pos-

sible to mine the extant footage for traces of anthropology's preser-
vationist politics, or a depiction of the "real" folk community that the
New Negro movement claimed as the gateway to transformative black
aesthetics. Yet I am interested in how Hurston approached film as an
experimental medium, one that might relay the temporal structure of
black life. If in the social survey figures like Alain Locke and W. E. B.
Du Bois saw an avenue for representing a fugitive blackness, one that
escaped the "watch and guard" of realist technologies, and in various
modes of photographic performance reformers aimed to visualize the
longue durée of racial violence, then Hurston asked whether film could
ever convey the ephemeral, contingent, and highly vital world of black
folk culture. As Hurston understood it, black folk life was not simply at
risk of being lost, as anthropologists feared. Rather, the difficulty was
in recording what she identified as the durational and active characteristics of black cultural production. "Black folk life is still in the making,
a new kind is pushing out the old," she famously espoused.[12]

Over the course of this chapter, film, like the social survey and photography, figures as a medium and technology that produced racial
data. As will become clear, by the 1920s when Hurston was recording,
anthropology's shifting attention to social customs and cultural be-
liefs posed a challenge for film, which had previously been co-opted
into the discipline as a tool of measurement and classification.[13] Thus,
while anthropologists were decidedly ambivalent about whether and
how film would feature as a medium for data collection, it nevertheless gains a foothold as a technology that could produce verifiable and
objective data. Film's role in a data regime is not only routed through
anthropology and its long genealogy of anthropometric film and ethnographic image making in which the people documented were perceived as data. At the same time, and to return to a central premise
of this book, throughout the first decades of the twentieth century,
film also joined debates about the "Negro Problem." As Allyson Nadia
Fields has shown, film emerged as a crucial medium from which the
tenets of racial uplift were articulated and circulated.[14] Advanced as a
corrective to the relentless tide of racial data that insisted on confirming black pathology, what Fields calls "uplift cinema" doubled as a survival strategy. Read as a medium that was deeply conversant with what
I describe in chapter 1 as the terrain of "antisocial data" that insisted on
black peoples enduring proximity to abjection and death, film asserts
itself as an alternative data source. Whether taken up by anthropolo-

gists, albeit with hesitancy and apprehension, or boldly forwarded by race theorists, what I want to emphasize here is that film shares data's organizing ethos: black life as eminently available.

At stake in prioritizing the role of film to Hurston's aesthetics and politics, but also routing a discussion of film through Hurston, is an account of early black film and cinema that centralizes experimental practices over oppositional politics. As she turned to the sights and sites traversed by her mostly white male counterparts, Hurston was never simply concerned with correcting their gross methodological and historical errors. As she noted in a January 1937 letter to Henry Allen Moe, Guggenheim Foundation adviser, even after spending time in La Gonâve and discovering that "the supposed kingdom of Workus's [sic]" claims to royalty were entirely invented, she resolved to "say nothing about it on my return." Privileging collegiality over a dramatic exposé, she simply noted, "I like Workus [sic]."[15] Never one to shy away from the power of invention, Hurston was likely disturbed by Wirkus's gross fabulations, even if she remained tight lipped. However, Hurston *was* impressed by what Wirkus might have been able to say and see with his camera. In 1932 she wrote to the Columbia University anthropologist Ruth Benedict to enlist her help contacting Wirkus with the hope of gaining a foothold in Haiti, where she planned to travel. Hurston's eager request is underpinned by an interest in his technological holdings. "He is a valuable man and eager to do something. *He has equipment and everything,*" she exclaimed.[16] When Hurston and Wirkus finally met she was most excited about the footage, reporting to Benedict, "He has some motion-picture films of dances and two conjure ceremonies that I know you want to see." Even as she recognized Wirkus's lack of formal training—"he has no formal preparation for the work," she lamented—she was nevertheless energized by the access to technology that their budding relationship might afford.[17]

Undoubtedly, Hurston's interest in Wirkus's footage and camera was a carryover from her own personal relationship to film and experience as a filmmaker. Between 1927 and 1930 she recorded at least twenty-seven minutes of footage of Southern black life, including children playing games, a baptism, a church picnic, and a Florida lumber camp; the most artistically ambitious was *Kossula: Last of the Takkoi Slaves,* a five-minute silent film featuring Kossula (also known as Cudjo Lewis), the eighty-eight-year-old man whom many believed to be the last survivor of the Middle Passage. Hurston also amassed footage of Bahamian dances that would serve as the choreographic blueprint for the theater performances she directed in the early 1930s, most notably *The Great Day* (1932), although this footage has not been recovered. The incorporation of film into her multigeneric wheelhouse began on the eve of her second field trip to the American South. As part of her exhaustive and constraining contract with her white benefactress Charlotte Osgood Mason, Hurston was equipped with a 16 mm camera, a car, a $200 monthly stipend, and the directive to collect "all information, both written and oral, concerning the music, poetry, folk-lore, literature, hoodoo, conjure, manifestations of art and kindred subjects relating to and existing among North American negroes" (see fig. 3.2).[18]

It is impossible to know whether the idea of incorporating the camera into her toolkit was Mason's or Hurston's. To be sure, the handheld camera was perfectly suited for gathering visual accompaniments to Hurston's written findings. For Mason, a collector of black "exotica" who is often charged with uncritically amassing black ephemera, it is easy to see how the camera's promise to record "pure" motion would operate as the visual equivalence to Hurston, who Mason also held up as an enlivened cultural object.[19] Mason's emotional and economic investment in Hurston's pursuit of black folk culture was at least in part a holdover from her own work as an ethnographer. Before taking up the mantle as one of the most influential financial backers of black writers and artists of the 1920s, a role that earned her the moniker "Godmother," Mason conducted fieldwork among the Indigenous populations of the American Plains. Yet by the 1920s, Mason's approach was losing traction. As Deborah Gordon has explained, against the new banner of cultural relativism that was structuring the period's aesthetic and disciplinary debates, Mason's primitivism was outdated. Whereas Hurston's Columbia University professor and mentor Franz Boas had long emphasized that "folklore should be cast as part of a larger whole called 'culture,'" Mason remained less interested in situating her findings within a broader cultural context than in simply gathering "a collection of diverse materials."[20] In theory, the camera's necessarily limited frame and its technological constraints—Hurston was not shooting with sound, for instance—were perfectly suited for Mason's goals. Recorded in the American South and viewed from the

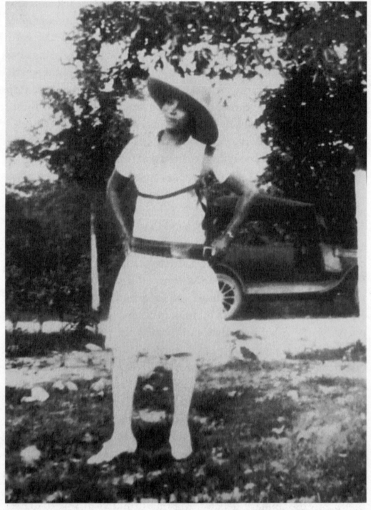

FIGURE 3.2 Zora Neale Hurston with car in Florida, ca. 1920s (George A. Smathers Library, University of Florida)

comfort of her home, Hurston's footage could be easily extracted from its cultural surroundings and isolated as a discrete artifact.

Yet granting Mason a starring role in Hurston's filmic origin story risks erasing her own enduring curiosity in technology and its aptitude for comporting with black social living. It is just as likely that Hurston requested the camera after experiencing the difficulty that came with collecting and collating information by hand. In early 1927 she traveled through the South on a research trip under the sponsorship of Carter G. Woodson and the direction of Franz Boas. Halfway through the trip Hurston lamented to Boas that she was having difficulty transcribing material quickly and accurately. Sandwiched between an account of a missed deadline and an appeal for more funds, Hurston wrote, "I am sorry that I have kept you waiting, I have a great deal of material in pencil, and I am transcribing it in odd moments. The reason it is not typed, is that it is hard for me to lug a machine along country roads in addition to my bag."[21] Hurston would ultimately request an additional $300 to purchase a car to help transport a typewriter and bolster her precision, although the funds never came through. Yet even if Boas had supplied Hurston with the means to buy a car, her explanation registers a technological dissonance between anthropology's representational forms, like the ethnographic report, and the temporality of black cultural expression. In this regard, the camera emerges alongside the typewriter as a technology of transcription and inscription, a medium from which she could fulfill Boas's mandate to "record, record, record." Hurston's request is also for unencumbered movement, movement that could ostensibly keep pace with her subjects.[22]

Thus, what I am naming as Hurston's preoccupation with film, one that exceeds her camerawork of the late 1920s, is not simply a function of her desire for efficient data collection. Nor can we solely understand it as an effect of her willingness to appease Mason and fulfill the terms of her contract; after all, Hurston regularly found ways to circumvent the creative and professional prohibitions that Mason imposed. Rather, in film Hurston found a training ground for exercising and experimenting with theories of blackness, aesthetics, and value, as well as a modality for querying the terms and conditions under which black life becomes legible to social scientists and the general public, both of which had an insatiable appetite for black life. From this vantage point Wirkus's "value" to Hurston was not so much the opportunity to access filmic data about black life in Haiti that would remain out of Hurston's reach for at least a few more years. Instead, Hurston was expressly interested in how film could orient and reorient the relationship between realism and black life that the camera purported to secure—that is, black life as an object whose value was transparent, recordable, and consumable. As it turned out, film provided the conceptual apparatus that made perceptible the idea of blackness as relational, contingent, and highly active, what she would describe as its always transforming and transformative capacity. But perhaps most important, for Hurston film and filmmaking were sites of active thinking and creative experimentation. This approach runs counter to dominant readings that treat film as a technology that collapses the space between referent and representation, the very qualities for which it emerged as a favorite tool of documentary realism.

Turning to a close analysis of Hurston's untitled films of children playing games and everyday life and the five-minute *Kossula: Last of the Takkoi Slaves*, I ask how the films might produce a visual grammar that challenges or shifts the existing logic of intelligibility governing the possibilities for what it means to see and be seen. And what cultural history of black cinema in general and Hurston as filmmaker in particular do Hurston's films make visible when we shift our focus away from a politics of representation that takes for granted the representability of black social life and reorient our concerns around what visual technology can and cannot convey? Answering these questions means exploring the formal, aesthetic, and technical dimensions of Hurston's filmmaking, aspects that have been glossed over in favor of reading her films as exercises in ethnographic recording or a thoroughly conceived project produced by a well-trained filmmaker. In critically reassessing Hurston's filmic oeuvre, taking into account the kinds of subjects, reading practices, and historical narratives these films produce even as they attest to Hurston's ethnographic endeavors, I argue that Hurston's filmic practice anticipates Michael B. Gillespie's recent provocation to suspend what he calls the "fidelity considerations of black film." Encouraging us to approach black film as an idea rather than a material object, Gillespie insists that we must dismantle the "presumption that the primary function of this brand of American cinema entails an extradiegetic responsibility or capacity to embody the black lifeworld or provide answers in the sense of social problem solving."[23] Hurston does not necessarily advocate for black film's status as art as Gillespie does. Yet in spite of her relative silence around cinema and filmmaking, her films evince an investment in treating film as more than an exercise in data gathering or an opportunity to revise the deep archive of distorted racist imagery, although she often moves dangerously close to both principles. Indeed, time and again Hurston's films reveal a constant struggle to reconcile the filmic medium with its subject: black folk life.

Recast as a comment on the interface of blackness and filmic technology, rather than an exercise in ethnographic documentary style, Hurston's films illuminate a social terrain that exceeds extant epistemological frameworks of cinematic representation. A cursory glance at the films begins to make this point. The twenty-four minutes of footage recorded between 1927 and 1930 are riddled with technical imperfections and inconsistencies: the film is frequently overexposed or underexposed, the lens is often obstructed, and subjects regularly come in and out of focus. The film historian Elaine Charnov describes this as Hurston's method of "pushing the medium to its limit" so that the film itself is as much a subject of the recording as black life is.[24] Extending Charnov's insightful observation, this chapter spotlights the variable technical quality in Hurston's films in order to become attuned to an understudied aspect of her aesthetic practice, one that I term "overexposure."

My use of the word "overexposure" draws directly on the technical sense of the term. Within the realm of film production, overexposure means exposing the film to too much light, which creates an effect that can be either minor (resulting in washed-out images) or extreme (producing blinding brightness). At the same time, overexposure registers the limit of film's representational capacity, the threshold at which visibility collapses into invisibility and light doubles back on its promise of elucidation and transparency. In what follows, I extend this definition and deploy overexposure to name instances of excess (light, motion, bodies) that disrupt film's basic conditions (synchronization, narrative coherence, embodied movement) and interrupt spectatorial expectations. Through encounters with overexposure, filmic experience is transformed from one of detached immersion to a persistently shifting relation between viewer and subject, so that overexposure's formal and visual effects undercut the widely held assumption that cinema can organize an otherwise unruly and chaotic social world.[25]

While film materializes overexposure as a praxis for blackness and black aesthetics, it ultimately exceeds the medium itself. Stretching beyond the material boundaries of the camera and bleeding out from the film stock, overexposure finds articulation in black everyday practice and literary output. This chapter tracks multiple iterations of overexposure across Hurston's work, from her first published essay "Drenched in Light" to the films themselves to her 1934 manifesto "Characteristics of Negro Expression." In each case overexposure names a disruptive force that elides legibility to reorder the visual economy in which illumination is a pathway to access, commodification, and visibility. Before drawing out overexposure's relationship to literary aesthetics, the remainder of this section draws out the stakes of overexposure for thinking about black visuality in general, and black film in particular.

Like social surveys and photography, film has historically functioned as a medium whose claims to referentiality enable it to both articulate and resolve the "problem" of black life. In black film studies the problem of black life has been historically theorized as one of representation, wherein the relationship between viewer, film, and filmed subject has been structured by values of realism, authenticity, and a politics of representation. It is a relationship that, as Wahneema Lubiano notes, enforces an "authoritarian perspective" to imply "that our [African American] lives can be captured by the presentation of enough documentary evidence or by the insistence on another truth."[26] In addition to rendering an accessible image for the viewer, the conflation of precision, documentary, and transparency also structures the process of racial identification that hinges on an encounter between a seeing subject and a visible (racial) object. It is from this vantage point that exposure gets mobilized and linked with the hegemony of hypervisibility and the violence of the gaze, part of a hostile scopic regime from which retreat is impossible. As Nicole Fleetwood notes, normative accounts of hypervisibility register "both historic and contemporary conceptualizations of blackness as simultaneously invisible and always visible, as underexposed and always exposed."[27] These accounts figure the visual sphere as a hostile domain wherein to be seen is to submit oneself to epistemic, physical, and psychic violence, a domain that sustains "the invisibility of blacks as ethical enfleshed subjects so that blackness remains aligned with negation and decay."[28]

But if normative accounts of black visual culture mobilize various kinds of exposure to register a putative relationship between visibility and subjectivity, then through overexposure Hurston's films destabilize the chain of association linking visibility, authenticity, and atomization by producing too much evidence while withholding other, expected knowledge. For example, the footage contains countless sustained close-ups of the body, and frames are often overloaded with gestic and historical referents. In much of her footage, figures come in and out of focus; one scene depicts a group dance that abruptly zooms in to isolated movements of feet, and another reveals children with hands clasped, knees bent, and weight evenly distributed spinning in circles until they dissolve into a blur (fig. 3.3). It is possible that Hurston recorded such fragments as cutaways for integration into a more "polished" film during editing; it is just as possible that she was experimenting with this novel technology's capacity. In either case the result is a filmic grammar that oscillates between the recognizable and the uncontrollable, producing visually discordant and disruptive effects at the very moment when coherence is at stake. In the face of an excess of "facts," the films clear a space for the emergence of social formations, political narratives, and ways of seeing that move outside the terms of positive, good, and real that are traditionally deployed to assess black film and that unhinge the authoritarian perspective of both camera and spectator. The payoff of what we might term the "overexposure effect" is a kind of visual frustration generated by what appears to be an unhampered overload of visual information combined with disappointment at these short, sketch-like films, which remain open-ended and unresolved and in which nothing much seems to transpire.

This ambiguity is not entirely surprising when we recall that Hurston neither wrote about nor publicly screened her films, even though she repeatedly returned to filmmaking at different points during her career. After her experiments of the late 1920s, she tried her hand at screenwriting and was briefly employed as a story editor by Paramount Studios. By 1940, and with the assistance of Jane Belo (an anthropologist also interested in film), Hurston set out to produce a sound film of the Commandment Keeper Church in Beaufort, Alabama. Yet even these later efforts are underpinned by the sense that film technology and the forms of black life appearing before the camera are not necessarily compatible. In a letter to Belo dated May 20, 1940, Hurston emphasized this disconnect: "We've been shooting, shooting, and shooting. . . . Not all that we planned worked out—We don't have synchronization because our motor lay down on us before we started—so we were hand cranking all the four hundred rolls using the spring on the 100 foots. . . . Had we attempted to synchronize the

FIGURE 3.3 Film still of children holding hands and spinning, ca. 1927–1929 (Used with the permission of the Zora Neale Hurston Trust)

sound the flexibility of the jumping from place to place would have been impaired—We find that after having gone through it once that there are a number of things we'd have liked to do that our equipment did not permit."[29] In this rich account, Hurston draws attention to what the cinematic apparatus cannot do ("jump from place to place" or coordinate sound and motion), and in doing so, she unsettles the long-held notion that black life was necessarily amenable to the camera and, likewise, that the camera could reveal a "real" and "accurate" picture.[30] As Hurston frames it here, more than anything, film's technical limitations actually attest to what black cultural life is: a continually moving networking of relations requiring a level of dexterity and flexibility that exceeds the capabilities of a camera, let alone an entire crew and their arsenal of modern equipment. Part of what overexposure registers is this tension between film, Hurston's vision (both real and imagined) of black folk life, and the cultural practices that were actually transpiring in front of the camera. That is, in spite of her best efforts, Hurston could not synchronize the technical working of film with the practices constitutive of black life.

In what follows I track overexposure in Hurston's filmic and literary practice by closely reading correspondence, essays, and the films themselves. To begin, I show how even before Hurston experimented with film we can find an aesthetic of overexposure operating in her short story "Drenched in Light." The second part of the chapter draws out the theory of overexposure through a close reading of a series of films of children playing games and the 1928 essay "How It Feels to Be Colored Me." From there I turn to the five-minute film *Kossula: Last of the Takkoi Slaves* to consider the film as articulating Hurston's enduring effort to identify the medium that might convey the afterlife of slavery. The final part of the chapter argues that Hurston's films and their announcement of overexposure provide the theoretical architecture for her 1934 essay "Characteristics of Negro Expression." Additionally, while "Characteristics" has been theorized as a foundational work to performance studies, when read in relationship to film it also announces a nascent theory of black cinema, one that takes gesture as its primary organizing principle. I stage a dynamic reading between "Characteristics" and the films, arguing that the key ideas of angularity, ephemerality, and contingency render textually and aesthetically what Hurston encountered through the camera. In each case overexposure registers the way that black life lives in excess of the frameworks and visual technologies that were meant to secure its value (financial and disciplinary) as real, recordable, and consumable.

"Drenched in Light"

The conceptual force that light exerts across Hurston's work is difficult to overlook. In "Drenched in Light," overexposure's filaments take hold as a literary strategy that comments on the interface of race, value, and visibility. While overexposure materializes in her films as a technical working that has aesthetic aftereffects, in "Drenched in Light" overexposure operates as a mode of critical retreat from the visual sphere in which blackness is rendered available for consumption and readily disposable. At stake in reading this early short story as an expression of overexposure is the emergence of a long road map that directs us to understand how, on the one hand, Hurston was always preoccupied with visuality's technical workings and, on the other hand, how exposure, saturation, and excess were enduring rubrics through which she would wrestle with the meaning of blackness. "Drenched in Light" thus establishes the terms and aesthetic concerns that would stretch across Hurston's work.

"Drenched in Light" appeared in the December 1924 issue of *Opportunity*, the official organ of the National Urban League. Although its origins were as a sociologically oriented magazine, beginning in 1924 Charles Johnson decided to prioritize literature's role within the development of a distinct "New Negro aesthetic" by establishing the magazine's famed literary contest. Invoking a well-rehearsed discourse of representational politics and insisting that black writers need not pander to white readers' interest in the exotic and the primitive, the announcement for the literary contest charged black writers with "replac[ing] their worn out representations in fiction and faithfully and incidentally mak[ing] themselves better understood."[31] Within a year, *Opportunity*'s annual writing prize and its acclaimed dinner parties secured its status as a formidable institutional force within the New Negro Renaissance.[32] Likely encouraged by Alain Locke, whom she met while studying at Howard University, Hurston submitted "Drenched in Light" for publication in *Opportunity*. Within weeks of its release, she arrived in New York City. Emboldened by an *Opportunity* byline, Hurston's emergence onto New York's literary and cultural scene was celebrated, if not entirely unexpected. Although "Drenched in Light" paved the way for her professional ascent, Hurston was already familiar with the racial dynamics and commercial demands dictating New York's artistic world. In Washington, she was a permanent fixture in Georgia Douglass Johnson's literary salons, a gathering that regularly attracted the likes of Du Bois, Jean Toomer, Marita Booner, and Locke.[33] And at Howard she was a member of the Stylus, "the small literary society" that was "limited to 19 members"; Locke was the "presiding genius."[34] Hurston's experience in Washington provided a cursory introduction into the racial politics of the 1920s cultural and literary marketplace, one in which white and black consumers clamored for access to "real" black culture. As Gordon has articulated, the compulsion to access authentic black life, whether framed as pure African past or untainted Southern folkway, was the latest instantiation of the ever-present "Negro Problem." Like its ideological predecessor, the rebranded "New Negro" named a "cultural and political problematic" that was concerned with "how to make citizens and cultured people out of former 'savages.'"[35] With an eye toward literary and visual art, race theorists and cultural thinkers argued that mining the roots African American culture would uncover a genealogy of black creative expression and sketch a rubric for a future of unique black aesthetic contribution. At the same time, the compulsion to possess black cultural production was a distinct facet of modernist primitivism, what Anne Cheng describes as the "entwined crises of race, style, and subjecthood," articulated and resolved through modern technologies, including film, photography, and architecture.[36] "Drenched in Light" enters into this cultural market to ask whether blackness—and its presumed visibility—can ever be fully consumed and, if so, at what cost.[37]

Set in Eatonville, Florida, Hurston's birthplace and the location of many of her future texts, "Drenched in Light" orbits around Isis, or "Isie," Watts, a young girl whose tenacity frustrates her grandmother and attracts the attention of the town's black residents and white tourists. Filmic in nature, "Drenched in Light" opens on what Lena Hill usefully describes as a "a site of observation": Isis, the "little brown figure," is perched on a gatepost.[38] Situated at a remove from her own social world, the gatepost affords a privileged perceptual position from which Isis watches the embodied racial drama that organizes the color line. Four years later Hurston would return to the trope of the gatepost, elaborating it in her 1928 essay "How It Feels to Be Colored Me" as a "gallery seat," a "proscenium box for a born first-nighter."[39] A site of detached spectatorship, Isis's patently black domestic outpost in the historically black town situates her at the nexus of competing gazes and geographies: "[Isis] looked yearningly up the gleaming shell road that led to Orlando, and down the road that led to Sanford and shrugged her thin shoulders." The site of (visual) racial encounters and disorienting racial reflection, the "shell lined road" facilitates Isis's slippage between performer and spectator, between object of desire and consuming subject, or to return to Du Bois's phrasing, the position of a black subject who is always seeing herself through the eyes of others. Both the ground of spectacle entertainment—it is a "great attraction"—and the location from which she draws the attention of "everybody in the country," the road emerges as performance thoroughfare where racial encounters are staged and negotiated.[40] In this regard it is significant that Isis's post is located at a crossroads, one direction leading farther south, and ostensibly deeper into the Black Belt, and the other north, closer to modernity. Yet Isis remains ambivalent about moving in either direction, preferring to remain unmoored from geographic and racial coordinates.

As in much of her early writing, Hurston draws up well-rehearsed racial tropes and conventions to construct her young heroine. Isis's decision to shave her grandmother's "whiskers," for instance, recalls the slapstick performances popular in early twentieth-century actuality films, but also Topsy, Harriet Beecher Stowe's popular prankster whose iconography exceeded the literary boundaries of *Uncle Tom's Cabin*. But Hurston is not especially concerned with the entertainment function of Isis's capers. Rather, the stunts are exercises in acts of self-making and remaking in which she draws on an expansive repertoire of racial and gender emblems. Undertaking what Daphne Brooks describes as the work of "suturing together hybrid and sometimes profane cultural materials to rewrite categories of self-presentation," Isis's theatrical rehearsals are tutored study for what will amount to a reappraisal of the value assigned to blackness in a visual economy.[41] The gatepost is not Isis's only theatrical habitat. Evading her grandmother's disciplining arm and skirting her chores, she also finds refuge in a makeshift, subterranean theater. Sequestered beneath a table and safe from her grandmother's prying eyes, Isis hides behind a "red plush cover with little round balls for fringe." Under the table-turned-stage, Isis transcends the limits of girlhood and blackness to fashion herself "various personages"; at times she wears "trailing robes, golden slippers with blue bottoms" and at others she "rode white horses with flaring pink nostrils to the horizon, for she believed that to be land's end."[42] Prepared to mobilize as a visually intransigent performer who can re-regulate the racial market, Isis is drawn from her theatrical refuge by the "sounding brass and tinkling cymbal" from a passing parade and moved to dance. For "music to Isis meant motion" and her "feet were gifted—she could dance most anything she saw."[43] Isis completes the passage from rehearsal to performance by procuring her grandmother's prized red tablecloth, transforming it into an elaborate racial costume. With the linens draped around her body and a daisy wedged "between her teeth," she crafts a "Spanish shawl," morphing from "brown" girl to "gipsy" whose "brown feet twinkled in and out of the fringe" until "little by little the multitude had surrounded the brown dancer."[44]

Isis's impromptu choreography draws the ire of her grandmother and the attention of a car of two "indifferent" white men and one captivated white woman, Helen, who drive her home after her crowd-pleasing solo. Only when they arrive at Isis's doorstep, Helen is reluctant to release her. Recognizing in Helen a mix of hesitancy and desire, Isis offers her own body as consolation, simply asking, "Do you wanta keep me?" The invitation instantiates Isis's transformation from entertainment spectacle to currency, a shift cemented by her new role as a "shiny little morsel."[45] Determined to "keep" her possession, Helen offers Isis's grandmother $5 to offset the price of the costume under the condition that Isis will go to their hotel "and dance in that tablecloth."[46] With Isis en route to her performance duties, Helen relishes in the benefits of the newfound partnership. As Isis "snuggled up to her new benefactress," Helen tightens her grip on her new purchase and draws the "little red draped figure at her side."[47] With their hands clasped, Helen drifts into a state of pure contentment: "She looked hungrily ahead of her and spoke into space rather than to anyone in the car. 'I want a little of her sunshine to soak into my soul. I need it.'"[48]

"Drenched in Light" is most often read as a highly autobiographical text. As her biographer Valerie Boyd notes, without much of a well-developed plot, "Drenched in Light" is an "unapologetic tribute to the impudent, unrefined child she [Hurston] once had been."[49] Here, the story is read less for its literary attributes than for what it tells readers about Hurston. It is, writes Boyd, essentially "a self-portrait—an extended character sketch of Isis Watts, clearly Zora Neale Hurston's embodied memory of her own girlhood."[50] Echoing this position, Robert Hemenway maintains, "Zora's identification with Isie Watts is almost total," with the story finally functioning as "a belligerent, combative statement of independence, intended to portray the value of an Eatonville memory for Zora Neale Hurston."[51] There are certainly unmistakable overlaps between Isis and Hurston's life, including the setting of Eatonville and the fact that the work's fictional grandmother is given Hurston's own grandmother's name. Likewise, in her 1945 autobiography *Dust Tracks on a Road*, Hurston recounts how she "used to take a seat on the top of the gate-post and watch the world go by," a posture that mirrors Isis's opening stance.[52] Moreover, Isis's characterization as a "visually minded child" is in keeping with Hurston's enduring commitment to visuality, what Lena Hill theorizes as her "fascination with pondering visual dexterity, the ability to understand the world through rigorous looking."[53] Just as "Drenched in Light" animates Hurston's childhood and underlines her investment in visual culture, scholars have been equally compelled by its predictive qualities. As Hemenway and Michael North note, Isis's relationship with her white benefactress, Helen, anticipates Hurston's vexed relationship with white patronage. For North, the overlaps are impossible to ignore: "The way that Isis is picked up and cosseted by a patronizing white traveler oddly predicts the way that Hurston herself, arriving in New York hard on the heels of 'Drenched in Light,' was virtually adopted, first by Fannie Hurst and then by the grimly philanthropic Mrs. Charlotte Osgood Mason."[54]

While "Drenched in Light" is unmistakably autobiographical, if not clairvoyant, it is also a remarkable meditation on the crisis of racial value and visual legibility that cohere at the site of black embodied performance. The title is particularly telling. Beyond either symbolically encoding her with the qualities that "endear her to everyone," as Hemenway notes, or signifying on her last name, a play on the electrical unit "watts," as Boyd suggests, "Drenched in Light" occasions a meditation and reordering of the value accorded to blackness and light within a visual economy in which the racialized body was paradoxically located outside the pale of humanity, even as it was positioned as symbol of authenticity. Deborah Poole has described the visual economy as three-pronged network of production, circulation, and exchange value, which collectively function to produce a "broad range of representational practices and discourses" that determine how we perceive and assess the social world.[55] Although Poole is especially concerned with the traffic patterns of graphic and photographic renderings, as Krista Thompson points out, visual economy "also stresses the way aesthetic qualities or ephemeral visual effects," effects like light (and for Thompson, shine), function as a representational practice and discourse that tender exchange value according to a scale that associates worth with levity, illumination, and purity. But if light circulates within a visual economy, then it also can redistribute social, aesthetic, and racial (exchange) value. Extending the foundational insights of Richard Dyer, who explicates a racialized "cult of light" that was standardized by Hollywood icons and encoded in cinematic technology, Cheng argues that in addition to its capacity to denote tenderness, femininity, and purity, luminescent and feminized light performs as a protective layering, a sheath that interrupts the transmutation from body to commodity fetish. Less a soft finish that invites touch than an inorganic material that projects the sheen of metal, when cast on the black female body, light is shiny, more plastic than gauzy, with a property that at once "attracts and repels vision."[56] Expressive of an acute awareness of light's multiple iterations, its status as both a violent technology that might obliterate racial value or protect it from the voyeuristic gaze, "Drenched in Light" coordinates a visual economy in which light is the occasion for both reordering racial capitalism's elements and imaging new possibilities for racial relation that might occur under the condition of complete illumination.

Here, Hurston's deployment of light occasions a strident critique of what Anthea Kraut has described as the "commercialization of the folk," the cultural phenomenon that monetized African American Southern life by offering it up as a historically and geographically evacuated pathway to racial purity. Emerging largely from postwar nostalgia for a cultural milieu of seemingly fixed and controllable racial and social hierarchies, white and black cultural producers crafted and consumed an image of a "premodern" black folk culture that was untainted by the corrupting influence of the marketplace.[57] Untouched by "outside" (white and Northern) influences, in music, literature, and visual culture the "folk" were "desirable as 'raw material' for consumption by the commercial mainstream."[58] Hurston's deployments, as well as critiques, of black folk culture are not without their problems. The vexed construction of black folk culture in Hurston's work has been well documented, most forcefully by Hazel Carby, who argues that Hurston "assumed that she could obtain access to, and authenticate, an individualized social consciousness through a utopian reconstruction of the historical moment of her childhood in an attempt to stabilize and displace the social contradictions and disruptions of her contemporary moment."[59] In turn, "the rural black folk become an aesthetic principle, a means by which to embody a rich oral culture." The rhetorical move has the effect of a "discursive displacement" that situates the "folk as outside of history."[60] The fictional spaces that Hurston often prepared advanced a fantasy of "authentic" black life, one that functioned to revise the popular constructions that funneled blackness through the terms of minstrelsy or primitivist fantasies. While Carby has invited us to consider how the folk operate as an "aesthetically purified version of blackness," Kraut, a dance studies scholar, isolates theater and performance as sites where Hurston forcefully, if problematically, yokes the value of authenticity to the folk. Thus, when in the early 1930s Hurston began to stage a series of performance revues, "she promised to deliver a theatrical performance purportedly free of the 'taint' of commodification."[61] Recognizing that "there has been a sharp trend towards genuine Negro material," in *Dust Tracks on a Road* Hurston explains that by embracing theater production, "I aimed to show what beauty and appeal there was in genuine Negro material, as against the Broadway concept."[62]

That Isis's performing body fulfills Helen's desire for "some brightness," "for a little sunshine to lighten her soul," confirms her status as a marker of "real" black culture. Against what Hurston described as the "taint" of commercialization and the "artificially polished" world of popular, mainstream theater, Isis's choreography fulfills the promise of purity and illumination. Even the stage itself, a picnic, is cast an improvisational, and thus authentic, site of black sociality. But if in her transformation from the dreaming "brown" figure to a "shiny morsel" Isis becomes inscribed as an "authentic" folk object, then this is also a scene of gross misrecognition and high-risk miscalculation. As Isis emerges as a commodity fetish, she also overproduces racial ornamentation. Far from the stripped-down and raw "folk," Isis sells a performance of sartorial excess that cannot be easily incorporated into the racial market. After all, Isis's costume mimics a Spanish dancer, complete with a flower and a healthy dousing of lemon essence. Even so, Helen consumes the surfeit of racial stereotypes as authentic so that when Isis's grandmother offers to comb her hair before sending her to the hotel, Helen protests: "No, no, don't bother. I like her as she is."[63]

In the end, Isis is purchased for a surplus of $4, the ruined tablecloth was just $1. Layering her clothes, donning the tablecloth, Isis undertakes the labor of what Hurston would later describe as "decorating a decoration."[64] Nevertheless, Helen obtains Isis in a bid to, at least temporarily, access the purity and levity that is scripted into black folk culture. But as the title suggests, Helen does not only purchase access to the light; she becomes overburdened by it. Unable to distinguish what is authentic from mere performance, Helen fails to properly perceive the "real" racial object. In lieu of the authentic "thing," Helen receives a "shiny morsel," the very stuff of which Hurston was critical and that disrupts the racial calculus that determines the value of blackness.

Importantly, Hurston does not make Isis the object of the narrative's vexation, as she would in her critique of black popular culture. In this earlier moment her concern is with black performance's capacity to produce an overwhelming surplus of visual symbols under the guise of authenticity. Here, Isis does not only manufacture "originality as commodity," as Michael North would put it; she overproduces it.[65] Ultimately, the racial overflow cannot get incorporated into the economic engine in a way that is profitable, even if profit is being extracted. While Hurston offers a sly reflection on the value system that accords value to the "authentic" and the "real," she brokers a new visual economy by staging confrontations with a series of light-emitting surfaces. Indeed, "Drenched in Light" is less interested in monetary value than in the way that Isis, as a bright object, interacts with other bright objects.

In the moment that Isis confronts Helen, the one an abundance of light and the other the kind of romantic whiteness to which Dyer is attuned, both figures confront their mutual desire for an elsewhere. For Isis this is made possible by a commitment to racial performance that gains her access to a modern car; for Helen this is a desire for blackness. But rather than arrival or actualization, the confrontation produces blindness. In the moment of ocular impairment, social value is not only suspended but also temporarily reordered. In the midst of misrecognition, it is not clear who is exercising power. Is Isis, with her newfound access to modernity (money, a car, and a possible exit from Eatonville) the recipient of Helen's (white) light, or is Helen overcome by Isis's racial surplus? For as Helen's white male companion comments, "There Helen, you've been adopted."[66]

Over the course of her career, Hurston would repeatedly theorize the relationship of racial value, performance, and authenticity, most notably in her 1934 essay "Characteristics of Negro Expression," which I discuss at some length later in this chapter. That Hurston begins by channeling this argument through visual consumption and visuality—how visual objects gain social meaning in a highly racialized economy—registers as crucial the interplay of perception, excess, and black cultural life, which would come to the forefront of her filmmaking. "Drenched in Light" is finally a meditation on what Joseph Roach has described as the impressions that black and white performing bodies make on one another as they weigh the possibilities for interaction and exchange.[67] As she turned to film, Hurston would grapple with the material consequences of these questions as she considered whether technologies of illumination actually produce legibility or whether light provides the conditions for retreat, inaccessibility, and new modes of black sociality.

Recording Racial Feeling

On March 8, 1928, Zora Neale Hurston wrote to Langston Hughes, her friend and collaborator, updating him on her trip through the American South. At the time Hurston was just three months into what would turn out to be a three-year trip, yet she was already making tremendous strides. Between gathering "several very good modern stories" ("as many now as I got on my entire trip last year"), reading excerpts from Hughes's poetry volume "Fine Clothes to the Jew," and intercepting love letters for a potential project, Hurston was undergoing a perceptual transformation. "I am really getting inside of Negro art and lore," she exclaimed, "I am beginning to see really and when you join me I shall point things out and see if you see them as I do."[68] Hurston never elaborated the precise nature of her visual revelation; nor did she ever comment on filmmaking or announce an explicit theory of cinema. Yet if she struggled to articulate the contours of her visual transformation, the 16 mm handheld camera undoubtedly contributed to her new visual stance, even if she avoided directly describing it.

The evasive phrasing is in keeping with Hurston's general silence regarding her camera work. Across her countless letters, notes, and unpublished and published works, Hurston mentions film only a handful of times. Aside from her interest in Wirkus's footage, she briefly mentions screening films for Mason: "She summoned us when one or the other returned from our labors. Miguel [Covarrubias] and I would exhibit our movies."[69] Years later and in a letter to Boas, Hurston lamented that the rise of consumer culture, especially popular film, was leading to a decline in folklore: "While a large number of tales were found, not nearly so many are current as before the literate era of the Negro. The bulk of the population now spends its leisure in motion picture theaters or with the phonograph and its 'blues.'"[70] But if Hurston's relationship to film and cinematic representation is ambivalent, then her phrasing emphasizes the camera's significance as a tool that was equal parts technology and conceptual framework, a mechanism that could produce visual epistemologies and elucidate a previously opaque black lifeworld. In producing rather than merely reflecting a social landscape and coordinating a mode of seeing, Hurston's phrasing signals what Kara Keeling, elaborating on Gilles Deleuze, outlines as cinema's status as a "mode of thinking, that is, of creating concepts."[71] The payoff of attending to cinema's capacity for knowledge production, Keeling explains, is the awareness of "the extent to which our knowledges of the world are increasingly mediated by images but also the ways in which our sensory apparatus is accustomed to receiving and forming images according to the parameters put in place by cinema."[72] Assuming this critical position, one that is both attuned to film's hegemony and its capacity to engender new epistemes, she continues, holds open the possibility for identifying "kernels of perceptions that might be capable of supporting alternate forms of sociality."[73] Thus, when Hurston reports that she is "beginning to see really," while also wondering whether Hughes will be able to see as she does, she registers the formation of perceptual practice that can espy new formations and names the camera as a technology that can, in Keeling's words, "support," or hold, black sociality.

That Hurston approached the camera as a tool for thinking and imagining and not simply a referential technology to capture and record what was already evident cuts across the predominant way that her professional peers, most notably Franz Boas and Margaret Mead, utilized film. Hurston's relationship to Boas has been well documented, most notably by black feminist anthropologists who have recovered her formative role in modern ethnography. From her willingness to participate in atomizing assignments—like taking anthropometric measurements of African Americans' skulls on the streets of Harlem—to her declaration that Boas was "the greatest Anthropologist alive," Hurston's commitment to Boas was also largely fueled by professional adoration.[74] Boas's scientific ethos, what she described as an "insatiable hunger for knowledge and then more knowledge," that was sated without compromising "pure objectivity," gave disciplinary credence to Hurston's method of indiscriminate gathering, of "collecting like a new broom" whatever she could get her hands on.[75] What Hurston theorized as an ethical orientation that prioritized unrestrained collecting over regulatory systems of classification, explains

Robert Hemenway, would have been an especially attractive "taxonomy for her childhood memories" of black folk culture. As Hurston recalled in *Dust Tracks on a Road*, Boas's defense of the culture concept and his approach to simply collect cohered in the directive to "go out and find what is there."[76]

Although Boas was well versed in the workings of visual anthropology—he regularly incorporated ethnographic photographs into his research and was deeply committed to the value of visual evidence to the study of culture—he began incorporating film into his repertoire only in 1930. As the historian of visual anthropology Allison Griffiths explains, the utility of film was "its evidentiary status and practical utility, including the fact that Boas could return to them again and again to refresh his memory or assist him in his interpretive work."[77] Here, narrative coherence was not the goal. Instead, the films comprised loosely linked sequences, "the equivalent of visual field notes."[78] Although Boas used film to record the human body, which he understood as the signifier of cultural norms and patterns, in the early part of the twentieth century, film was not a standard tool for anthropologists, and it was certainly not a regular part of the field's curriculum. Thus, while early movement studies and motion pictures set the disciplinary tone, creating a grammar that would shape a visual economy of race that submitted racial difference as an immutable fact inscribed in and on the body, in the classroom, film was a nascent ethnographic strategy that Hurston was not likely to have encountered. In this regard, Boas shares Hurston's filmic reticence. Describing the remarkable absence of any reflections on film as something of a black hole in Boas's research and writing, Jay Ruby explains that he "wrote nothing about film as a scientific tool or even about his views of the role of cinema in our society."[79] What film did afford, Ruby speculates, was a medium especially well suited to his ideological framework, one that prioritized a "bits of pieces method" of gathering cultural data, a "theory of culture which allowed him to remove bits of behavior from their normal context for purposes of recording and analysis."[80] Conversely, and as Hurston's phrasing to Hughes lays bare, film did not bolster an extant ideology; rather, it was the very basis for exploding and reconstituting the ideological architecture structuring racial knowledge.

The dearth of information surrounding Hurston's films means that scholars most often turn to *Mules and Men* to make sense of her footage. Advancing an argument for the film's status as ethnographic evidence, these interpretative efforts ground their analysis in Hurston's metaphor of the spyglass. Invoked in the introduction to *Mules and Men*, the spyglass describes the process whereby social science equipped her with the tools to penetrate the otherwise opaque world of black folk culture. Hurston begins *Mules and Men* with a note of gratitude: "I was glad when somebody told me, 'You may go and collect Negro folklore.'" The enthusiasm, however, is quickly tempered by the realization that identity is not the same as knowledge. Waging an early critique of what decades later would be described as identity politics, Hurston explains:

> In a way it would not be a new experience for me. When I pitched headforemost into the world I landed in the crib of negroism. From the earliest rockings of my cradle, I had known about the capers Brer Rabbit is apt to cut and what Squinch Owl says from the house top. But it was fitting me like a tight chemise. I couldn't see it for wearing it. It was only when I was off in college, away from my native surroundings, that I could see myself like somebody else and stand off and look at my garment. Then I had to have the spy-glass of Anthropology to look through at that.[81]

A black female social scientist struggling to negotiate her liminal position as outside observer and insider who, as she explains, was born in the "crib of negroism," the spyglass succinctly metaphorizes Hurston's status as a "participating observer" simultaneously detached from and deeply involved with the folk community.[82] Through its mediating lens, Hurston perceived a dynamic picture of black folk life, a community that was neither outside of modernity nor in rapid decay, as both Franz Boas and Charlotte Osgood Mason believed. Rather, Hurston espied a wellspring of cultural production and innovation, a black folk culture that was, as Fatimah Tobing Rony argues, a "highly visual world" of active transformation.[83]

Although the spyglass is useful for theorizing Hurston's filmic output, formulations equating the spyglass with the camera risk confining Hurston and her films to a limiting paradigm of oppositional image making, but they also risk circumscribing readings of her films within her anthropological labor. Within this script, Hurston is cast as bold camerawoman who confidently takes up the film to correct negative (false) images of the black folk with positive (accurate) representations of a vibrant folk community.[84] With the aid of the spyglass turned camera, critics suggest, both Hurston and her subjects reverse the atomizing gaze of white scientists, emerging as fully embodied black folk subjects who are endowed with the cultural authority to re-present the "truth" or "reality" of black life. Such positions reflect a broader critical tendency to assess early black film within the terms of accuracy, objectivity, and documentary. Although visual scholars have outlined the dangers of reading black images, specifically films, within a positive-negative binary, early black films rarely factor into these debates. Thus, while contemporary black films and black filmmakers are theorized for their capacity to disturb the visual field or reconceive the very terms of cinema and the cinematic, far too often black films from the first decades of the century are, as Jacqueline Stewart cautions, evaluated within preexisting paradigms and value systems, eclipsing the more complicated and complex narratives taking shape on the screen and behind the camera.[85]

When we suspend the spyglass metaphor, the footage itself begins to reveal a visual world that gives way to new modes of seeing and engenders equally novel racial epistemologies, those "kernels of perceptions" that Keeling speaks of.[86] From this perspective, the Hurston who surfaces is far from a master camerawoman who deployed her "cinematic eye" with a perfect balance of confidence and dexterity; instead, she is a woman who managed the camera with the clumsiness of an amateur and the skepticism of an artist who was unconvinced of cinema's documentary powers.[87] Entering into the films as Hurston did, without training, preconceived notions, or a firm ideology in place, we encounter an impossible visual subject, one whose cinematic intransigence renders black kinesthetic motion as an aesthetic principle and racial praxis.

This is not to suggest that Hurston's entire approach to film was ad hoc and disordered. On the contrary, the footage reveals her sustained interest in a series of themes, most notably, dance, games, and everyday labor, particularly life at turpentine and lumber camps. In fact, films of children playing games make up nearly half of the twenty-four minutes of footage recorded during the 1927–1930 trip. Ranging from mere seconds to just under two minutes (or half of a four-minute roll of 16 mm film), the films shift between footage of highly organized schoolyard games and spontaneous play. In one film, girls and boys face off in a loosely choreographed social dance, each one taking turns showing off in the center of a circle; in another clip, a toddler dressed in a formal white dress stands among a group of preteens who circle her in some version of ring around the rosy. Like many of her other films, this footage encapsulates the tension between the codes of cinema and the forms of black social life taking shape before the camera's lens. It is during this footage, for example, that we see the children spinning at a dizzying rate or rushing toward the camera with a force that overwhelms Hurston and her equipment, both of which end up knocked over. In these moments, the camera's promise to record and convey movement buckles under the weight of its subject, as if black sociality's temporality is at odds with the camera's directive to capture embodied motion. The kinesthetic overload corporealizes the theory of overexposure that is literalized in "Drenched in Light." Where Helen is blinded by the synchronicity of Isis's racial performances, staged as the layering of costumes, props, and gesture, here the camera also folds under the force of black embodied motion.

Interspersed throughout the scene of play are five independent shots of young boys and girls standing before the camera and holding up a large white rectangular piece of paper (figs. 3.4–3.8). Just as they bear out the conceptual and theoretical workings of overexposure, the films of children holding up the white pieces of paper also demonstrate overexposure's productive working in a technical sense. Tracking the technical occurrences of overexposure reveals how the footage can recalibrate a visual grammar of race that, as evidenced in the films of schoolyard games, hinges on the idea that visual technology can quantify, document, and distill some otherwise imperceptible racial essence. Even more, overexposure invites us to return to moments in the scholarly record that have unwittingly blinded us to the intricacies of Hurston's recordings. In her foundational reading of Hurston as visual anthropologist, Fatimah Tobing Rony reads these films as evidence of Hurston's conservative scientific training with Boas, who had a particular investment in objective and distanced observation. From the early motion studies of Eadweard Muybridge to Boas's and Mead's later ethnographic cinema, this was a positivist tradition predicated on the idea that embodied motion was the locus of racial essence, film was an indexical medium that recorded and transmitted reality, and tools like identifying placards and measuring grids ordered racial meaning.[88] Within a rubric of atomization through visualization, Rony assumes the white placards that introduce the

FIGURES 3.4–3.8 Film stills of children holding white cards, ca. 1927–1929 (Used with the permission of the Zora Neale Hurston Trust)

film are anthropometric devices—identifying signs deployed by scientists, anthropologists, and eugenicists to record and classify racial difference as pathology. Reading Hurston squarely within a Boasian genealogy of racial quantification, Rony maintains that "Boas's interest in 'isolable actions' are reflected, for example, in Hurston's footage of children playing: they are made into types, holding up pieces of paper with their ages, filing past the camera frontally and then in profile."[89] Concurrent with readings of the spyglass as technology of both subjection and elucidation, as Rony frames it, the children holding white paper signal the subjecting power of scientific racism and its arsenal of truth-telling apparatuses while also providing the backdrop against which Hurston's critical ethnography sharpens. With the

ethnography's visual codes in place, Rony argues, we can make sense of the "marked disruptions from the normal iconography" of early twentieth-century visual anthropology.[90]

On closer inspection, the white cards do not actually record identification data; they contain production information. On one film, a young boy walks toward the camera clutching a white card to his chest with the letters "E-E-L" faintly etched across it (see fig. 3.4). As he advances into the foreground, the scene abruptly ends. In the next shot the boy reappears, assumes the same pose (eyes forward, white paper clutched to his chest) and again begins to advance toward the camera. As he approaches the foreground it becomes clear that this is a second card inscribed with the number 1 (see fig. 3.5). Although the initial letter of the first card is indecipherable, it is safe to assume that together they read "Reel 1," with the boy marking the start of a roll of footage. Over the course of the footage, children appear holding white cards three more times on different reels. Except for the number 5, the writing on the other cards is impossible to make out. However, I assume they also document production information.

On the one hand, Rony's misclassification of the cards, a reading that has been restaged by almost all Hurston film scholars, is entirely understandable. The footage is old, it is often difficult to see, and as noted, Hurston was a filmmaker who, whether intentionally or not, frequently over- and underexposed her film. Yet this scholarly misstep also demands that we pause to consider with Tavia Nyong'o the techniques and technologies that, in the words of Frantz Fanon, fix the "historico-racial schema."[91] This stance insists that concepts and theories, whether liberatory or repressive, must "not to be considered apart from, but rather entangled with, the material qualities of the recording apparatus."[92] Even as we accept that the placard signifies on the anthropometric device, one that carries an impossibly violent weight as it conscripted black bodies into the project of bodily management and racial categorization, the cards also direct us away from the classificatory grammar and instead spotlight the technical workings of the camera. Indeed, the card's illegibility is due to the internal limits of early film technology. Because white objects reflect more light than black ones, and thus require less exposure time, and because cinematic technologies, from aperture settings to film stock, were calibrated to take the white face or object as their focal point, balancing blacks and whites in a single frame posed a formidable challenge for early filmmakers.[93] Under the intensity of glaring rays of sunlight and against the brown of the young boy's skin, the white paper is compelled to repel the natural light, endowing the standard prop with a nearly fluorescent glow that at once enraptures us and makes it nearly impossible to decipher its inscription. In the most technical sense of the term, the white card is undeniably overexposed.

The misreading of the films registers as much about our own critical predisposition to read early black films through the lens of objectivity and truth as it does the mechanical capacities of filmic technology. For Rony, the mere presence of the cards on the screen is enough to situate Hurston and her films within a visual discourse that privileges cinema as an unimpeachable record of racial essence and legitimates a racial classification schema by which black subjects are flattened into mere objects. What is more interesting about the long-standing misreading of the cards, however, is not so much the error itself, but the way that Hurston's efforts are at odds with film's technical capabilities. Even though Hurston cast the boy as an active participant in the film production, and not a specimen of scientific inquiry, because it is nearly impossible to make out the inscription on the white card, the seemingly empowered role is undercut by the illegibility proffered by overexposure. Furthermore, although it is likely that Hurston took notes or remembered the order in which she shot her footage (which is certainly possible, given her inclination for meticulously documenting everything), in this brief instant, the films fail to make legible cinema's intended project of order, control, and intelligibility. The footage of children's games begins to destabilize the correlation between filmic representation and objectivity embraced by early twentieth-century ethnography and oppositional black image makers alike while pointing to the limits of cinema's representational techniques.

As the films unfold, overexposure extends out from the white cards and pushes our vision toward the frame's material and conceptual margins. In addition to the white cards, these two short films featuring the boy also contain other compositional elements that make it difficult to situate them in a recognizable interpretive paradigm. For example, in the first film in which the boy holds the card with the letters "E-E-L," his body (dis)organizes a visual field that teases viewers into thinking we have entered a space of racial data production. Yet this project is complicated by a group of boys and girls playing various schoolyard games behind him. As he approaches the camera, his body creates four distinct fields of vision (the space between his bent elbow and his ear on either side of his head, and the space to the left and right of his body). The individual spaces function like apertures through which different bodies and objects and scenes come into focus: through one perspective a buckle on a boy's overall is visible; the opening carved out by the space between the elbow and ear gives view to a raucous game among a group of boys (of whom one remains off-screen, one on-screen, while a third darts in and out of the frame); elsewhere a group of girls plays a hand-clapping game. With his body taking up the entire frame, the boy emerges as the conceptual and physical link connecting the otherwise disparate activities taking place behind him.

In his transmutation from a possible object of analysis to an object designed to anchor and organize knowledge, the boy conjures another image linked to the production of racial data: a grid. The term "grid" draws us back to film's instrumental practices of regulation and surveillance. Muybridge's chronophotographs, for example, regularly deployed grids to suture fictions of race to the body. As Shawn Michelle Smith has explained, "schooled on discourses of 'savagery' that sought to dehumanize men and women of color, scientists employed the grid to rein in the body perceived to be not quite fully human. They [race scientists] used the grid to manage the black body's perceived excess."[94] Rather than provide an entry point for coveted racial data, as a grid come to life, the boy's body unleashes a cacophony of undisciplined "data" and summons hierarchical ways of seeing, only to dissolve them. In lieu of the measurable units designed to calcify the supposedly excessive racial body, each perspective gives way to partially exposed limbs, indecipherable movements, and, together, an entirely out-of-focus tableau. At just thirty seconds, the film concludes before viewers can realize the scope of the action or where to direct their gaze, leaving us with the awareness that we have seen too much and yet nothing at all. Although it is tempting to read this film as simply signifying upon scientific conventions, together the boy's symbolic transformation from subject to grid and the intense activity behind him produce an interpretative frenzy that interrupts viewers' consumption of any racial data. Through his paradoxical performance as subjecting technology, the boy holding the card at once anticipates and refuses the compulsory fragmentation that his very presence before the camera would seem to invite. Although each of the viewpoints created by his body draws viewers in, they are greeted with starts, stops, and dead ends. What eventually emerges as an impossible attempt to "get" the films doubles as metaphor for what the films imply is the impossibility of capturing blackness as a quantifiable object of knowledge.

Whereas the first film leaves viewers at a visual impasse, the second film momentarily promises to locate subjects and viewers on steadier ground. Starting closer to the camera and in the center of the frame, the boy's stance produces the impression of a symmetrical image that might be easier to apprehend. But as if anticipating the viewer's comfort, the boy's movement forward shifts the shot in and out of focus, yanking away the hope of a stable perspective. Stationed thus, the boy's position creates three distinct fields of vision, his body acting as a focal point that actually draws viewers' attention back to the distant horizon. Although his body occupies most of the frame, again all efforts to capture or isolate him are undermined by a flurry of actions transpiring in the background. A few feet from his starting position, several young girls stand near the left edge of the frame, one of whom seems to be captivated by the camera; just behind them another figure dances into the right corner. Meanwhile boys and girls playfully dart on and off the screen, again producing indecipherable blurs. The fleeting bodies draw our attention away from the central figure (the boy) and toward the fringes of the frame. With each flash of a limb or glimpse of a piece of clothing, the boys and girls test the camera's capacity to capture their movements for posterity. But if this is a test, it is one that utterly fails. Not only is it impossible to recognize exactly what we are seeing on the screen, but even were the film to be slowed down or frozen, methods popular among early scientific filmmakers who wanted to decompose movement, the bodies always remain just beyond the reach of Hurston's filmic apparatus.

In both short films, Hurston's camerawork grants the visual and affective illusion of approaching living black culture, an illusion that Nicole Fleetwood reminds us always "returns implicitly or unwillingly to 'the real' and the compulsion to get it 'right.'"[95] Although both the camera's and the viewer's inability to "get it right," or at least familiar, proves unnerving for viewers, for the filmed subjects the effect of this perceptual conundrum is nothing short of liberating. Unable to be fully captured by viewers, the young children are symbolically emancipated from their duty to produce truths, knowledge, and data. Likewise, if these films index anything, it is not black life as a discrete and consumable "object," or the black folk as embodied subjects who reverse the scientific gaze and whose actions illustrate the dynamic life pulse of "real" or authentic black life. On the contrary, blackness emerges as an always-shifting network of relations and movements that, despite cinema's best efforts, are impossible to sync up. And although the films are certainly not lacking in a proliferation of black embodied movement, the significance of the physical body to the film is figured as ambiguous, so blackness must be defined in its tension with filmic technology.

From this perspective, the philosophy of race that emerges in these short films manifests the practice of racial formation that Hurston analogizes in her short essay "How It Feels to Be Colored Me." Published in the *World Today* in 1928, Hurston composed the essay while shooting these films, an overlap that I suggest is far from coincidental. The brief autobiographical essay promises unmitigated admittance into the emotional and psychic experience of blackness, of how it "feels." While the films purport to offer unimpeded entryway to the highly coveted terrain of racial knowledge, the essay goes one step further and extends an invitation into the depths of Hurston's own psyche. In this groundbreaking work, which many consider to be her most vague and revealing articulation of black identity, Hurston assembles and rejects a linear narrative structure in favor of a snapshot aesthetic described by one critic as a "collage of scenes."[96] As Shane Vogel writes, "from her childhood performances in the front porch of her Eatonville home, to the very white campus at Barnard, to a mixed-race basement cabaret, to a stroll down Seventh Avenue . . . the juxtaposition of these scenes suggests that racial feeling for Hurston is contextual and relational."[97] Hurston's racial feelings certainly shift according to where she is and whom she is with, so while she admits, "I do not always feel colored," at other moments her "color comes" when she "sit[s] in the drafty basement of the New World Cabaret with a white person" listening to jazz.[98] Elsewhere in the essay, Hurston confesses, "at certain times I have no race," only to later explain, "I feel most colored when I am thrown against a sharp white background."[99] In addition to being "contextual" and "relational," racial feeling is also ephemeral or, recalling Du Bois's description of Zora in *The Quest of the Silver Fleece*, what we might describe as "formless" and "boundless."

Coming and going, appearing and disappearing, the feeling of blackness moves in excess of extant categories of identification, racial idioms, or visual signifiers. By the end of the essay Hurston rejects history, genealogy, and music as frameworks for imaging or imagining the particularities of blackness. Instead, she writes: "But in the main, I feel like a brown bag of miscellany propped against a wall. Against a wall in the company with other bags, white, red, and yellow."[100] Here, the "little colored girl" who became brown the moment she left her home in Eatonville is refigured as an inanimate, portable, and exceedingly banal "brown bag of miscellany" offered to the reader for inspection; "in your hands is the brown bag," she writes. As it turns out, the only thing the bag contains is a "jumble of small things priceless and worthless."[101] Without a key or decoding device, the contents can exist only as a series of loosely affiliated objects: "A first-water diamond, an empty spool, bits of broken glass, lengths of string, a key to a door long since crumbled away, a rusty knife blade, old shoes saved for a road that never was and never will be, a nail bent under the weight of things too heavy for any nail, a dried flower or two, still a little fragrant."[102] If there is any organizing principle it is disorder; the parts are in a jumble, "heaped" and "dumped" together. Anticipating the frustration of her viewers, Hurston ends the essay with a sort of resignation: "On the ground before you is the jumble it held—so much like the jumble in the bags, could they be emptied, that all might be dumped into a single heap and the bags refilled without altering the content of any greatly. A bit of colored glass more or less would not matter. Perhaps that is how the Great Stuffer of Bags filled them in the first place—who knows?"[103] A repository that collects and records random objects but cannot and does not order its elements—here, blackness is a position best articulated in the impossible-to-answer question, Who knows? Like the paper bag, in Hurston's hands the camera is a technology at the base of which we find blackness to be graspable only as an unstable term.

Contraband Flesh

That Hurston's films manifest the theoretical moves of "How It Feels to Be Colored Me" suggests that ephemerality and syncopation are at the heart of cinema and black cultural life. Yet if Hurston's filmic work is organized around an aesthetic of overexposure, one that produces a subject that is perpetually inaccessible within the bounds of cinematic realism and that finds its literary analogue in "How It Feels to Be Colored Me," then the footage that was edited as *Kossula: Last of the Takkoi Slaves* bears this theory out in explicit terms. *Kossula* at once summons and challenges the extensive and varied visual culture of slavery in which the deeply imbricated themes of objectivity, race, and visuality are intensified. While "Characteristics of Negro Expression" arranges a racial logic around an open question, it also announces an outlook on what contemporary scholars describe as slavery's psychic afterlife.[104]

Toward the beginning of "How It Feels to Be Colored Me," Hurston refuses to identify with the "school of sobbing Negrohood," an affiliation that would reduce her to the abject role of "tragically colored." Defiant, she rejects the option of routing her identity toward slavery's dispossessive force, "No, I do not weep at the world," and instead prepares for planning—"I am too busy sharpening my oyster knife."[105] Thus, if slavery is an enduring *habitus*, it is not so much as a racial calculus that structures black life, as contemporary scholars would have it, but as an unwelcome historical relic that intrudes on Hurston's radical dreaming. "Someone is always at my elbow reminding me that I am the granddaughter of slaves," she writes. The genealogical scripting, however, does not produce a melancholic response. Instead, as Hurston explains, "it fails to register depression with me. Slavery is sixty years in the past. The operation was successful and the patient is doing well, thank you."[106] If, according to Hurston, the affective experience of slavery is a thing of the past, then she would nevertheless confront its enduring corporeal legacy in Cudjo Lewis. Thus, for Hurston slavery did not occasion a psychic dilemma, but it did prompt a visual and aesthetic one. Like the conceptual and representational challenges posed by Lavinia Baker and her surviving children discussed in chapter 2, in Lewis, Hurston grappled to communicate endurance and survival with a media toolkit that privileged either historical progression or temporal arrest.

Shot in 1928, just as she was recording her footage of children playing games, what would become the five-minute silent film *Kossula* is structured around Cudjo Lewis, also known as Kossula, the man believed to be the last living survivor of the Middle Passage. In May 1859, Lewis, along with 110 other Africans, was captured by the Dahomey, held captive in Ouidah, and sold to William Foster (a ship captain) and Timothy Meaher, an Alabama slaveholder who, along with his two brothers, had recently transitioned from owning to importing slaves. The acquisition of the slave ship *Clotilda* and its journey through the Middle Passage confirmed their new role. Three months later, the *Clotilda* docked in Mobile Bay, where the newly enslaved individuals were sold. Because the transatlantic slave trade had been abolished some fifty years earlier, once the Meahers landed on US soil, the ship was "scuttled and fired": its remains were left to sink to the bottom of Mobile Bay.

Although we can only speculate about the order in which Hurston recorded these films, it is likely that *Kossula* was among the last footage recorded. In a December 9, 1927, letter to Hughes, outlining the preliminary itinerary for her impending trip, Hurston underscored her desire to get to Lewis quickly: "I am leaving for the South on Wed. 14th on the 3:40 from the Penn Station enroute to Mobile. I shall see Cudjoe Lewis first as he is old and may die before I get to him otherwise."[107] However, Hurston didn't arrive in Alabama until the summer of 1928. This would not be Hurston's first encounter with Lewis. In July 1927 she met and interviewed Lewis while working under the sponsorship of Carter G. Woodson and Franz Boas. Three months later, Hurston's findings appeared in the October 1927 issue of Woodson's *Journal of Negro History* as "Cudjo's Own Story of the Last African Slaver." The short essay, which details Lewis's story of capture, the Middle Passage, and enslavement, turned out to be suspiciously similar to Emma Langdon Roche's account of Lewis printed in *Historic Sketches of the Old South* (1914). Although the overlap was neither discovered nor addressed during her lifetime, Hurston's return to Alabama can be understood as an attempt to, as Genevieve Sexton suggests, "confront the task of recording this story once again."[108] Her strategy was certainly different the second time around. While the first trip lasted just a few days, this time Hurston spent several months routinely visiting Lewis, sharing meals with him, accompanying him to church, and recording his story.[109] Yet Hurston's interest in revisiting Lewis and filming him, combined with the curious writing decisions, also registers a larger formal and aesthetic challenge, one that returns to questions of realism, representation, and cinema; that is, how to render legible the story of enslavement?

This challenge was not limited to the years Hurston actually spent with Lewis. Over the course of her career, Hurston grappled with locating a formal and aesthetic mode capable of conveying the nuances and complexities of Lewis's life. Hurston's unpublished manuscript "Negro Folk Tales of the Gulf States" includes an index of 482 stories, called "Kossula Told Me," and in the early 1930s she considered dedicating the final chapters of *Mules and Men* to "Kossula's little parables," although they never made it into the final draft.[110] Hurston spent much of the 1930s editing and revising a full-length narrative version of Lewis's story called *Barracoon: The Story of the Last Black Cargo*, although this too remained unpublished until 2018. In the context of these cross-genre efforts, *Kossula* speaks to Hurston's continued effort to negotiate the limits of available forms and narratives to conceptualize the story of what she would call the "last Black cargo." Drawing this point out, Sexton notes that *Barracoon* "shows a conflict between looking to testimony in order to access the atrocity of the past as a means of recovering [the rupture of slavery] . . . and the simultaneous recognition that the past is interminably closed off as inaccessible and intangible."[111] Extending Sexton's insightful reading, both Lewis's story and his embodied presence can be said to blur the commonplace conception of history as a progressive movement between past, present, and future, and to insist instead that the past, specifically enslavement and the Middle Passage, continues to condition the historical present. Hurston's efforts to account for Lewis index the persistent struggle to register a story that exists at the "precipice of loss" and dispossession, or to return to the brown bag metaphor, a history that is only graspable as unknowable, ephemeral, while dismantling the idea of a past that is distinct from the present.

That *Kossula* is the only formal experiment on which Hurston never commented, mentioned, or reflected, even as she detailed her daily activities with Lewis in works like *Barracoon*, reveals the added layer of complexity posed by cinema's narrative and technical limits. Most scholars insist that Hurston's decision to record *Kossula* was at the behest of her patron Charlotte Osgood Mason, whose interest dovetails with that of 1920s and 1930s organizations like the Works Progress Administration and Woodson's *Journal of Negro History*, which labored to document first-person accounts of antebellum slavery. Yet as the only publicly recognized survivor of the Middle Passage, Lewis's account rests somewhere between conventions of testimony, slave narrative, and first-person witness, a status that posed a conceptual and formal challenge.[112] Even so, Lewis's status as the supposed last corporeal link to a romanticized African past would have been sure to draw a captive audience. By the early twentieth century, Cudjo (or Cudjoe, or Kossula) Lewis was, to borrow a phrase from Hurston's biographer Hemenway, a "major scientific resource." Anthropologists and historians, eager to hear a firsthand account of slavery and the Middle Passage, clamored to meet him. Alain Locke included "T'appin (Terrapin)" and "Br'ere Rabbit Fools Buzzard," transcribed versions of two of Lewis's folktales, in his seminal *New Negro Anthology*. As the anthropologist Arthur Huff Fauset, who collected and recorded Lewis's stories and also contributed an essay to the volume, explained, "There is a strong need of a scientific collecting of Negro folklore before the original sources of this material altogether lapse." Lewis, it follows, was an exemplary original source. In denoting Lewis a scientific resource, Hemenway and Fauset's phrasing has the effect of evaluating him and his stories as a data source. Although it is impossible to know whether Hurston made the film (or any of these films) for Mason's private viewing or for screening in some other public forum, Charnov speculates that *Kossula* symbolizes her "transition from creating 'objective' records for research purposes to making films intended for a non-academic audience," a move that would have put her efforts at odds with the moment's trends.[113] At the same time, her attempts at narrative coherence and technical finesse with the film *Kossula* suggest an investment in experimenting with cinema as the most viable medium for representing the *whole* of Lewis's life, even as this investment quickly revealed itself to be precarious.

From its earliest moments, *Kossula* slips between the terms of source material and filmic experiment. It begins with a series of title cards introducing Lewis as "Kossula," "Full of Vigor at 89" and "Cheerful and Dignified; Always Gracious and Courtly," which parallels the film's simple three-part narrative structure. The film opens with a full-body shot of Lewis dressed in overalls, a worn jacket, and a rumpled hat. Seated on the porch of his cabin, he smiles "graciously" at the camera before he begins to tell what we can assume is his story. Lewis's mien within this mise-en-scène recalls the figuration of the "old plantation Negro" Joel Chandler Harris made famous in his Uncle Remus tales that turn-of-the-century racist cinema subsequently spectacularized. The opening setting and the literary and historical worlds it evokes seek to establish the title's promise of opening a window onto a coveted relic of the past: the "last" *African* slave. In the next shot, Lewis has relocated to a clearing on his property where he begins to chop wood, and then he sits down and continues telling the story of his life. In the third and final scene Lewis has returned to the porch, where the film ends.

Despite these straightforward and easily decipherable visual strategies and narrative cues, *Kossula* contains a number of technical missteps that inadvertently point to the aesthetic and practical limitations of rendering a narrative of black survival within the generic bounds of cinematic realism. Three minutes into the five-minute film an object (perhaps Hurston's finger) covers half the lens for nearly thirty seconds. During this time, the top of Lewis's body fades in and out of focus, the bottom half is obscured, and eventually nothing but rustling treetops are visible (see fig. 3.9). When his entire body comes back into view near the four-minute mark, it is clear that Lewis has finished his story: he stands up, stops speaking, and circles back to his porch. In a move that would seem to mark a transition into the next segment, Lewis looks at the camera, takes off his hat, and gestures to viewers to follow him indoors. At this moment, the scene begins to fade out, as a glow of whites and grays washes the screen for a full minute. Thus, the film culminates in this oversaturation of light, producing a bathetic effect that renders both Lewis and his narrative illegible. As a technical "error," this protracted moment of overexposure disrupts narrative cohesion and closure. Conceptually, however, the overexposure in *Kossula* reflects cinema's inability to provide the representational frame with which to reconstruct Lewis's African past. Constitutive of the film's fragmentary and jarring amalgam of genres, techniques, and visual cues, overexposure betrays cinema's own promise to synchronize sight, sound, and motion in order to (re)present black life. That is, even when overexposure amounts to a technical "failure," it is ultimately an epistemologically productive one in that it calls into question cinema's fitness to capture and convey a "true" account of enslavement, or to gather "scientific information" from a living person.

In her brief treatment of *Kossula*, Charnov designates the incongruity between the film's technical strivings and its final form as "ironic." Describing it as the most formally sophisticated and the most techni-

FIGURE 3.9 Film still of Cudjo Lewis, ca. 1927–1929 (Used with the permission of the Zora Neale Hurston Trust)

cally "poor" of her early footage, Charnov argues that the subject, "a silent film whose theme is that of a man story-telling," is fundamentally at odds with Hurston's goal of presenting an accurate portrayal of black Southern life. What Charnov names as the film's "irony" triggers a series of important, if impossible to answer, questions. "Why" she asks, "would one make a silent film of folklore? . . . Why was the segment edited, with titles and intertitles? For whom was this film intended?"[114] But there is also a way to read the overexposure in *Kossula* as a failure of realist techniques that reveals the limits of these very kinds of queries. That is, if overexposure registers an incongruity between filmic medium and Lewis, then it is because the technical failure demands that we ask what it even means to see an "accurate" portrayal of enslavement when, as the film of the boy holding the card implies, a "complete" image always depends upon the elision of something else. In an exaggerated manner overexposure reveals how "properly" registering the details of one filmic subject is to necessarily lose information about another. The sustained overexposure suggests that film is never accurate or authentic, and instead the product of a series of decisions that are often out of the hands of even the filmmaker.[115]

The representational challenges wrought by *Kossula* and amplified in the extreme instances of overexposure demand that we think of cinema's particularities in relation to the formal, aesthetic, and political limitations that subtend any attempt to visualize an account of slavery. Thinking the visual alongside accounts of slavery is at best difficult, and more often than not, impossible within the bounds of realist techniques. As Krista Thompson and Huey Copeland have shown, this formal and aesthetic struggle derives from slavery's slippery place in historical records and archives that depend on the assumed visibility of the slave experience and also on its visual absence. Even as antebellum slavery depended on tools of visual subjection from the scientific daguerreotype to more diffuse forms of visual technology circumscribing the plantation as a space of continual surveillance, slavery nevertheless posed, and continues to pose, artistic challenges for artists, historians, and scholars. At the heart of such political and artistic quandaries, write Thompson and Copeland, is the question of rendering visible an account of slavery without reinscribing the forms of violence that "occlud[e] her [the enslaved's] subjectivity at the very moment of representation."[116] Although slavery is cast as a highly visible and visual institution, it nevertheless strains against the boundaries of available modes of representation. As a survivor of the Middle Passage, enslavement, and the (failure of) Reconstruction policies, Lewis contributes additional layers of complexity to this formal and generic conundrum by demanding that we ask, How to visualize a story about slavery that has not yet come to an end?

Filmic representations of slavery that get valued as "real" or "true" accord with a temporal precision (their ability to confirm that slavery happened in the nineteenth century and ended with emancipation), as well as their ability to present the subject of slavery in objective and truthful terms. Slavery's visual power is dependent on the figuration of slavery as a remote historical event, which underscores the conception of time as progressive and continuous, which itself, as I showed earlier, is fundamentally at odds with Lewis and his story. By nature of his status as a survivor of the Middle Passage and witness to the transatlantic slave trade, Lewis throws this temporal order into crisis. At least symbolically, then, the moments of dramatic overexposure in *Kossula* demand that we think of the technical limitations that arise when we try to synchronize time and motion into a coherent document when its subject continues to resonate with and in the present. Put another way, if, as Natalie Zemon Davis suggests, the "coming together" of sound, motion, narrative, and cuts of film "has implications not only for the coherence and beauty of a film but also for the account it gives of the past," then together, the inability of *Kossula* to come together (either commercially as a publicly screened film or technically) suggests that the historical past of slavery remains open and incommensurable.[117] In this sense, overexposure not only raises important ethical questions about what it means to visually re-present an account of enslavement; by shedding light on the disparate temporalities that define slavery, overexposure demands that we consider how any account of black survival is fundamentally at odds with the workings of film.

Like its strange mix of ostensibly competing visual idioms, the dramatic moments of overexposure in *Kossula* index Hurston's urgent attempt to reconcile Kossula's status as survivor of the Middle Passage with the visual grammar of cinema. These moments in the film insist that viewers occupy the space of incommensurability and contingency that also structures the brown bag of miscellany and organizes the footage of the children playing games. If the films of children playing games suggest a black social life that is taking shape in excess of filmic technology, a life that is at odds with the filmic technology itself, then the moments of overexposure in *Kossula* announce a visual logic that is not governed by veracity, truth, or realism but by fragmentation, contradiction, and generic diversity.

Cinematics of Negro Expression

If Hurston's camerawork—understood as the visual world that emerges from her own confrontation with the 16 mm camera, as well as the camera's encounter with black Southern life—advances an aesthetic praxis of overexposure, then it also provides the architecture for her theory of black gesture. The smallest component of movement, gesture is the corporeal enactment of the fragment, the break, and the pause, the constitutive elements of Hurston's films. Gesture is also, to follow Giorgio Agamben's influential formulation, pure mediality. Here, gesture leads not to a complete narrative or closure but signals the ongoing process of making and a landscape of limitless possibilities. "What characterizes gesture," he writes, "is that in it nothing is being produced or acted, but rather something is being endured and supported."[118] In the hands of black feminist practitioners, gesture has also been theorized as deeply collaborative and citational. "Constituted in, through, by and with communities," gestures, writes Christina Sharpe, are "relational and (ac)cumulative."[119] Adopted, adapted, and constantly changing, gestures are also always in process.

Agamben's gesture-oriented ethics emerges in the context of a violent media history in which gesture is taken up by a modern biopolitical regime in the name of social management and efficiency. "By the end of the nineteenth century, the Western bourgeoisie had definitely lost its gesture," begins *Notes on Gesture*. After being collapsed within a political order premised on bodily regulation, gesture was reanimated by cinema; "cinema has its center in the gesture," he concludes.[120] Where the chronophotographic motion studies of Muybridge, the same ones that influenced ethnographic cinema, co-opted gesture in the name of breaking the body down into units to improve efficiency, modern cinema endeavored to release it from its instrumental workings. Hurston's films were produced at the very moment that, as Agamben sketches it, the fight over the right to gesture was under way (the 1920s), where it was simultaneously composed into a discourse of bodily biopolitical management and liberated through modern dance, theater, and cinema, spaces that returned gesture back to the provenance of the body. As it is for Agamben, for Hurston, film and gesture were mutually informing domains, even if they were not always compatible. Hurston's perceptual discoveries, the "kernels" that she culled from her camerawork, structure a theory of black embodied expression and issue forth an aesthetics of overexposure, which is also always already gestural. Reading gesture through Hurston's films extends Agamben's seminal formulation, but it also asks us to take seriously what it would mean to situate Hurston near the beginning of a history of black filmic and cinematic expression.[121] At stake here is a reading that continues to show how Hurston's literary aesthetic and racial logic were born of her filmmaking. But perhaps more important, at this point in the chapter we can begin to see her status as progenitor of critical theory and literary studies' central formulations. In this vein, this final section thinks alongside Sonya Postmentier, who,

in positioning Hurston at the very forefront of the disciplinary formations of cultural studies and black studies, insists that Hurston anticipated what we take to be late twentieth-century pedagogical methods,
critical approaches, and scholarly debates.[122] Expanding on Postmentier's insight that Hurston authored new theories for thinking poetics and race together long before literary studies cohered as a formal
discipline, I suggest that her work also generates a new vocabulary
for considering how the intersecting terms of race, film, and gesture
charted a course that many radical black filmmakers would follow.

Shortly after admitting to Hughes that she was "beginning to see
really," and just before completing "How It Feels to Be Colored Me,"
Hurston sketched an outline for her landmark essay "Characteristics
of Negro Expression." Between reflecting on visual revelation and historical dispossession, Hurston theorized black cultural life in gestural
terms. In an April 12, 1928, letter to Hughes, Hurston boiled down
her research observations and notes into a digestible schema: "I am
working hard & broadening some. I have come to 5 general laws," she
wrote.[123] Across the "laws" (of which ultimately there are seven, not
five) gesture features prominently. The first law asserts: "The Negro's
outstanding characteristic is drama. That is why he appears so imita-
tive. Drama is mimicry. *note gesture is place of words.*" Gathering drama,
gesture, and language into an interlocking chain of association, Hurston challenges us to consider gesture, with Elin Diamond, "not as sup-
plementary to language ... but rather the inverse: language as a kind of
gesture."[124] To think of language as gesture, Diamond argues, is to consider gesture's "semantic register," its capacity to "transmit characteristic rhythms, spoken, danced, and sung, of a specific cultural group,
in this case rural African Americans in their everyday labour and leisure."[125] But for Hurston, gesture is not purely a techne that transmits
cultural knowledge. When gesture surfaces again in the fifth law it is
as an enactment of overexposure, an illusory entry point to black authenticity: "Restrained ferocity in everything. There is a tense ferocity
beneath the casual exterior that stirs the onlooker to hysteria. note
effect of negro music, dancing, gestures on the staid Nordic." Constitutive of a black performance repertoire, gesture names the interface between whites' desire for racial consumption (and the frenetic
responses it compels) and black privacy. In a more oblique fashion,
gesture orients the third and fourth laws. "3. Angularity in everything,

sculpture, dancing, abrupt story telling 4. Redundance. Examples: low-down, Capn high sheriff, top-superior, the number of times—usually three—that a feature is repeated in a story. Repetition of single simple strain in music."[126] In a last-minute decision that is in keeping with Agamben's notion that gesture is pure endurance, Hurston closes the letter with a postscript: "Discovery 7. Negro folk-lore is still in the making a new kind is crowding out the old."[127] Here, Hurston insists that gesture is not only deeply performative, the embodied expression of black cultural life; it is, to borrow again from Diamond's phrasing, "constantly renewing its gestures."[128] Against modernity's impulse to regulate the social body by extracting and abstracting its gestures, Hurston formulates an impossible gestural subject, one whose constantly evolving embodied language is at odds with modern technology's temporality.

Six years later Hurston revised and expanded her taxonomic sketch as "Characteristics of Negro Expression," one of two essays that appeared in Nancy Cunard's anthology *Negro* (1934). As in her 1928 letter to Hughes, gesture orients the theory of black cultural performance in "Characteristics." "Characteristics" begins with one of Hurston's well-known formulations: "The Negro's universal mimicry is not so much a thing itself as an evidence of something that permeates his entire self. And that thing is drama."[129] An updated version of her first law ("The Negro's outstanding characteristic is drama"), in its insistence that performance is originality, the declaration could just as easily be read as summary of "Drenched in Light." "Characteristics" replaces the word "gesture" with a detailed description of black men's and women's gestural language, what she terms the world of "action words." Thus, it is through gesture that a "robust young Negro chap posing upon a street corner" can communicate his virility without uttering a word; through "languid posture, there is no mistaking his meaning."[130] And in response to such gestural provocations, "A Negro girl strolls past the corner lounger. Her whole body panging and posing. A slight shoulder movement that calls attention to her bust, that is all of a dare. A hippy undulation below the waist that is a sheaf of promises tied with conscience and power."[131] A sly lean, a subtle sway of the hips, a shoulder roll, the woman's gestural repertoire offers a quiet, even restrained, response to her suitor, what Hurston later described as dancing's "dynamic suggestion" and "compelling insinuation."[132] The purposefully misaligned choreography—hips undulating while shoulders roll—ushers in Hurston's bold claim that one of the most "striking manifestations of the Negro is Angularity." As Hurston articulates, angularity is both an inherited legacy and an unavoidable aesthetic gift. "Everything that he touches becomes angular," she explains.[133] Although African art is one place that evinces an angular aesthetic, it is in dance that the theory is fully elaborated. "Anyone watching Negro dancers will be struck by the same phenomenon," she writes. "Every posture is another angle. Pleasing, yes. But an effect achieved by the very means which a European strives to avoid." At work in the theory of angularity is active disinterest in a recognizably coherent narrative or a progressive plot that smooths over the seams, the fractures, or the breaks. Or, to return to filmic idioms, Hurston's angularity is at home in unedited fragments and the overexposure effect. In addition to angularity, black dance also incubates the related concept of asymmetry, a meeting ground of "modernity's discontinuities."[134] "The presence of rhythm and lack of symmetry are paradoxical, but there they are. Both present to a marked degree. There is always rhythm, but it is the rhythm of segments. Each unit has a rhythm of its own, but when the whole is assembled it is lacking in symmetry," she explains. Segments, breaks, poses, and postures; "insinuations" and "suggestions"—the Negro's characteristic is gesture.

As it unfolds, "Characteristics" itself devolves into a kind of segmented, asymmetrical essay, formally articulating what Cheryl Wall has described as its "jagged harmonies," a phrase she draws from Hurston's essay "Spirituals and Neo Spirituals." With this stance in mind, Wall treats "Characteristics" as emblematic of Hurston's compulsion for rejecting "consistent and orderly wholes" in favor of "variations around a theme—variations that are as often as not dissonant."[135] Thus, what she identifies as the essay's inharmoniousness— "its jagged harmonies"—accounts for its abrupt shift in tone, its typographic style ("deep indentations and acute projections"), and its "dialogic form which strives to produce the effect of the spontaneous, the tentative, and the open-ended."[136] Yet as I have been suggesting over the course of this chapter, film, like music, is an organizing mechanism that lends itself to the very kind of angularity, abruptness, and fragmentation that is constitutive of black gestural life and Hurston's aesthetic principles. Relayed on film, a technology that was never intended to enliven blackness, black life could only ever appear as open-ended, segmented, suspended, and disruptive—or simply gestural.

This is not to suggest that the 16 mm camera's technical capacity—its short reel length, somewhat bulky weight, status as an amateur's technology, and unpredictable speeds (spring-wound camera motors run at erratic speeds and record uneven pacing)—were responsible for generating Hurston's theory of gesture. Rather, in light of Hurston's notes, we might understand gesture and film as mutually constitutive. What Hurston perceived through the camera's frame and how she experienced black life mediated by and represented on film structured her theory of black expressive practice. Put another way, tracking a theory of gesture through film, and a theory of film through the gestural, situates "Characteristics" as an early expression of black cinema and the role of gesture therein.

Both the 1928 draft and the published version of "Characteristics" could double as scripts for the early footage. A scene of children dancing with arms akimbo while their legs move at a different rhythm embody the theory of angularity and asymmetry (see fig. 3.10). Likewise, Hurston's own embodied relationship to the camera is often askance, producing scenes that are skewed to the diagonal, or a perspective that is slightly too wide, cutting off the landscape at various angles. Hurston is also particularly attuned to black female comportment. For Hurston, as the embodiment of angularity and asymmetry, black women's gestural life is especially instructional. But as it turns out, it also houses a theory of black aesthetic practice and blackness more broadly that its confrontations with film amplify. A segment recorded at an outdoor social gathering is especially instructive here. The footage opens with a nearly bird's-eye view of the social gathering. Shot from a distance, in the scene we see a throng of black folks seated in bleachers, hanging around their cars, and quietly moving their bodies to some unseen and unheard music source. In the next shot Hurston and her camera have inched further into the crowd, narrowing the focus on a man who performs a series of impressive dance stunts in front of a saxophonist. The very embodiment of asymmetry, he jumps backward and forward while hinging his chest and legs in opposite directions, before finishing by proudly thrusting his cane into the ground. Despite his theatrics, Hurston's gaze reaches beyond his extraordinary moves and lands on a solitary dancing woman. In a bright dress and matching hat that produce a near blinding cascade of light, the woman casually sways back and forth in a modified two-step before raising her hands above her head and shimmying her hips (fig. 3.11). When she notices that Hurston is recording, she abruptly stops, looks directly at the camera, and raises her hand to her mouth in a gesture that is at once bashful and prideful. In the next shot she has moved closer to Hurston and confidently performs her signature move: hands up, hip shimmy. Unlike her male counterpart's practiced choreography, hers is spontaneous and improvisational. Compelling in its subtlety, her movements draw Hurston closer and closer.

This dancing woman is just one example of many Hurston records. Together they register as an archive of black female comportment as "dynamic suggestion." An ensemble of gesture, the films create what the dance studies scholar Jasmine Johnson describes as a "representational storehouse with which to challenge a narrow spectrum of black woman's ambulant embodiment."[137] This gestural repertoire is not about measuring the "presumed degree of labor" required to achieve virtuosity, as in the male showstopper; nor is it concerned with summoning a gaze or instantiating a kind of gestural call-and-response, as in the man and woman whom Hurston deploys in "Characteristics."

FIGURE 3.10 Film still of children dancing, ca. 1927–1929 (Used with the permission of the Zora Neale Hurston Trust)

FIGURE 3.11 Film still of a woman dancing at picnic, ca. 1927–1929 (Used with the permission of the Zora Neale Hurston Trust)

Following Johnson, this gesture "demands a different kind of viewing—it requires spectatorial poise; it lets you in but makes clear the inconsequentiality of your looking."[138]

Although Hurston's looking, and by extension, that of the empirically trained specialists who were perhaps patiently waiting to view the footage, may remain inconsequential, I want to wager that there is filmic consequence to this quietly choreographed exercise. Through Hurston's lens, the camera produces a scene of black gestural life, a scene that is asymmetrical, jagged, and improvisational, a scene of movement that refuses to cohere into a progressive narrative. In so doing, Hurston's film directs us to a theory of cinema and gesture that cuts through Agamben's seminal formulation. For his genealogy takes for granted black life's status as an object that can be captured on film. After all, to liberate gesture from biopolitical structures means that it must be incorporated into those systems, a process that requires that the technologies can capture it in the first place. However, as I've been arguing and as Hurston helps us see, black life is that which moves in excess of the camera's technologies of capture. From this stance we can trace a different genealogy of the black gestural and film, one in which the camera's internal and physical limits produce the corporeal language of the gesture around which Hurston would coordinate her aesthetic practice. Hurston's film produces a radical gestural grammar of blackness, one that cannot be apprehended or codified into the terms of social control; it is, as Hurston put it, "still in the making."[139]

Coda

RACIAL DATA'S AFTERLIVES

On December 16, 1928, Zora Neale Hurston wrote to Alain Locke from Mobile, Alabama, warning him not to utter a word about the "hazy dreams of the theater" that they had recently shared. After a stern warning from Charlotte Osgood Mason, who considered Locke, Hurston, and Langston Hughes her "three children," the theatrical plans were put on hold indefinitely.[1] In the meantime, Hurston continued recording footage of Southern black life, using the camera as practice arena for the theories and themes that would eventually make their way into her early 1930s dramatic oeuvre. If theater and drama afforded Hurston another arena where she could, once more, try to reconcile the epistemological crisis that film made visible, then at the very moment that Hurston was posting her letter, Locke was also facing a racial data crisis. Locke was preparing to attend the National Interracial Conference in Washington, DC, a three-day symposium dedicated to "construct[ing] a faithful contemporary picture of Negro life and relationships with the white race in the United States."[2] Although symposia and meetings focusing on the study of black life were routine in the 1920s, the conference structure reflected a new epoch in the meaning and production of racial data, one motivated by the realization that, despite decades of social research, the "Negro Problem" had yet to be solved. As they wrestled with a protracted "Negro Problem," one that remained as intransigent to new tools of analysis as its nineteenth-century iteration, conference organizers were less interested in a formal gathering than in curating an occasion that would require social scientists, historians, reformers, social workers, and philanthropists to rigorously engage in sustained research on US race relations. As they described it, the conference would allow "a long prefatory period in which the results of social studies and the meaning of official statistics would be formulated for discussion."[3] Implicit in the charge was the claim that, although there was certainly no shortage of material diagnosing race relations in general, and black life in particular, contemporary perspectives were fractured. Lacking a unified and actionable horizon, the organizers brainstormed an innovative research incubator.

At the conference, Locke was joined by Kelly Miller and W. E. B. Du Bois, who was set to deliver remarks on "The Negro Citizen." That Miller, Du Bois, and Locke gathered is certainly not surprising. As we have seen, over of the course of their intersecting careers, the three men were consistently enmeshed in social-scientific debates about the "Negro Problem," which, by 1928, had been replaced with seemingly less offensive "race problem." And although the overlap between Hurston, Locke, Miller, and Du Bois sketched here offers a neat way to end this book, my decision to conclude this study with a glance at the National Interracial Conference has everything to do with the way that the meeting's call to data harkens back to its late nineteenth- and early twentieth-century usage while anticipating the very kinds of labor that empirical forms are still compelled to perform in our contemporary moment.

Two years after the conference, participant presentations were reprinted in *The Negro in American Civilization: A Study of Negro Life and Race Relations in Light of Social Research*. In his capacity as research secretary, Charles Johnson, former editor of *Opportunity*, prepared for the conference by gathering an expansive body of "scientific data concerning actual conditions in the relations of white and Negro races today, so that the participating organizations may come to understand more accurately the problems with which they are confronted."[4] Somewhere along the very long line of research, the diverse research collective was dubbed the "data factory." Supported by Fisk University, where Johnson had been appointed to the sociology department, the data factory's "vital task" was "analyzing social data and forming it into synthesis" for the December conference.[5] The assembled research was coined the "Data Book" and distributed to each presenter ahead of his or her scheduled talk. The 244-page document was the result of the work of dozens of economists, lawyers, social workers, criminologists, historians, and sociologists, and that work comprises at least two-thirds of the published text (the remaining third consists of printed talks and a summary of the question-and-answer portion of the convening).

Evoking the terms of industrialization and the production of a surplus of disembodied knowledge, the data factory recalls the racial data revolution with which I began this book. We might also read the Data Book as an analog database, a storehouse that is searched and mined by researchers eager to bolster their work with the credibility of data. Metonymy aside, the productivity of the data factory had everything to do with the institutionalization of social-scientific disciplines that began in the final years of the 1920s and was solidified by 1930. With the professionalization of social science came a shared sense of what constituted data and to which ends it should be put. By 1930, the year that the Data Book was published as *The Negro in American Civilization: A Study of Negro Life and Race Relations in Light of Social Research*, data was disciplined.

Even as sociology fortified its disciplinary boundaries and anthropology refined its methods, including the use of film, African American cultural producers continued to critically engage with social science and data throughout the twentieth century. Richard Wright's introduction to *Black Metropolis*, Katherine Dunham's ethnographic recordings of black diasporic choreography, Ralph Ellison's transformational critique of sociology in *Invisible Man*, and Toni Morrison's *Beloved*, to name just a few, are all deeply engaged with revising and rewriting the relationship between data's regimes (photography, sociological studies, film) and black life.[6] Yet these works are different from the exercises in undisciplining data that I have elaborated in this book, not least because they were responding to the nebulous character of postbellum racial thought rather than a formalized institutional setting. The skepticism, doubt, and frustration that underscores *The Philadelphia Negro*, for instance, emerges in a form like the social survey, one that was being routinely taken up and then cast aside by a motley crew of reformers and social scientists eager to exploit its novel potential for recording the social. Likewise, Hurston's filmic practice surfaces in the context of technical missteps and ambivalence. What propelled each study was not so much the production of a counterarchive of data or a more accurate body of facts, but the question whether black life could even be rendered legible within the regulatory grammar of data. On the contrary, the work of the data factory concedes to the givenness of data, to the idea that data will always already make itself available for analysis, incorporation, or research.

It has been said that we are in the midst of a twenty-first-century racial data revolution, one in which we bear witness to the onslaught of data churned out by a sophisticated twenty-first-century data factory that, like its predecessors of the late nineteenth and early twentieth centuries, promises to solve the "problem" of African American life.[7] Here, data, facts, and the world of administrative information continues to be positioned as the threshold to both freedom and social control. For evidence of this we need look no further than the way that data continues to be called on as both evidence of the problem of black life and the first available solution by groups as diverse as social justice workers, government officials, social scientists, and everyday individuals. We see this, for instance, in President Barack Obama's 2014 public address in response to the uprisings that took shape in the aftermath of a grand jury's decision not to indict the police officers charged with murdering Michael Brown in Ferguson, Missouri. As Obama called for collective healing and entreated us to remember "how this started" ("we lost a young man, Michael Brown, in heartbreaking and tragic circumstances"), he summoned a familiar discursive repertoire. Harkening back to his progressive antecedents, he framed social movement as a problem for social-scientific research, explaining: "What we need to do is to understand them [protestors] and figure out how do we make more progress. And that can be done.... And I am confident that if we focus our attention on the problem and we look at what has happened in communities around the country effectively, then we can make progress not just in Ferguson, but in a lot of other cities and communities around the country."[8] The solution was a commission of policing, a state-sponsored data factory.

Just a few months later, the *New York Times* announced the Equal Justice Initiative's groundbreaking lynching report and its accompanying data visualization project. The report published the most comprehensive list to date of victims of racial terror, and an interactive map used small red squares to indicate the volume of lynching by county; the more saturated the area was with squares, the more deadly the racial terror. Grazing your cursor over a terrain would indicate the total number of lynchings and a click would transport you to a short biographical film of the victim that juxtaposes archival documents (usually photographs) to contemporary footage of the location. In their own effort to make data move, photographs of the 1893 lynching of Henry Smith in Paris, Texas, for instance, are edited with a photo-grammetry technique that renders the photograph three-dimensional and in motion. As Brian Stevenson, the project's founder, put it shortly after the website launched, "The project is intended to force people to reckon with the narrative through-line of the country's vicious racial history, rather than thinking of that history in a short-range, piecemeal way."[9] Espousing an unshakable commitment to the politically trans-formative power of facts and truth, Stevenson offered enumeration as the pathway to racial reconciliation. "We cannot heal the deep wounds inflicted during the era of racial terrorism until we tell the truth about it," he explained.[10] In the summer of 2020, the project announced a new report whose focus is the period of racial terror bookended by the beginning and end of Reconstruction. In the updated iteration, histor-ical information and archival fragments from the press and advertise-ments contextualize the death toll, which took center stage in the 2015 report. Perhaps encountering the very limits of statistical accounting, Stevenson reasoned: "It's important that we quantify and document violence. . . . But what's more important is that we acknowledge that we have not been honest about who we are, and about how we came to this moment."[11] Notwithstanding the Equal Justice Initiative's self-conscious reflection that documentation and data alone could never account for the entirety of racial violence, both projects stage an ap-peal to the transformative power of data, whether visually rendered in numerical figures or in narrative film. And yet the labor that data are compelled to perform is not simply toward a political awakening. Rather, seeing and (at least digitally) feeling the force of anti-black vio-lence is tasked with the work of rupture and repair. If the data of racial terror are charged with illumining the historical overlaps that index the *longue durée* of black disfranchisement and precarity, then they are also tasked with providing a road map to a more just future.

The impulse to map a relationship between past and present repre-sents a dominant philosophy of history, one that insists on historical continuities rather than ruptures and that attends to resonances across institutions, ideologies, policies, and economic structures traditionally assigned to discrete historical epochs. In the past decade, this critical orientation has gathered under the heading "afterlife of slavery." In this framework, the persistent denial of black civil and social rights, the longing for an unattainable past, and the unfulfilled promise of emancipation demonstrate slavery's enduring presence in the twenty-first century. As Saidiya Hartman reflects: "If slavery persists as an issue in the political life of black America, it is not because of an antiquarian obsession with bygone days or the burden of a too-long memory, but because black lives are still imperiled and devalued by a racial calculus and a political arithmetic that were entrenched centuries ago. This is the afterlife of slavery—skewed life chances, limited access to health and education, premature death, incarceration, impoverishment."[12] More than simply drawing comparisons between past and present, a nuanced engagement with slavery and its afterlife is concerned with that which endures across time and space but cannot be assimilated into narrow definitions of past and present; it is a framework that investigates how dominant modes of knowledge production relegate certain injustice, injuries, and inconsistencies to the past in order to construct a progressive narrative of history and freedom.

If we are living in the afterlife of slavery, then this condition is just as much owing to continued assaults against black life—both the spectacular and the mundane—as it is to the work that data are compelled to perform, both toward ordering and managing blackness and toward actualizing freedom and social justice. Put another way, if the afterlife of slavery draws attention to the epistemological workings of anti-blackness, then we must consider how the continued construction of black life as a problem of and for data undercuts this work. Here, we can look to the ease with which black life is conscripted to a data problem and a problem for data. We can also consider the ease with which our elected officials conscript black life as an object of study while masquerading data-driven reports and new surveillance systems as the thoroughfare to social equity.

Just as data continue to be harnessed as a tool of racial subjection, it paradoxically is also what we reach for—statistical, visual, and graphic—to evidence the precarity of black living and the long arm of state-sanctioned violence and the deep roots of systemic racism. For evidence of this, we need look no further than the political labor that cell phone footage of the murder of George Floyd was compelled to perform in the summer of 2020. Take, for instance, an interview in early August on WNYC with the *Hamilton* actor Okieriete Onaodowan. During the segment Onaodowan called for a "reckoning" in theater, one that would amplify black voices, expanding what producers understood as "successful" theater by diversifying actors, producers, and dramatic themes. To make this point, Onaodowan summoned the recently recorded video of Floyd's murder as "data." In his punctuating statement, he explained: "The fact is that what Black people and people of color have been saying for centuries is actually true. We have technology of cell phone footage where it's undeniable now, eight minutes, you can sit down from top to bottom we saw what happened. So, there's no question of what happened before or whether this is not true. It's just data and it's just facts."[13] That data are so quickly and often uncritically recruited to both index the problem (of anti-blackness, in all its permutations) and solve it reflects a central strand of this book, one that, as we have seen, animated and encouraged the work of African American cultural producers intent on imaging and imagining a new relationship between black life and data.

But I want to chart a different connection between past and present while holding onto the utility of thinking about the ongoing manifestation of black precarity and the way it continues to shape our contemporary moment. Rather than take for granted the givenness of data—that is, the imminent availability of data and the assumption that black life enters a consensual and productive relationship with its regimes—might we train our attention to the ambivalent, the anxious, and the altogether experimental engagements with data, those experiments tracked over the course of this book? Following this line of thinking means considering Johnson's data factory as always already destabilized by Hurston's plans for an innovative black theater. It also requires taking seriously the aesthetic innovations and visual transformations that emerge when we approach Sutton Griggs's 1899 novel *Imperium in Imperio* as a social survey, or when we encounter Zora Neale Hurston's filmic experiments that ultimately conditioned a theory of blackness in general and black gestural practice in particular. It is also to read lynching photography as an endeavor that is neither self-assured nor ontologically secure, but persistently punctured by performances of black embodied motion (the stakes of which we discovered in chapter 2).

With these archival touchstones as our guide, I conclude by staging a rereading of racial data, one that develops when we begin from the experimental and often messy confrontations between black life and data regimes elaborated in this book. At stake in this project is shifting and texturing the archival anchors that orient our embrace of history's recursiveness.

In July 2016 the *New Yorker* printed "American Exposure," the historian Jill Lepore's reflection on the widely circulated video of Philando Castile's deadly encounter with police officers that his girlfriend, Diamond Reynolds, recorded and uploaded to Facebook. Lepore's decision to watch the footage of Castile's death sets in motion a sustained reflection on the thorny role of visual media in the long African American freedom struggle, a meditation that leads her directly from Reynolds to Frederick Douglass. Recounting her viewing experience, Lepore writes: "So I forced myself to watch. And, as I did, the screen went black—the police had thrown down Reynolds's phone, and put her in handcuffs—and you could only hear voices, the muted, distant sound of Reynolds crying and praying, and closer, the urgent voice of her four-year-old daughter, and right then I remembered that photograph of Douglass."[14] The image in question, "that" particular photograph, is a mid-1850s daguerreotype. In 1968 the portrait reappeared as the cover of *Life* magazine's special issue "The Search for a Black Past," printed a few months after the assassination of Martin Luther King Jr. and the subsequent riots during which police violently faced off with mostly black protestors. The 1968 cover, Lepore maintains, was the magazine's attempt to sketch a historical trajectory that, with Douglass as its starting point, would map a future devoid of racial violence and the continued repudiation of black life. In contradistinction to photographs taken right after King's death (also published in *Life*) and press coverage of violent encounters between police and protestors, Douglass's image of embodied subjectivity was a visual reminder of blacks' capacity to embody citizenship, even if their so-called unruly behavior across US cities suggested otherwise. Although she cannot account for her involuntary move from Reynolds's video to Douglass's daguerreotype—"I don't know how to explain why I thought of that photograph while watching Diamond Reynolds's Facebook video of the police shooting of her boyfriend," she writes—like the editors of *Life*, Lepore endeavors to reconcile an incomprehensible black "present" with its homologous "black past." This is a present characterized by relentless assaults against black life and the wide circulation of visual evidence of anti-black violence in the name of political reform. For although more than a century separates Douglass's and Reynolds's camerawork, Lepore is most concerned with their shared confidence in visual technology's capacity to incite political transformation, even as, she argues, "the overwhelming evidence of history" instructs us that visual media have never been able to undermine the workings of anti-black violence. In Lepore's assessment, Reynolds's quick camera work, the immediacy with which she began to record the encounter between Castile and police, and the forethought to livestream the video to Facebook are a continuation of Douglass's own ethos that visual revelation is the key to political transformation. Or, as Reynolds put it during her testimony in the trial of the police officers accused of manslaughter, "I wanted to make sure if I was to die in front of my daughter, someone would know the truth."[15]

Even as it was produced to present the "truth," Reynolds's recording also emerges from the encounter between black life and the technological apparatus of the camera phone. In this case, the force, what Hurston described as the always already dynamic nature of black living, and what Lavinia Baker embodied as an irruptive choreographic solo that could disintegrate a perfectly produced performance cycle, is precisely what posed a threat to the officers. The genealogy that this book traces emerges out of the recognition of the necessity of a visual grammar that can recognize the forms of black life that fall out of the camera's field of vision, those figures who, like Reynolds, lurk in the "black space" of the frame where they can never be fully visualized, documented, or easily composed into data. The "black space" indexes an overreliance on data to articulate and account for anti-black violence, even if we realize that there is no amount of data that can account for black death. If the black space illuminates anything, it is certainly not the violence that police mete out, which the state routinely forgives. Rather, what is made visible in this unmappable and unquantifiable lacuna is that white supremacy is never captured at the same level of intricacy as anti-black violence. This is what the poet Dawn Lundy Martin has recently described as the "darkness of whiteness" and what Zora Neale Hurston understood to be the terrain of overexposure.[16] More than a technical hiccup or an advertent misstep, might we think of the black space as a site from which we rescript the relationship between blackness and data? From this perspective, the past and present continue to be yoked together by a necessarily open question: how to document the sociality of black life?

Acknowledgments

This book is emerging on the other side of years working alongside a sprawling archive that defied disciplinary bounds and demanded a capacious methodology to match its contours. As I learned early on, the archive of late nineteenth- and early twentieth-century life and literature is nothing if not overwhelming, and I have often felt that this book's archive outpaced me. For this reason, I am indebted to countless friends, interlocutors, mentors, and archivists who helped me clear a pathway to complete a book that, I hope, holds on to the complexity, asymmetry, and, most important, beauty of turn-of-the-century black living.

This project took shape across multiple academic institutions and in as many cities. In each space, I've been lucky to find colleagues, friends, and collaborators who have nourished this study, offering social mooring, steady encouragement, and countless moments of joy. At Columbia University, where the kernels of this book surfaced, I discovered the importance of ethical archival research, responsible reading, and, most important, what it means to take intellectual risks. Brent Hayes Edwards and Saidiya Hartman were ideal advisers and mentors who continue to model what it means to move through this profession with grace, integrity, and sheer brilliance. They saw the value of this project, and although it has developed in important ways, their incisive and insightful questions continue to stay with me. My thinking about late nineteenth-century black life was enriched by Hartman's seminar "Du Bois and His Circle," where my notional ideas about social science and literary practice began to cohere. This book was also buoyed by her unwavering support, guidance, and inspiration. Elizabeth McHenry embraced me as an advisee, offering her time and generous feedback at every turn. Monica Miller and Tina Campt also provided important feedback at an early stage, much of which has found its way into this final book. At Columbia, I was graced with an incredible cohort who remain some of the smartest people I know. Jean-Christophe Cloutier, Nijah Cunningham, John Hay, Jang Wook Huh, Jenny James, Jarvis McGinnis, Sherally Munshi, Imani Owens, Mariel Rodney, and Jessica Teague were crucial teammates, collaborators, and friends. For its deep attention to literary history, this project is indebted to the training I received as a master's student at the University of Maryland. Gene Jarret, Robert Levine, Carla Peterson, and Mary Helen Washington offered a collective master class in African American literature and instilled in me the very earliest inklings of what it would mean to take this career on, and all the exciting intellectual rewards that it might yield. Anita Baksh, Christopher Brown, Rewa Burnham, Nina Candia, Schuyler Esprit, Ariana Austin Makonnen, Lakisha Odlum, and Anna Steed showed me what friendship and collegiality in the academy might look like. At the time, I did not realize what a gift it was to take a graduate class with eight other scholars who were also working in African American and diasporic studies. Were it not for Jennifer James, with whom I took my very first class in African American literature as an undergraduate at George Washington University, I would never even have dreamed of attending graduate school; thank you.

As a postdoctoral fellow in African American literature at Rutgers University, I was lucky enough to learn alongside Cheryl Wall. Being able to develop this project in her proximity was an honor and a gift. That I could even dream up this book is owing to her fearless commitment to African American studies and her tireless presence in the academy. Cheryl's force is manifest in the Rutgers faculty who encouraged and supported this project. Elin Diamond, Brad Evans, Nicholas Gaskill, Carter Mathis, Stephane Robolin, and Evie Shockley were especially generous, offering both their time and their intellectual insights. This project was also supported by a faculty fellowship from Penn State University's Center for the History of Information. Eric Hayot's seminars pushed me to consider "data" as a complex and capacious term. I am especially grateful to Laura Helton, who not only encouraged me to think about my work in terms of the rich field of data and information but also continues to teach me so much about archival work and information systems.

The University of Pittsburgh was an ideal place to nurture this project. I am especially grateful to Don Bialostosky, Tyler Bickford, Nancy Glazner, Cory Holding, Dawn Lundy Martin, Gayle Rogers, and William Scott for their friendship and encouragement. At Princeton I am fortunate enough to work with scholars in African American studies and English. In African American studies, Anna Arabindan-Kesson, Wendy Belcher, Ruha Benjamin, Wallace Best, Eddie Glaude, Reena Goldthree, Joshua Guild, Tera Hunter, Naomi Murakawa, Kinohi Nishikawa, Chika Okeke-Agulu, Imani Perry, and Keeanga-Yamahtta Taylor are incredible colleagues whose commitment to the field inspires me at every turn. April Peters, our fearless department manager, keeps everything in order, and without her none of this archival research would have been possible. In English, Christina León, Monica Huerta, Paul Nadal, and Sarah Chihaya are ideal colleagues who offer levity and comradery, bringing light to the basement of McCosh Hall. Christina León and Monica Huerta, in particular, have been crucial sounding boards, reading key parts of the manuscript and reminding me when I was closer to being finished than I imagined. Russ Leo is a scrupulous reader, and I am grateful for the time and patience that he gave this book during its final push to the finish line. My colleagues in English have supported and encouraged this book from the very beginning. Anne Cheng, Simon Gikandi, Bill Gleason, Josh Kotin, Meredith Martin, Susan Stewart, and Tamsen Wolff have offered encouraging words and invaluable wisdom. I am especially grateful to my students of Blackness and Media, Experimenting in Dark Times, and Nineteenth-Century African American Literature who, in the end, shared my enthusiasm for all things nineteenth century. Thank you for coming along for the ride. Research for this book was also enabled by grants from the Princeton University Committee on Research in the Humanities and Social Sciences, the Department of African American Studies, and the Humanities Council, including the Data in Humanities Working Group. For the peace and productivity, I am especially grateful to a writing retreat at the Foundation Valparaiso, whose staff and fellows reignited my love for this book and all of its actors.

Priscilla Wald, Gene Jarrett, and Imani Perry generously participated in a manuscript workshop. Their feedback helped me begin to see the individual pages of this manuscript as a book. Both Priscilla and Gene offered nuanced and detailed feedback and invited me to produce a project that matched its aspirations. This book has also been enriched by conversations at University of Wyoming, University of Maryland, New York University, the American Antiquarian Society, Bowdoin College, and Haverford College. The formidable Kimberly Juanita Brown and the members of the Dark Room are a consistent source of energy and brilliance, and I am incredibly honored to have shared parts of this book in its symposia. The anonymous readers at the University of Chicago Press read this book exactly as I intended and offered the reader reports of my dreams. Their feedback encouraged me to take authorial risks and embrace the full force of this project's argument. At the University of Chicago Press, Alan Thomas has been an absolute pleasure to work with and an ideal editor and interlocutor. Thank you for seeking out this book, for believing in the project from the very beginning, and for championing it every step of the way.

It is impossible to imagine this book without the friends who have also become my most respected readers and my greatest source of inspiration. Janet Neary has been a voice of reason, a stellar thinking partner, and the very best friend. Lindsay Reckson recognized the value of this project before anyone else and has offered incisive, thoughtful feedback along the way. Jasmine Johnson transcends the categories of friendship and collaborator. For her feedback and her comradery, her generosity and her precision, I am equal parts grateful and in awe. Emily Hainze is my coworker in everything Progressive Era and one of the few people who also find joy sifting through case files and social surveys; thank you for fielding all of my crazy questions and reading so much of this book. Kemi Adeymi, Nijah Cunningham, Anoop Mirpuri, C. Riley Snorton, and Nik Sparks read parts of this book at critical moments, pushing my thinking into directions that I didn't necessarily know it needed to go. Angie Cruz opened her home and her family to me, all while reminding me to dream and write big. Sampada Aranke, Josh Begley, Ashon Crawley, Laura Fisher, Sarah Haley, Leigh Raiford, and Arielle Zibrak are important interlocutors and friends whose work always teaches me something new. To live and write in proximity to New York is to always move beyond the academy proper. Nada Ayad, Alexandra Bell, Ashleigh Brown, Katie Engst, Armando Garcia, Douglas Jones, Helen Kim, Neville Louison, Matthew Morrison, Lakisha Odum, Harrison Perry, Elana Safar, and Gavin Steingo have nourished me with necessary escapes and the reminder that there is always a life outside of this book. I am thankful for the spontaneous dinner dates and countless museum trips, picnics, baby playdates, and, most important, fun.

For their patience and assistance, I am deeply indebted to the work of the archivists and librarians at the Library of Congress; the University of Florida, Gainesville; the University of Chicago; Howard University's Mooreland Spingarn Research Center; the New York Public Library; and the Museum of Modern Art. The Library of Congress's Print and Photographs Division allowed me to sift through every cabinet card in search of photographic traces of the Baker family. Using archives to write about the lives of real people in literary and aesthetic terms is a difficult endeavor, one that I've tried to approach ethically and respectfully. Much shorter versions of chapter 2 appeared as "Lynching's Afterlife," *J19: The Journal of Nineteenth-Century Americanists* 6, no. 1 (2018): 204–11; and "Object Lesson(s)," *Women and Performance* 27, no. 1 (2017): 59–66. Parts of chapter 3 appear as "'The Brown Bag of Miscellany': Zora Neale Hurston and the Practice of Overexposure," *Black Camera: An International Film Journal* 7, no. 1 (2015): 115–33. And parts of the coda appear as "Visuality, Surveillance, and the Afterlife of Slavery," *American Literary History* 29, no. 1 (2017): 191–204. My thanks to the journals for permission to reprint parts of these articles.

This book is unthinkable without the support of my family. My parents, Charity and James, nurtured my love of nineteenth-century life and were confident enough to let me chart my own relationship to reading and learning. Thank you for trusting me to make my own life decisions and for being there every step of the way. My sister, Makeeda Holley, is my forever coconspirator, especially when it comes to imagining new words and reconstructing old ones; this project is simply unimaginable without you. Tray Womack, Marc Holley, and Ella and Xander Holley regularly reminded me to slow down, have fun, and say yes. Mary Marshall has always offered reading breaks and beautiful places to write. My canine companions, Greyson and Larry, are the very embodiment of unconditional love, always keeping an eye on me when I write. Finally, this book is dedicated to the memory of my grandmother, Rosemary Marshall, one of the most brilliant women I've known. Thank you for always reminding me that thinking is never done, that curiosity is a lifelong project, and that reading is a respite, a privilege, and a reward.

Notes

Introduction

1. W. E. B. Du Bois, *The Quest of the Silver Fleece* (New York: Pine Street Books, 2004), 44.

2. See Tufuku Zuberi, *Thicker Than Blood: How Racial Statistics Lie* (Minneapolis: University of Minnesota Press, 2001). For a discussion of the particularly late-nineteenth-century explosion of racial data in the name of delimiting free black life, see Khalil Muhammad, *The Condemnation of Blackness: Race, Crime, and the Making of Modern Urban America* (Cambridge, MA: Harvard University Press, 2011). I return to Muhammad's phrase "the racial data revolution" later in this chapter. Importantly, while Muhammad argues that the census heralded a racial data revolution, in this book I argue that photography, film, and sociological studies also fueled and fed this data frenzy.

3. W. E. B. Du Bois, "The Study of the Negro Problems," *Annals of the American Academy of Political and Social Science*, January 1898, 23; Du Bois, "My Evolving Program for Negro Freedom," in *What the Negro Wants*, ed. Rayford Logan (Chapel Hill: University of North Carolina Press, 1944), 57. Importantly, Du Bois does not give language to this tension until the mid-1940s. Yet one of the arguments of this introductory chapter, and this book, is that his empirical ambivalence was alive and well within his late nineteenth- and early twentieth-century oeuvre. Moreover, the task of seeking to reimagine social-scientific territory while also arguing for inclusion is the tension that I track across each chapter.

4. Du Bois, *The Quest of the Silver Fleece*, 13. For a reading of the relationship between *Quest* and "Negro Labor in Lowndes County, Alabama," see Maria Farland, "W. E. B. Du Bois, Anthropometric Science, and the Limits of Racial Uplift," *American Quarterly* 58, no. 4 (2006): 1017–44. See also Emily Hainze, "'Wayward and Untrained Years': Reforming the 'Wayward Girl' in 'The Quest of the Silver Fleece' and 'Jennie Gerhardt,'" *Studies in American Fiction* 46, no. 2 (2019): 341–72.

5. For a careful and nuanced reading of the swap as a site of ecological excess that also conditions new social and sexual formations, see C. Riley Snorton, *Black on*

Both Sides: A Racial History of Trans Identity (Minneapolis: University of Minnesota Press, 2017); Du Bois, *The Quest of the Silver Fleece*, 14.

6. Du Bois, *The Quest of the Silver Fleece*, 15.

7. Daphne Brooks, *Bodies in Dissent: Spectacular Performances of Race and Freedom, 1850–1910* (Durham, NC: Duke University Press, 2006), 105.

8. Brooks, *Bodies in Dissent*, 103.

9. W. E. B. Du Bois, *The Souls of Black Folk* (1903; New York: Norton, 1999), 156.

10. As I show in chapter 1, even as scholars normally mark Du Bois's break with formalized sociology with the 1903 publication of *The Souls of Black Folk*, he continued to mobilize and experiment with social science's methodological tools well into the twentieth century. Most notable are the Atlanta University Studies that he directed and the economic reports he produced for the US Department of Labor. One of my arguments here is that by imagining Zora, the very kind of subject who, from the position of social-scientific reform, excited and maddened him, Du Bois is experimenting with the different mediums and media that might actually be able to hold and convey her.

11. This reading of Zora, *Quest*, and Du Bois is deeply indebted to Saidiya Hartman's account of Du Bois's formal frustrations in *Wayward Lives, Beautiful Experiments: Intimate Histories of Social Upheaval* (New York: Norton, 2019). I detail the coherence of race, data, and modernity later in this introduction, but it is worth indexing the body of literature on the emergence of social science as a particularly modern enterprise. On this history of social science and modernity, see Dorothy Ross, *The Origins of American Social Science* (New York: Cambridge University Press, 1991); Robyn Wiegman, *American Anatomies: Theorizing Race and Gender* (Durham, NC: Duke University Press, 1993); Muhammad, *The Condemnation of Blackness*. This book is also more obliquely engaged with a body of literature that has been especially attentive to the relationship of modernity, literary realism, and the place of disciplines and technology therein. This book is conversant, then, with works such as Jacqueline Goldsby's *A Spectacular Secret: Lynching in American Life and Literature* (Chicago: University of Chicago Press, 2006) and Nancy Bentley's *Frantic Panoramas: American Literature and Mass Culture, 1870–1920* (Philadelphia: University of Pennsylvania Press, 2009). Finally, and as this book argues, turn-of-the-century writers themselves theorized the relationship of modern black life, technology, and data in meaningful and nuanced ways. We might turn to Ida B. Wells's powerful indictment of statistics and sociology in her 1893 *A Red Record: Tabulated Statistics and Alleged Causes of Lynching in the United States*.

12. Vilashini Cooppan, "Move on Down the Line: Domestic Science, Transnational Politics, and Gendered Allegory in Du Bois," in *Next to the Color Line: Gender, Sexuality, and W. E. B. Du Bois*, ed. Susan Gillman and Alys Eve Weinbaum (Minneapolis: University of Minnesota Press, 2007), 49. Cooppan argues that even as Du Bois authored a sociological method that, in revising the Spencerian perspective, insisted on producing and analyzing facts and data, he continued to reproduce antiquated gender categories: "Du Bois's sociological studies can nonetheless be seen to rely for their racial newness upon a certain kind of gendered oldness" (51).

13. Shawn Michelle Smith, *Photography on the Color Line: W. E. B. Du Bois, Race, and Visual Culture* (Durham, NC: Duke University Press, 2004), 11.

14. W. E. B. Du Bois, *The Georgia Negro: A Social Study*, 1899, plate 1.

15. Saidiya Hartman, *Wayward Lives, Beautiful Experiments: Intimate Histories of Social Upheaval* (New York: Norton, 2019), 113.

16. See Hartman, *Wayward Lives, Beautiful Experiments*, 110.

17. This line of thinking depends on a relationship between data and information that I develop in more detail later in this introduction, where data becomes information through mediating technologies. See also the Toni Morrison epigraph.

18. Du Bois, *The Souls of Black Folk*, 9.

19. On the relationship between double consciousness and psychology, see Shamoon Zamir, *Dark Voices: W. E. B. Du Bois and American Thought, 1888–1903* (Chicago: University of Chicago Press, 1995).

20. The formal innovation of *Souls*, from its mobilization of the slave narrative's signal rhetorical maneuvers to the pairing of traditional African American music with European masterpieces that frame each chapter, has been theorized by an important body of scholarship. See, e.g., Robert Stepto, *From Behind the Veil: A Study of Afro-American Narrative* (Urbana: University of Illinois Press, 1991); Alexander Weheliye, *Phonographies: Grooves in Afro-American Modernity* (Durham, NC: Duke University Press, 2005), esp. chap. 3.

21. This line of thinking engages with Leigh Raiford, who writes, "To examine the dialectics between movement and medium, between (cultural) visibility and (political) invisibility, we are required to ask how and why African American activists chose to enlist photography as part of their political struggle." Although Raiford is writing in the context of photography in particular, her provocation is especially pertinent to black cultural producers working across a range of visual modalities and time periods. See Raiford, *Imprisoned in a Luminous Glare: Photography and the African American Freedom Struggle* (Chapel Hill: University of North Carolina Press, 2011), 7.

22. For a discussion of documenting and documentary's status as a tool of self-regulation, discipline, and instrumental power, see John Tagg, *The Burden of Representation: Essays on Photographies and Histories* (Minneapolis: University of Minnesota Press, 1993); Lindsay Reckson, *Realist Ecstasy: Religion, Race, and Performance in American Literature* (New York: New York University Press, 2020), 3.

23. "Do Black Lives Matter? Robin D. G. Kelly and Fred Moten in Conversation," December 14, 2015, Vimeo video, posted by Critical Resistance, https://vimeo.com/116111740.

24. Carla Kaplan, *Zora Neale Hurston: A Life in Letters* (New York: Doubleday, 2002), 115; Theodora Krober, *Alfred Kroeber, a Personal Configuration* (Berkeley: University of California Press, 1970), 51.

25. Dorothy Ross, "Changing Contours of the Social Science Disciplines," in *The Cambridge History of Science*, vol. 7, *The Modern Social Sciences*, ed. Theodore Porter and Dorothy Ross (Cambridge: Cambridge University Press, 2003), 207.

26. On the disciplinary workings of fields, like sociology, but also institutions,

like the university, see Roderick Ferguson, *Aberrations in Black: Toward a Queer of Color Critique* (Minneapolis: University of Minnesota Press, 2013).

27. Eddie Glaude, *In a Shade of Blue: Pragmatism and the Politics of Black America* (Chicago: University of Chicago Press, 2007), x; Saidiya Hartman, *Lose Your Mother: A Journey along the Atlantic Slave Route* (New York: Farrar, Straus & Giroux, 2008), 6.

28. Fred Moten, "Taste Dissonance Flavor Escape (Preface to a Solo by Miles Davis)," *Black and Blur (consent not to be a single being)* (Durham, NC: Duke University Press, 2017), 68.

29. Maurice Lee, *Overwhelmed: Literature, Aesthetics, and the Nineteenth-Century Information Revolution* (Princeton, NJ: Princeton University Press, 2019), 8.

30. Simone Browne, *Dark Matters: On the Surveillance of Blackness* (Durham, NC: Duke University Press, 2015); Zuberi, *Thicker Than Blood*.

31. Katherine McKittrick, "Mathematics Black Life," *Black Scholar* 44, no. 2 (2014): 20.

32. Kimberly Juanita Brown offers an especially cogent reading of "refuse" as excess and resistance in *The Repeating Body: Slavery's Visual Resonance in the Contemporary* (Durham, NC: Duke University Press, 2015).

33. Evelyn Ruppert, Engin Isin, and Didier Bigo, "Data Politics," *Big Data and Society* (2017): 2.

34. Ruppert, Isin, and Bigo, "Data Politics," 3.

35. Lee, *Overwhelmed*, 4.

36. Colin Koopman, *How We Became Our Data: A Genealogy of the Informational Person* (Chicago: University of Chicago Press, 2019).

37. Browne, *Dark Matters*.

38. Lisa Gitelman and Virginia Jackson, introduction to *Raw Data Is an Oxymoron*, ed. Lis Gitelman (Cambridge, MA: MIT Press, 2013).

39. Toni Morrison, "The Origin of Others, The Literature of Belonging," The Charles Elliot Norton Lectures, Harvard University, March 8, 2016.

40. Alan Sekula, "The Body and the Archive," *October* 39 (1986): 3–64.

41. McKittrick, "Mathematics Black Life," 19.

42. McKittrick, "Mathematics Black Life," 17.

43. See Caitlin Rosenthal, *Accounting for Slavery: Masters and Management* (Cambridge, MA: Harvard University Press, 2018).

44. Browne, *Dark Matters*.

45. Stephen Jay Gould, "American Polygeny and Craniometry before Darwin: Blacks and Indians as Separate, Inferior Species," in *The Racial Economy of Science*, ed. Sandra Harding (Bloomington: Indiana University Press, 1993), 102.

46. Gitelman and Jackson, introduction to *Raw Data Is an Oxymoron*, 12.

47. Johanna Drucker, *Graphesis: Visual Forms of Knowledge Production* (Cambridge, MA: Harvard University Press, 2014), 20.

48. Nicholas Mirzoeff, *The Right to Look: A Counterhistory of Visuality* (Durham, NC: Duke University Press, 2014).

49. Alan Sekula, "The Body and the Archive."

50. The body of scholarship on race and photography in the nineteenth century is extensive, and this list doesn't begin to scratch the surface. By no means exhaustive, the following titles register texts that have been particularly crucial to my thinking in this book: Shawn Michelle Smith, *American Archives: Gender, Race, and Class in Visual Culture* (Princeton, NJ: Princeton University Press, 1999); Smith, *Photography on the Color Line*; Brian Wallis, "Black Bodies, White Science: Louis Agassiz's Slave Daguerreotypes," *Journal of Blacks in Higher Education* 12 (1996): 102–6; Nicholas Mirzoeff, "The Shadow and the Substance: Race, Photography, and the Index," in *Only Skin Deep: Changing Visions of the American Self*, ed. Coco Fusco and Brian Wallis (New York: International Center for Photography, 2004); Laura Wexler, *Tender Violence: Domestic Visions in the Age of US Imperialism* (Chapel Hill: University of North Carolina Press, 2000); Deborah Willis and Carla Williams, *The Black Female Body: A Photographic History* (Philadelphia: Temple University Press, 2002). There is also a large body of work that focuses primarily on twentieth-century black visual culture and photography but nevertheless draws important lines of connection to the nineteenth century's photographic ethos. Examples include Nicole Fleetwood, *Troubling Vision: Performance, Visuality, and Blackness* (Chicago: University of Chicago Press, 2011); Tina Campt, *Image Matters: Archive, Photography, and the African Diaspora in Europe* (Durham, NC: Duke University Press, 2012).

51. Smith, *American Archives*, 163.

52. Fred Moten, *In the Break: The Aesthetics of the Black Radical Tradition* (Minneapolis: University of Minnesota Press, 2003), 1.

53. Frederick Douglass, *My Bondage and My Freedom* (1855; New York: Barnes and Noble Classic, 2005), 269.

54. Uri McMillian has thoroughly elaborated the concept of objecthood in *Embodied Avatars: Genealogies of Black Feminist Art and Performance* (New York: New York University Press, 2015).

55. Britt Rusert, *Fugitive Science: Empiricism and Freedom in Early African American Culture* (New York: New York University Press, 2017).

56. For a nuanced reading of Ida B. Wells's mathematic manipulations, see Goldsby, *A Spectacular Secret*, esp. 80–88.

57. Nathaniel Shaler, "The Negro Problem," *The Atlantic*, November 14, 1884.

58. Shaler, "The Negro Problem."

59. Shaler, "The Negro Problem."

60. Muhammad, *The Condemnation of Blackness*, 19.

61. Alan Sekula, "The Body and the Archive."

62. This is by no means an exhaustive list, but a brief overview of these titles begins to make this point: Michael Chaney, *Fugitive Vision: Slave Vision and Black Identity in African American Literature* (Bloomington: Indiana University Press, 2008); Jasmine Cobb, *Picture Freedom: Remaking Black Visuality in the Early Nineteenth Century* (New York: New York University Press, 2015); Rusert, *Fugitive Science*.

63. Avery Gordon, *Ghostly Matters: Haunting and the Sociological Imagination* (Minneapolis: University of Minnesota Press, 2008); Ferguson, *Aberrations in Black*.

64. Brooks, *Bodies in Dissent*, 5.

65. Brooks, *Bodies in Dissent*, 5.

66. Moten, *In the Break*, 201.

67. Moten, *In the Break*, 201.

68. On the place of the ecstatic in turn-of-the-century literary productions and racial imaginaries, see Lindsay Reckson, *Realist Ecstasy: Religion, Race, and Performance in American Literature* (New York: New York University Press, 2020).

69. For an account of the vibrancy of this literary period, see Barbara McCaskill and Caroline Gebhard, eds., *Post-Bellum, Pre-Harlem: African American Literature and Culture, 1877–1919* (New York: New York University Press, 2006).

70. Interestingly, even though this period ends in 1919, more often than not James Weldon Johnson's 1910 *Autobiography of an Ex-Colored Man* signals the end of our postbellum interests.

71. Saidiya V. Hartman, *Scenes of Subjection: Terror, Slavery, and Self-Making in Nineteenth-Century America* (New York: Oxford University Press, 1997).

72. McCaskill and Gebhard, *Post-Bellum, Pre-Harlem*, 2.

73. On the periodization of social science, see Theodore Porter, "Statistics and Statistical Methods," in *The Cambridge History of Science*, vol. 7, *The Modern Social Sciences*, ed. Porter and Ross, 238–50. Porter explains: "Statistics assumed its recognizable modern disciplinary form during the period from 1890 to 1930. These dates are also comparable for the formation of disciplines in the leading fields of social science" (238). See also Dorothy Ross, *Modernist Impulses in the Human Sciences, 1870–1930* (Baltimore: Johns Hopkins University Press, 1994).

74. For a careful analysis of how biopower cohered through discourses of racial and gendered difference, see Kyla Schuler, *The Biopolitics of Feeling: Race, Sex, and Science in the Nineteenth Century* (Durham, NC: Duke University Press, 2018).

75. Amanda Anderson and Joseph Valente, "Discipline and Freedom," in *Disciplinarity at the Fin de Siècle*, ed. Amanda Anderson and Joseph Valente (Princeton, NJ: Princeton University Press, 2002), 1–18.

76. Hartman, *Scenes of Subjection*, 117.

77. In its attention to the aesthetic forms and creative practices that emerged to disentangle black life from its status as manageable data, *The Matter of Black Living* sits alongside Nihad Farooq's work, which also follows this moment's generative disorder: *Undisciplined: Science, Ethnography, and Personhood in the Americas, 1880–1940* (New York: New York University Press, 2016).

78. Tavia Nyong'o, *Afro-Fabulations: The Queer Drama of Black Life* (New York: New York University Press, 2019), 49.

79. See, e.g., Nahum Dimitri Chandler, *X—The Problem of the Negro as a Problem for Thought* (New York: Fordham University Press, 2014); Aldon Morris, *The Scholar Denied: W. E. B. Du Bois and the Birth of Modern Sociology* (Oakland: University of California Press, 2015); Whitney Battle-Baptiste and Britt Rusert, *W. E. B. Du Bois's Data Portraits: Visualizing Black America* (Princeton, NJ: Princeton University Press, 2018); Alexander Weheliye, "Diagrammatics as Physiognomy: W. E. B. Du Bois's Graphic Modernities," *CR: The New Centennial Review* 15, no. 2 (2015): 23–58.

Chapter One

1. W. E. B. Du Bois, *The Philadelphia Negro* (1899; Philadelphia: University of Pennsylvania Press, 1996), 1.

2. W. E. B. Du Bois, "The Study of the Negro Problems," *Annals of the American Academy of Political and Social Science* 11 (January 1898): 3.

3. Nathaniel Shaler, "The Negro Problem," *The Atlantic*, November 1884.

4. As we shall see, like "Art," Du Bois repeatedly capitalized "Truth" in his discussions of the social survey and sociology.

5. Du Bois, "The Study of the Negro Problems," 6.

6. W. E. B. Du Bois, *Dusk of Dawn: An Essay Toward an Autobiography of a Race Concept* (1940; New York: Oxford University Press, 2007), 134–35. For an analysis of *The Quest of the Silver Fleece*'s relationship to the Atlanta University Studies and Du Bois's own economic theories, see Maria Farland, "W. E. B. Du Bois, Anthropometric Science, and the Limits of Racial Uplift," *American Quarterly* 58, no. 4 (2006): 1017–45; Jarvis C. McInnis, "'Behold the Land': W. E. B. Du Bois, Cotton Futures, and the Afterlife of the Plantation in the US South," *Global South* 10, no. 2 (2016): 70–98.

7. Herbert Aptheker, *The Literary Legacy of W. E. B. Du Bois* (New York: Krauss International Publications, 1898), 109.

8. W. E. B. Du Bois, "The Atlanta Conferences," *Voice of the Negro* 1, no. 3 (March 1904): 88.

9. Du Bois, "The Atlanta Conferences," 88. Du Bois's vision for a continuously unfolding and developing "record" also articulates the tension between movement and medium that is at the heart of late nineteenth-century black experimental practice. His evocation of the record as a form of animate documentation is, of course, also in conversation with Ida B. Wells's 1895 *A Red Record*, which I briefly discuss in chapter 2.

10. Brent Hayes Edwards, "Late Romance," in *Next to the Color Line: Gender, Sexuality, and W. E. B. Du Bois*, ed. Susan Gillman and Alys Eve Weinbaum (Minneapolis: University of Minnesota Press, 2007), 124.

11. Shane Vogel, *The Scene of the Harlem Cabaret: Race, Sexuality, Performance* (Chicago: University of Chicago Press, 2009).

12. W. E. B. Du Bois, "Conference for the Study of the Negro Problems Atlanta, Georgia," *Report of the first conference of Negro land-grant colleges for coordinating a program of social studies: Convened at Atlanta University, Atlanta, Ga., April 19, 20, 1943, as the Twenty-sixth Atlanta University Conference to Study the Negro Problems*, Atlanta.

13. Kevin Gaines, *Uplifting the Race: Black Leadership, Politics, and Culture in the Twentieth Century* (Chapel Hill: University of North Carolina Press, 1991), 157.

14. Following turn-of-the-century terminology, over the course of the chapter I use "social study," "social survey," and "survey" interchangeably.

15. Roderick Ferguson, *Aberrations in Black: Toward a Queer of Color Critique* (Minneapolis: University of Minnesota Press, 2004), 27.

16. On the flexibility of sociology at the turn of the century, see Mia Bay, "The World Was Thinking Wrong about Race: W. E. B. Du Bois and Nineteenth-Century Racial Science," in *W. E. B. Du Bois, Race, and the City: The Philadelphia Negro and Its Legacy*, ed. Michael B. Katz and Thomas J. Sugure (Philadelphia: University of Pennsylvania Press, 1998), 41–61.

17. In *The Pittsburgh Survey*, widely celebrated as the paradigmatic expression of the survey, Paul Kellogg identifies surveyors as social engineers. This relationship is discussed in Stephen Turner, "The Pittsburgh Survey and the Survey Movement: An Episode in the History of Expertise," in *The Social Survey in Historical Perspective, 1880–1940*, ed. Martin Bulmer, Kevin Bales, and Kathryn Kish Sklar (New York: Cambridge University Press, 1991), 269–91.

18. Brent Hayes Edwards, *The Practice of Diaspora* (Cambridge, MA: Harvard University Press, 2003), 23.

19. Fred Moten, "Nowhere, Everywhere," *Black and Blur (consent not to be a single being)* (Durham, NC: Duke University Press, 2017), 164.

20. Carol Aronovici, *The Social Survey* (Philadelphia: Harper Press, 1916), 2.

21. Aronovici, *The Social Survey*, 2.

22. Bay, "The World Was Thinking Wrong about Race," 42–44.

23. Dorothy Ross, *The Origins of American Social Science* (New York: Cambridge University Press, 1991), 227.

24. Du Bois, "Conference for the Study of the Negro Problems," 8.

25. Countless slave narratives made recourse to this phrasing in the titles or prose of their work. In the preface to Frederick Douglass's 1845 *Narrative*, William Lloyd Garrison highlights the slave narrative's currency as objective evidence: "I am confident that it is essentially true in all its statements; that nothing has been set down in malice, nothing exaggerated, nothing drawn from the imagination; that I comes short of the reality, rather than overstates a single fact in regard to SLAVERY AS IT IS." Frederick Douglass, *Narrative of the Life of Frederick Douglass, an American Slave* (1845; New York: Penguin Classics, 2014), 7.

26. Laura R. Fisher, *Reading for Reform: The Social Work of Literature in the Progressive Era* (Minneapolis: University of Minnesota Press, 2019), 34.

27. Shannon Jackson, *Lines of Activity: Performance, Historiography, Hull-House Domesticity* (Ann Arbor: University of Michigan Press, 2001).

28. Bulmer et al., "The Social Survey in Historical Perspective," in *The Social Survey in Historical Perspective*, ed. Bulmer, Bales, and Sklar, 2–3.

29. Robert Ezra Park, "Notes on the Social Survey," June 17, 1919, box 5, folder 1, Special Collections Research Center, University of Chicago Library.

30. Paul U. Kellogg, "The Spread of the Survey Idea," *Proceedings of the Academy of Political Science in the City of New York* 2, no. 4 (1912): 2.

31. Carl C. Taylor, *The Social Survey: Its Histories and Its Methods* (Columbia: University of Missouri Press, 1919), 476.

32. Taylor, *The Social Survey*, 5.

33. Taylor, *The Social Survey*, 27.

34. Jackson, *Lines of Activity*, 11.

35. Mark Seltzer, "Statistical Persons," *Diacritics* 17, no. 3 (1987): 84.

36. *Hull-House Maps and Papers* (New York: Thomas Y. Crowell & Company, 1895), vii; *The Negro in the Cities of the North*, 5.

37. Carl Taylor, "The Social Survey and the Science of Sociology," *American Journal of Sociology* 25, no. 6 (1920): 745–46.

38. Thomas Riley, "Sociology and Social Surveys," *American Journal of Sociology* 16, no. 6 (1911): 818.

39. Taylor, *The Social Survey*, 50.

40. Paul Kellogg to W. E. B. Du Bois, June 17, 1905, W. E. B. Du Bois Papers (MS 312), Special Collections and University Archives, University of Amherst Libraries, Amherst, MA.

41. Taylor, *The Social Survey*, 62. It is also worth drawing out the antebellum lines of connection between the microscope and this pseudomicroscope that Britt Rusert details in *Fugitive Science: Empiricism and Freedom in Early African American Culture* (New York: New York University Press, 2017). I also have in mind here Du Bois's construction of the "megascope" in his recently recovered short story "The Princess Steel," as well as his enduring commitment to the pageant. On Du Bois and the pageant, see Soyica Diggs Colbert, *The African American Theatrical Body: Reception, Performance, and the Stage* (New York: Cambridge University Press, 2011). For an analysis of Du Bois's megascope, see Adrienne Brown, *The Black Skyscraper: Architecture and the Perception of Race* (Baltimore: Johns Hopkins University Press, 2017).

42. Jean Converse, *Survey Research in the United States, 1890–1960* (Berkeley: University of California Press, 1987), 1.

43. Converse, *Survey Research*, 1.

44. Jonathan Crary, *Techniques of the Observer: On Vision and Modernity in the Nineteenth Century* (Cambridge, MA: MIT Press, 1990), 15, 20.

45. W. E. B. Du Bois, *The Autobiography of W. E. B. Du Bois: A Soliloquy on Viewing My Life from the Last Decade of Its First Century* (New York: Oxford University Press, 2007), 124.

46. Robyn Wiegman, *American Anatomies: Theorizing Race and Gender* (Durham, NC: Duke University Press, 1995).

47. Khalil Muhammad, *The Condemnation of Blackness: Race, Crime, and the Making of Modern Urban America* (Cambridge, MA: Harvard University Press, 2010), 19.

48. Vogel, *The Scene of the Harlem Cabaret*, 138.

49. Alexander Weheliye, "Diagrammatics as Physiognomy: W. E. B. Du Bois's Graphic Modernities," *CR: The New Centennial Review* 15, no. 2 (2015): 27.

50. James Weldon Johnson, *The Autobiography of an Ex-Colored Man* (1912; New York: Norton Critical Editions, 2015), 5.

51. Frederick Hoffman, *Race Traits and Tendencies of the American Negro* (New York: American Economic Association, 1896), xi.

52. Susan Mizruchi, *The Science of Sacrifice: American Literature and Modern Social Theory* (Princeton, NJ: Princeton University Press, 1998), 285.

53. Hoffman, *Race Traits*, 312.

54. Hoffman, *Race Traits*, 312.

55. Although subtle, Hoffman's phrasing, "of all the races for which statistics are obtainable," also implies that African Americans are particularly legible for statistical counting and that black life is reducible to information.

56. Frederick Starr, "Review of Race Traits and Tendencies of the American Negro, by Frederick L. Hoffman," *The Dial* 22 (January 1897).

57. Shaler, "The Negro Problem."

58. Muhammad, *The Condemnation of Blackness*, 31.

59. Maurice Lee, *Uncertain Chances: Science, Skepticism, and Belief in Nineteenth-Century American Literature* (New York: Oxford University Press, 2012), 104.

60. Margo J. Anderson, *The American Census: A Social History*, 2nd ed. (New Haven, CT: Yale University Press, 2015), 106.

61. Quoted in Melissa Nobles, *Shades of Citizenship: Race and the Census in Modern Politics* (Stanford, CA: Stanford University Press, 2000), 58.

62. Nobles, *Shades of Citizenship*, 57.

63. Nobles, *Shades of Citizenship*, 58.

64. Hoffman, *Race Traits*, v.

65. Ann Fabian, *The Skull Collectors: Race, Science, and Americans Unburied Dead* (Chicago: University of Chicago Press, 2010).

66. Hoffman, *Race Traits*, 310.

67. Hoffman, *Race Traits*, 310.

68. For a discussion of race and insurance, see Ian Baucom, *Specters of the Atlantic: Finance Capital, Slavery, and the Philosophy of History* (Durham, NC: Duke University Press, 2005).

69. Mizruchi, *The Science of Sacrifice*, 285.

70. W. E. B. Du Bois, *The Quest of the Silver Fleece* (1911; New York: Harlem Moon Books, 2004), 15; Avery Gordon, *Ghostly Matters: Haunting and the Sociological Imagination* (Minneapolis: University of Minnesota Press, 1997), 188.

71. Jacqueline Goldsby, *A Spectacular Secret: Lynching in American Life and Literature* (Chicago: University of Chicago Press, 2006), 83.

72. In his description of the Atlanta University Studies, Du Bois explained, "We wish not only to make the truth clear but to present it in such a *shape* as will encourage and help social reform." See *Conference for the Study of the Negro Problems*, Atlanta, 5; Johanna Drucker, *Graphesis: Visual Forms of Knowledge Production* (Cambridge, MA: Harvard University Press, 2014).

73. Hoffman, *Race Traits*, v.

74. Drucker, *Graphesis*, 88. The idea of the limit also squares with Alexander Weheliye's important analysis of diagrammatics.

75. Megan Wolff, "The Myth of the Actuary: Life Insurance and Frederick L. Hoffman's *Race Traits and Tendencies of the American Negro*," *Public Health Reports* 121, no. 1 (2006): 85.

76. Wolff, "The Myth of the Actuary," 85.

77. Drucker also makes a similar point in regard to late twentieth- and early twenty-first-century data visualization projects. But part of what this book aims to do is argue that these same questions underpin late nineteenth- and early twentieth-century engagements with statistics as well.

78. This is a riff on Katherine McKittrick's question, "Can we really count it out differently?" in "Mathematics Black Life," *Black Scholar* 44, no. 2 (2014): 23.

79. Hoffman, *Race Traits*, 312.

80. Alfred A. Moss, *The American Negro Academy: The Voice of the Talented Tenth* (Baton Rouge: Louisiana State University Press, 1981), 24.

81. Moss, *The American Negro Academy*, 40.

82. Moss's *The American Negro Academy* offers the most incisive analysis of the ANA, its history, and Kelly Miller's speech.

83. Moss, *The American Negro Academy*, 93.

84. See Muhammad, *The Condemnation of Blackness*.

85. "Friday Morning Session: Review of Mr. Hoffman's Book," *Southern Workman*, September 1897, 180.

86. Kelly Miller, "A Review of Frederick Hoffman's Race Traits and Tendencies of the American Negro," *American Negro Academy Occasional Papers Vol. 1* (Washington, DC: American Negro Academy, 1897), 34.

87. Miller, "A Review," 34.

88. Miller, "A Review," 35.

89. Miller, "A Review," 35.

90. Miller, "A Review," 5.

91. Miller, "A Review," 5.

92. Miller, "A Review," 6.

93. Miller, "A Review," 3.

94. Miller, "A Review," 6.

95. Miller, "A Review," 36.

96. A review of Du Bois's *The Philadelphia Negro* in the *Southern Workman*, Hampton University's official publication, also criticized the project for illuminating "ugly facts." Quoted in Gaines, *Uplifting the Race: Black Leadership, Politics, and Culture in the Twentieth Century* (Chapel Hill: University of North Carolina Press, 1996), 157.

97. "Friday Morning Session," 8.

98. Miller, "A Review," 1.

99. Paul Lawrie, *Forging a Laboring Race: The African American Worker in the Progressive Imagination* (New York: New York University Press, 2016), 33.

100. On aesthetics as a category that distributes the sensible, see Jacques Rancière, "The Aesthetic Dimension: Aesthetics, Politics, Knowledge," *Critical Inquiry* 36, no. 1 (2009): 1–19.

101. "Friday Morning Session," 8.

102. Peter Brooks, *The Melodramatic Imagination: Balzac, Henry James, Melodrama, and the Mode of Excess* (New Haven, CT: Yale University Press, 1976), 12–13.

103. Saidiya V. Hartman, *Scenes of Subjection: Terror, Slavery, and Self-Making in Nineteenth-Century America* (New York: Oxford University Press, 1997), 27.

104. Susan Gilman, *American Race Melodrama and the Culture of the Occult* (Chicago: University of Chicago Press, 2003), xvi.

105. W. E. B. Du Bois, "Review of *Hoffman's Race Traits and Tendencies of the American Negro*, by Frederick Hoffman," *Annals of the American Academy of Political and Social Science* (1897): 131.

106. Du Bois, "Review," 129.

107. Du Bois, *Autobiography*, 125.

108. Aldon Morris, *The Scholar Denied: W. E. B. Du Bois and the Birth of Modern Sociology* (Oakland: University of California Press, 2015), 47.

109. Du Bois, *The Philadelphia Negro*, 3.

110. Du Bois, *The Philadelphia Negro*, 3; Morris, 47.

111. Du Bois, *The Philadelphia Negro*, 63.

112. This argument extends Weheliye's claim that Du Bois's experimental graphics also combat the representative limits of tables and charts. My reading here departs from Weheliye's, however, in its attention to the social survey as whole rather than his specific focus on charts and graphs; Du Bois, "The Study of the Negro Problems," 10–11.

113. Saidiya Hartman, *Wayward Lives, Beautiful Experiments: Intimate Histories of Social Upheaval* (New York: Norton, 2019), 93.

114. Du Bois, *The Philadelphia Negro*, 64.

115. Du Bois, *The Philadelphia Negro*, 64.

116. See Tera Hunter, "The 'Brotherly Love' for Which This City Is Proverbial Should Extend to All': The Everyday Lives of Working-Class Women in Philadelphia and Atlanta in the 1890s," in *W. E. B. Du Bois, Race, and the City*, ed. Katz and Sugure; Hartman, *Wayward Lives, Beautiful Experiments*.

117. Du Bois, *The Philadelphia Negro*, 267.

118. Vilashini Cooppan, "Move on Down the Line: Domestic Science, Transnational Politics, and Gendered Allegory in Du Bois," in *Next to the Color Line*, ed. Gillman and Weinbaum, 55.

119. Du Bois, *The Philadelphia Negro*, 67.

120. In his unpublished autobiography, and likely in reference to *The Philadelphia Negro*, Miller writes, "[Du Bois and I] entertained almost identical views as to the place of education in the solution of the race problem, and from the sociological point of view saw many things eye to eye. We still have a more or less common vision on the race problem, although we do not view it through the same glasses." Kelly Miller, "Autobiography of Kelly Miller," series D, box 1, p. 5, Moorland Spingarn Research Center, Howard University.

121. Sutton E. Griggs, *The Story of My Struggles* (Nashville: Orion Publishing, 1916), 7.

122. Sutton Griggs, *The New Plan of Battle and the Man on the Firing Line* (Nashville: Orion Publishing, 1902), 6.

123. Griggs, *The Story of My Struggles*, 8.

124. Griggs, *The Story of My Struggles*, 9.

125. Griggs, *The Story of My Struggles*, 8.

126. Griggs, *The Story of My Struggles*, 8.

127. Sutton E. Griggs, *Guide to Racial Greatness; or, The Science of Collective Efficiency* (Memphis: National Public Welfare League, 1923).

128. Eric Curry, "'The Power of Combinations': Sutton Griggs' *Imperium in Imperio* and the Science of Collective Efficiency," *American Literary Realism* 43, no. 1 (2010): 26.

129. Pauline Hopkins, *Contending Forces: A Romance Illustrative of Negro Life North and South* (Boston: Colored Cooperative Publishing Co., 1900), 13–14.

130. Alain Locke, "The Negro's Contribution to American Art and Literature," *Annals of the American Academy of Political and Social Science* 140, no. 1 (November 1928): 421.

131. Locke, "The Negro's Contribution to American Art and Literature," 240.

132. Du Bois, *The Quest of the Silver Fleece*, 6.

133. Ferguson, *Aberrations in Black*, 55.

134. Seltzer, "Statistical Persons," 90.

135. Maeve Adams, "Numbers and Narratives: Epistemologies of Aggregation in British Statistics and Social Realism, c. 1770–1880," in *Statistics and the Public Sphere: Numbers and the People in Modern Britain, c. 1800–2000*, ed. Tom Crook and Glen O'Hara (Hoboken, NJ: Taylor & Francis, 2011), 104.

136. Eileen Janes Yeo, "The Social Survey in Social Perspective," in *The Social Survey in Historical Perspective*, ed. Bulmer, Bales, and Sklar, 50.

137. Toward the end of his career Griggs refocused his energy on sound recording and ministry. In 1928 he recorded his sermons, which were later released on the compilation album *Blues and Gospel Records, 1902–1943*. Grigg's (re)turn to oratory and his embrace of recording technology complete the disillusionment with visuality that he initially expresses in *Imperium in Imperio*. For a seminar discussion of his sound recordings, see Steven C. Tracy, "Saving the Day: The Recordings of the Reverend Sutton E. Griggs," *Phylon* 47, no. 2 (1986): 159–66.

138. Griggs, *Imperium in Imperio*, 10.

139. Griggs, *Imperium in Imperio*, 19.

140. Crary, *Techniques of the Observer*, 39.

141. Michael Chaney, "Mulatta Obscura: Camera Tactics and Linda Brent," in *Pictures and Progress: Early Photography and the Making of African American Identity*, ed. Maurice O. Wallace and Shawn Michelle Smith (Durham, NC: Duke University Press, 2012), 122–23.

142. Griggs, *Imperium in Imperio*, 20.

143. Carla Peterson, "Commemorative Ceremonies and Invented Traditions: History, Memory, and Modernity in the 'New Negro' Novel of the Nadir," in *Post-Bellum, Pre-Harlem: African American Literature and Culture, 1877–1919*, ed. Barbara McCaskill and Caroline Gebhard (New York: New York University Press, 2006), 42.

144. Shawn Michelle Smith, *American Archives: Gender, Race, and Class in Visual Culture* (Princeton, NJ: Princeton University Press, 1999), 189.

145. In *The Civil Contract of Photography* Ariella Azoulay makes the distinction between looking and watching as the basis for an ethical posture toward images that better respond and engage with injury but that also imbues the photographic image with a durational temporality: "Photography is much more than what is printed on photographic paper. The photograph bears the seal of the photographic event, and reconstructing this event requires more than just identifying what is shown in the photograph. One needs to stop looking at the photograph and instead start watching it. The verb 'to watch' is usually used for regarding phenomena or moving pictures. It entails dimensions of time and movement that need to be reinscribed in the interpretation of the still photographic image" (14). Although Azoulay is writing specifically of twentieth- and twenty-first-century photographs of human catastrophe, the idea that watching photographs as a site of political—and I would add affective—relations is instructive. For only when Belton tarries with the photographic album, watching it as a testament to the unfolding of an event, can he recognize his child. I elaborate on Azoulay in chapter 2. Ariella Azoulay, *The Civil Contract of Photography* (Boston: MIT Books, 2008).

146. Griggs, *Imperium in Imperio*, 171.

147. Wiegman, *American Anatomies*, 9.

148. Gaines, *Uplifting the Race*, xiv.

149. Gaines, *Uplifting the Race*, 21.

150. Du Bois, *The Souls of Black Folk*.

151. Gaines, *Uplifting the Race*.

152. Griggs, *Imperium in Imperio*, 97.

153. Shawn Michelle Smith, *Photography on the Color Line: W. E. B. Du Bois, Race, and Visual Culture* (Durham, NC: Duke University Press, 2004), 41.

154. Smith, *Photography on the Color Line*, 41.

155. Du Bois, *The Souls of Black Folk*.

156. Gaines, *Uplifting the Race*.

157. Du Bois, *The Souls of Black Folk*.

158. This argument is at the heart of Smith's reading of Du Bois's middle-class portraits in *Photography on the Color Line*.

159. Griggs, *Imperium in Imperio*, 100.

160. Griggs, *Imperium in Imperio*, 106.

161. Frantz Fanon, *Black Skin, White Masks* (1952; New York: Grove Press, 2008), 95; Hortense Spillers, "Mama's Baby, Papa's Maybe: An American Grammar Book," *Diacritics* 17, no. 2 (1987): 64–81.

162. Griggs, *Imperium in Imperio*, 29.

163. Paul Kellogg, 1905, 1, Kellogg, Arthur P. Letter from Arthur P. Kellogg to W. E. B. Du Bois, July 1, 1905. W. E. B. Du Bois Papers (MS 312). Special Collections and University Archives, University of Massachusetts Amherst Libraries.

164. Clarke Chambers, *Paul Kellogg and the Survey: Voices for Social Welfare and Social Justice* (Minneapolis: University of Minnesota Press, 1971).

165. Muhammad, *The Condemnation of Blackness*, 105.

166. *The Negro in the Cities of the North* (New York: Charities and Commons, 1905), 1.

167. Paul Underwood Kellogg to W. E. B. Du Bois, May 8, 1905, W. E. B. Du Bois Papers (MS 312), Special Collections and University Archives, University of Amherst Libraries.

168. Kellogg, May 8, 1905.

169. Paul Underwood Kellogg to W. E. B. Du Bois, June 17, 1905, W. E. B. Du Bois Papers (MS 312), Special Collections and University Archives, University of Amherst, Amherst, MA.

170. Paul Laurence Dunbar, *The Heart of Happy Hollow* (1904; New York: Dover, 2014), vii.

171. Andrea N. Williams, *Dividing Lines: Class Anxiety and Postbellum Black Fiction* (Ann Arbor: University of Michigan Press, 2012), 99.

172. Williams, *Dividing Lines*, 99.

173. It is worth noting that Paul Kellogg, who edited the 1905 special issue, was also the editorial force behind the 1925 special issue "Harlem: Mecca of the New Negro."

174. "Mission Sketches," in "The Negro in the Cities of the North," ed. Edward T. Devine, special issue, *Charities* 15, no. 1 (1905): 60.

175. Sarah Collins Fernadis, "Social Settlement in Washington," in "The Negro in the Cities of the North," ed. Devine, special issue, *Charities* 15, no. 1 (1905): 65.

176. Thomas Jesse Jones, "The Country at Large," in "The Negro in the Cities of the North," ed. Devine, special issue, *Charities* 15, no. 1 (1905): 88.

177. Jones, "The Country at Large," 92.

178. Alain Locke, "Harlem," in "Harlem: Mecca of the New Negro," special issue, *Survey Graphic* (1925): 630.

179. Locke, "Harlem," 630.

180. Alain Locke, "Enter the New Negro," in "Harlem: Mecca of the New Negro," special issue, *Survey Graphic* (1925): 631.

181. Anne Elizabeth Carroll, *Word, Image, and the New Negro: Representation and Identity in the Harlem Renaissance* (Bloomington: Indiana University Press, 2005), 56.

182. Carroll, *Word, Image, and the New Negro*, 59.

183. Crary, *Techniques of the Observer*, 6.

184. Jeremy Braddock, *Collecting as Modernist Practice* (Baltimore: Johns Hopkins University Press, 2012); Barbara Foley, *Spectres of 1919: Class and Nation in the Making of the New Negro* (Urbana: University of Illinois Press, 2008); George Hutchinson, *The Harlem Renaissance in Black and White* (Cambridge, MA: Harvard University Press, 1995).

185. One exception is Jeremy Braddock, who outlines the aesthetics of the 1925 Harlem issue in relation to the modernist's collecting impulse.

186. Jeffrey Stewart, *The New Negro: The Life of Alain Locke* (New York: Oxford University Press, 2017), 454.

187. Martha Jane Nadell, *Enter the New Negroes: Images of Race in American Culture* (Cambridge, MA: Harvard University Press, 2004), 48.

188. Nadell, *Enter the New Negroes*, 50.

189. "Survey Associates Appeals," *Survey* (1921): xii.

190. "Survey Associates Appeals," xii.

191. Locke, "Enter the New Negro," 629.

192. Locke, "Enter the New Negro," 630.

193. Braddock, *Collecting as Modernist Practice*, 175, 184.

194. Locke, "Enter the New Negro," 630.

Chapter Two

1. Sutton Griggs, *Imperium in Imperio* (1899; New York: Modern Library, 2003), 138.

2. Griggs, *Imperium in Imperio*, 149–50.

3. See Maria Karafilis, "Oratory, Embodiment, and US Citizenship in Sutton E. Griggs's 'Imperium in Imperio,'" *African American Review* 40, no. 1 (2006): 125–43.

4. Wilson Jeremiah Moses, "Literary Garveyism: The Novels of Reverend Sutton E. Griggs," *Phylon* 40, no. 3 (1979): 204.

5. Baker's name is alternately spelled "Frazier" and "Frazer." For the purpose of this chapter I retain the spelling "Frazier." However, the photographs stored at the Library of Congress record his name as "Frazer."

6. Harvey Young, *Embodying Black Experience: Stillness, Critical Memory, and the Black Body* (Ann Arbor: University of Michigan Press, 2010); John Tagg, *The Burden of Representation: Essays on Photographies and Histories* (Minneapolis: University of Minnesota Press, 1988), 76.

7. Tagg, *The Burden of Representation*, 66; Young, *Embodying Black Experience*.

8. "A Negro Postmaster Killed," *News and Courier*, February 23, 1898.

9. "Lake City Protests," *News and Courier*, February 12, 1898.

10. "Lake City Protests."

11. Kirk Fuoss, "Lynching Performances, Theaters of Violence," *Text and Performance Quarterly* 19, no. 1 (1999): 5; "A Negro Postmaster Killed."

12. "A Negro Postmaster Killed."

13. "A Negro Postmaster Killed."

14. William Baker is alternately referred to as Willie and Willis in newsprint and reviews. For the purposes of this chapter, I have chosen to refer to him by his full name as recorded in the 1900 census, William Frazier.

15. Griggs, *Imperium in Imperio*, 138.

16. Jacqueline Goldsby, *A Spectacular Secret: Lynching in American Life and Literature* (Chicago: University of Chicago Press, 2006).

17. See, e.g., Sandra Gunning, *Race, Rape, and Lynching: The Red Record of American Literature* (New York: Oxford University Press, 1996); Trudier Harris, *Exorcising Blackness: Historical and Literary Lynching and Burning Rituals* (Bloomington: Indiana University Press, 1984); Jacqueline Dowd Hall, *Revolt against Chivalry: Jessie*

Daniel Ames and the Women's Campaign against Lynching (New York: Columbia University Press, 1993).

18. Goldsby, *A Spectacular Secret*, 224.

19. Lindsay Reckson, *Realist Ecstasy: Religion, Race, and Performance in American Literature* (New York: New York University Press, 2020).

20. Leigh Raiford, *Imprisoned in a Luminous Glare: Photography and the African American Freedom Struggle* (Chapel Hill: University of North Carolina Press, 2011), 43.

21. Raiford, *Imprisoned in a Luminous Glare*, 34.

22. Griggs, *Imperium in Imperio*, 138.

23. See Koritha Mitchell, *Living with Lynching: African American Lynching Plays, Performance, and Citizenship, 1890–1930*; Deborah McDowell, "Viewing the Remains: A Polemic on Death, Spectacle, and the [Black] Family," in *The Familial Gaze*, ed. Marianne Hirsch (Hanover, NH: University Press of New England, 1999), 153–78; Raiford, *Imprisoned in a Luminous Glare*; Claudia Rankine, "The Condition of Black Life Is One of Mourning," *New York Times*, June 22, 2015.

24. Koritha Mitchell, *Living with Lynching*, 147, 151.

25. Saidiya V. Hartman, *Scenes of Subjection: Terror, Slavery, and Self-Making in Nineteenth-Century America* (New York: Oxford University Press, 1997).

26. Tina Campt, *Listening to Images* (Durham, NC: Duke University Press, 2017).

27. James Weldon Johnson, *Along This Way: The Autobiography of James Weldon Johnson* (New York: Viking Press, 1933), 170.

28. Rebecca Schneider, *Performing Remains: Art and War in Times of Theatrical Reenactment* (New York: Routledge, 2011), 7.

29. Kirk Fuoss, "Lynching Performances, Theaters of Violence," *Text and Performance Quarterly* 19, no. 1 (1999): 5.

30. Ariella Azoulay, *The Civil Contract of Photography* (Boston: MIT Books, 2008), 28.

31. Young, *Embodying Black Experience*, 169.

32. "A Negro Postmaster Killed."

33. J. L. Dart, *The Famous Trial of the Eight Men Indicted for the Lynching of Frazier B. Baker and His Baby, Late U.S. Postmaster at Lake City, S.C., in the U.S. Circuit Court at Charleston, South Carolina, April 10–22, 1899* (Charleston, SC: Charleston Normal and Industrial Institute, 1899), 5.

34. Arthur F. Raper, *The Tragedy of Lynching* (Chapel Hill: University of North Carolina Press, 1933).

35. Raper, *The Tragedy of Lynching*.

36. Shoshana Felman, *The Juridical Unconscious: Trials and Traumas in the Twentieth Century* (Cambridge, MA: Harvard University Press, 2002), 59, 65.

37. Felman, *The Juridical Unconscious*, 65.

38. For an analysis of lynching's relationship to spectacle in general and disaster spectacle in particular, see Goldsby, *A Spectacular Secret*; Amy Louise Wood, *Lynching and American Spectacle: Witnessing Racial Violence in America, 1890–1940* (Chapel Hill: University of North Carolina Press, 2010).

39. While scholars such as Amy Wood and Jacqueline Goldsby have located spectacle lynching's conditions of possibility in the rise of disaster spectacle entertainment that was popular at turn-of-the-century amusement parks, in melodramatic film, and the enduring history of public execution, we might also think of the courtroom as a stage that doubled as a site that extended lynching's cultural logic.

40. "Story of a Terrible Crime," *Charleston News and Courier*, April 12, 1899.

41. Goldsby, *A Spectacular Secret*, 224.

42. "Story of a Terrible Crime."

43. "Story of a Terrible Crime."

44. "Story of a Terrible Crime." Lavinia's performance echoes a genealogy of black female performers who also used bodily exposure to mount insurgent political claims. Most notable in this regard is Sojourner Truth, who famously offered her arm up as evidence of the materiality of the black female bodies. See, e.g., Carla Peterson, "Foreword: Eccentric Bodies," in *Recovering the Black Female Body: Self-Representations by African American Women*, ed. Michael Bennett and Vanessa D. Dickerson (New Brunswick, NJ: Rutgers University Press, 2001), ix–xvi; James B. Salazar, *Bodies of Reform: The Rhetoric of Character in the Gilded Age of America* (New York: New York University Press, 2010).

45. James Weldon Johnson, *The Autobiography of an Ex-Colored Man* (1911; New York: Penguin Classics, 1990), 136.

46. "Story of a Terrible Crime."

47. Daphne Brooks, *Bodies in Dissent: Spectacular Performances of Race and Freedom, 1850–1910* (Durham, NC: Duke University Press, 2006), 8.

48. Felman, *The Juridical Unconscious*, 85.

49. "Story of a Terrible Crime."

50. "Story of a Terrible Crime."

51. "Story of a Terrible Crime."

52. "Story of a Terrible Crime."

53. "Story of a Terrible Crime."

54. Nicholas Mirzoeff, "The Murder of Michael Brown: Reading the Ferguson Grand Jury Transcript," *Social Text* 34, no. 1 (Spring 2016): 54.

55. "Story of a Terrible Crime."

56. "Story of a Terrible Crime."

57. *The Crisis* 10, no. 2 (June 1915).

58. Young, *Embodying Black Experience*, 193.

59. Young, *Embodying Black Experience*, 193.

60. Ken Gonzales-Day, *Lynching in the American West, 1850–1935* (Durham, NC: Duke University Press, 2006), 57.

61. Peggy Phelan, "Atrocity and Action: The Performative Force of the Abu Ghraib Photographs," in *Picturing Atrocity: Photography in Crisis*, ed. Geoffrey Batchen, M. Gidley, Nancy K. Miller, and Jay Prosser (London: Reaktion Books, 2012).

62. This language of lynching and photography's fit is drawn from Jacqueline Goldsby's work in *A Spectacular Secret*.

63. Wood, *Lynching and American Spectacle*, 5.

64. Phelan, "Atrocity and Action," 53.

65. "Cause of the Negro Race," *Boston Herald*, July 29, 1899.

66. "Cause of the Negro Race."

67. "Cause of the Negro Race."

68. Ida B. Wells, *Crusade for Justice: The Autobiography of Ida B. Wells* (Chicago: University of Chicago Press, 1970), 40.

69. Patricia Schechter, *Ida B. Wells Barnett and American Reform, 1880–1930* (Chapel Hill: University of North Carolina Press, 2001), 22.

70. For a detailed account of the October 1892 "show," see Patricia Schechter's chapter "Talking through Tears" in her *Ida B. Wells Barnett and American Reform*.

71. "Lynchings," *Boston Herald*, July 17, 1899.

72. Amy Hughes, *Spectacles of Reform: Theater and Activism in Nineteenth-Century America* (Ann Arbor: University of Michigan Press, 2012), 25.

73. W. E. B. Du Bois, *Dusk of Dawn: An Essay Toward an Autobiography of a Race Concept* (1941; New York: Oxford University Press, 2007), 34.

74. "Lynchings," *Boston Herald*, July 17, 1899.

75. "Girl a Crusader against Lynchings," *New York Journal*, July 18, 1899.

76. "Girl a Crusader against Lynchings"; "Woman Champions the Negroes," *Baltimore Sun*, July 18, 1899.

77. "Providence Postered," *Boston Daily Advertiser*, August 7, 1899.

78. "A Red Hot Meeting," *Boston Herald*, August 1, 1899.

79. "Girl Crusader."

80. "All Acting Together," *Boston Herald*, July 19, 1899.

81. Laura Wexler, *Tender Violence: Domestic Visions in the Age of US Imperialism* (Chapel Hill: University of North Carolina Press, 2000).

82. "Miss Jewett and the Bakers Trip North."

83. "Providence Postered."

84. "Providence Postered."

85. "Baker Family in Providence," *Pawtucket (RI) Times*, August 8, 1999.

86. "Baker Family Central Figures in Providence Meeting," *Boston Post*, August 8, 1899.

87. "Liberty Land," *Boston Morning Journal*, August 8, 1899.

88. "Baker Family in Providence."

89. "Liberty Land."

90. "A Fee Charged," *Boston Daily Advertiser*, August 10, 1899.

91. "A Fee Charged."

92. "The Baker Family in Boston," *Pawtucket Times*, August 9, 1899.

93. Schneider, *Performing Remains*, 144.

94. "Miss Jewett," *Columbus Daily Enquirer*, August 11, 1899; "Showed Them How to Shout," *Columbus Daily Enquirer*, August 10, 1899.

95. "Showed Them How to Shout."

96. "Boston's Love for the Negro," *Charlotte Daily Observer*, September 28, 1899.

97. "Mrs. Baker Yields to Her Emotions."

98. "A Fee Charged."

99. Carla Peterson, *Doers of the Word: African American Women Speakers and Writers in the North (1830–1880)* (New York: Oxford University Press, 1995).

100. Ashon Crawley, *Black Pentecostal Breath: The Aesthetics of Possibility* (New York: Fordham University Press, 2016), 133.

101. Here the press's construction of the frenzied and frenetic black body is in keeping with what Kelina Gotman has identified as a "wider trend according to which African American dance signaled the 'potential to represent madness.'" Kelina Gotman, *Choreomania: Dance and Disordered* (New York: Oxford University Press, 2018), 272.

102. "Miss Jewett."

103. See Robert Levine, *Dislocating Race and Nation: Episodes in Nineteenth-Century American Nationalism* (Chapel Hill: University of North Carolina Press, 2008).

104. "Appeal," *Richmond Planet*, November 11, 1899.

105. B. O. Flower, "Photography: Its True Function and Its Limitations," in *The Arena* (Trenton, NJ: Brandit Press, 1907), 133.

106. Schneider, *Performing Remains*, 139.

107. Schneider, *Performing Remains*, 142.

108. Schneider, *Performing Remains*, 141.

109. Mary Chapman, "'Living Pictures': Women and Tableaux Vivants in Nineteenth-Century American Fiction and Culture," *Wide Angle* 18, no. 3 (1996): 22–52.

110. Schneider, *Performing Remains*, 141.

111. Ida B. Wells, *Southern Horrors: Lynch Law in All Its Phases* 1892 (New York: Bedford St. Martin's Books, 1997), 70.

112. Schechter, *Ida B. Wells Barnett and American Reform*, 19.

113. Christina Sharpe, *In the Wake: On Blackness and Being* (Durham, NC: Duke University Press, 2016).

114. David Levering Lewis, *W. E. B. Du Bois: Biography of a Race, 1868–1919* (New York: Henry Holt, 1993), 277.

115. Flower, "Photography," 136; Du Bois, *The Souls of Black Folk*, 5.

116. Lewis, *W. E. B. Du Bois: Biography of a Race*, 280.

117. Megan Ming Francis, *Civil Rights and the Making of the Modern American State* (New York: Cambridge University Press, 2014), 30.

118. W. E. B. Du Bois, *The Autobiography of W. E. B. Du Bois: A Soliloquy on Viewing My Life from the Last Decade of Its First Century* (New York: Oxford University Press, 2007), 162.

119. Wood, *Lynching and American Spectacle*, 183.

120. Raiford, *Imprisoned in a Luminous Glare*, 45.

121. Francis, *Civil Rights and the Making of the Modern American State*, 30–31.

122. In this regard, it is important to designate the NAACP's pre-1916 anti-

lynching strategies as experimental. For as Megan Ming Francis writes, the NAACP was "formulating a strategy for civil rights before there were actual civil rights in society." Any strategy, then, would not only be experimental but also necessarily speculative.

123. *The Crisis* 3, no. 3 (1912): 110.

124. *The Crisis* 3, no. 3 (1912): 110.

125. Russ Castronovo, *Beautiful Democracy: Aesthetics and Anarchy in a Global Age* (Chicago: University of Chicago Press, 2007), 170.

126. Goldsby, *A Spectacular Secret*, 84.

127. *The Crisis* 3, no. 2 (1911): 57.

128. "Triumph," *The Crisis* 2, no. 5 (1911): 195.

129. "The Gall of Bitterness," *The Crisis* 2, no. 3 (1912): 153.

130. "The Gall of Bitterness," 153.

131. "The Gall of Bitterness," 153.

132. Shawn Michelle Smith, *Photography on the Color Line: W. E. B. Du Bois, Race, and Visual Culture* (Durham, NC: Duke University Press, 2004), 9.

133. In his study of Du Bois's diagrammatics, Alexander Weheliye argues that, unlike photographs, which capture and arrest their referent, statistical charts and graphs visualize the "Negro" as a historical subject. Likewise, Saidiya Hartman's recent exploration of black life in the post-Reconstruction North makes the implicit argument that the pulse of black sociality characterizing cities like Chicago, New York, and Washington, DC, move in excess of photographic representation.

134. This is, of course, a riff of Du Bois's essay "Sociology Hesitant," posthumously published in *Boundary 2* 27, no. 3 (2000): 37–44.

135. Roland Barthes, *Image Music Text* (New York: Hill and Wang, 1977), 25.

136. An important exception is Amy Wood's brief overview of the story in *Lynching and American Spectacle*.

137. David Levering Lewis, *W. E. B. Du Bois: The Fight For Equality and the American Century* (New York: Henry Holt, 2000), 17.

138. Arnold Rampersad, *The Art and Imagination of W. E. B. Du Bois* (New York: Schocken Books, 1976), 180.

139. Wilson Jeremiah Moses, *Black Messiahs and Uncle Toms: Social and Literary Manipulations of Religious Myths: Social and Literary Manipulations of a Religious Myth* (University Park: Pennsylvania State University Press, 1993), 142.

140. Moses, *Black Messiahs and Uncle Toms*, 142.

141. W. E. B. Du Bois, "Jesus Christ in Georgia," *The Crisis* 3, no. 2 (1911): 70.

142. Du Bois, "Jesus Christ in Georgia," 73.

143. Du Bois, "Jesus Christ in Georgia," 72.

144. W. E. B. Du Bois, "The Church and the Negro," *The Crisis* 6 (October 1913): 290.

145. Du Bois, "Jesus Christ in Georgia," 73.

146. On the relationship between scenes of crucifixion and lynching see James Cone, *The Cross and the Lynching Tree* (New York: Orbis Books, 2011).

147. "Jesus Christ in Georgia," 74.
148. Phelan, "Atrocity and Action."

Chapter Three

1. Parts of this chapter were published as "'The Brown Bag of Miscellany': Zora Neale Hurston and the Practice of Overexposure," *Black Camera* 7, no. 1 (2015): 115–33. No part of it may be reproduced, stored in a retrieval system, transmitted, or distributed in any form, by any means, electronic, mechanical, photographic, or otherwise, without the prior permission of Indiana University Press. For education reuse, please contact the Copyright Clearance Center, http://www.copyright.com/. For all other permissions, contact IU Press at http://iupress.indiana.edu/rights/.

2. Kate Ramsey, *The Spirits and the Law: Vodou and Power in Haiti* (Chicago: University of Chicago Press, 2011), 168.

3. A. D. S., "King Faustin," *New York Times*, March 27, 1933.

4. The blurry line between exploitation and objectivity was, of course, a hallmark of early twentieth-century popular entertainment, as well as a core feature of ethnographic spectacle. See Fatimah Tobing Rony, *The Third Eye: Race, Cinema, and Ethnographic Spectacle* (Durham, NC: Duke University Press, 1996); "King Faustin."

5. Ramsey, *The Spirits and the Law*, 168.

6. Fatimah Tobing Rony explains this line of connection in *The Third Eye*. It is also worth noting that *Voodoo* appeared on the heels of the commercial success of *Tarzan*, a film that Rony argues exemplifies ethnographic spectacle's relationship to popular media.

7. Eve Dunbar, "Woman on the Verge of a Cultural Breakdown: Zora Neale Hurston in Haiti and the Racial Privilege of Boasian Relativism," in *Indigenous Visions: Rediscovering the World of Franz Boas*, ed. Ned Blackhawk and Isaiah Lorado Wilner (New Haven, CT: Yale University Press, 2018), 247.

8. Carla Kaplan, ed., *Zora Neale Hurston: A Life in Letters* (New York: Random House, 2007), 391.

9. See, e.g., Eve Dunbar, "Woman on the Verge of a Cultural Breakdown"; John Carlos Rowe, *Literary Culture and U.S. Imperialism: From the Revolution to World War II* (New York: Oxford University Press, 2000).

10. Dunbar, "Woman on the Verge of a Cultural Breakdown," 246.

11. Brian Hochman, *Savage Preservation: The Ethnographic Origins of Modern Media Technology* (Minneapolis: University of Minnesota Press, 2014), xii.

12. Kaplan, *Zora Neale Hurston*, 115.

13. Allison Griffiths, *Wondrous Difference: Cinema, Anthropology, and Turn-of-the-Century Visual Culture* (New York: Columbia University Press, 2002).

14. Allyson Nadia Field, *Uplift Cinema: The Emergence of African American Film and the Possibility of Black Modernity* (Durham, NC: Duke University Press, 2015).

15. Kaplan, *Zora Neale Hurston*, 391.

16. Kaplan, *Zora Neale Hurston*, 248.

17. Kaplan, *Zora Neale Hurston*, 252.

18. Robert E. Hemenway, *Zora Neale Hurston: A Literary Biography* (Urbana: University of Illinois Press, 1977), 109.

19. Hurston points to this in her autobiography *Dust Tracks on a Road*: "I must tell the tales, sing the songs, do the dances, and repeat the raucous sayings and doings of the Negro farthest down. She is altogether in sympathy with them, because she says truthfully, they are utterly sincere in living." Zora Neale Hurston, *Dust Tracks on a Road* (1942; New York: Harper Perennial, 1995), 145. This discussion of Mason is drawn from Jeffrey Stewart, *The New Negro: The Life of Alain Locke* (New York: Oxford University Press, 2018).

20. Deborah Gordon, "The Politics of Ethnographic Authority: Race and Writing in the Ethnography of Margaret Mead and Zora Neale Hurston," in *Modernist Anthropology: From Fieldwork to Text*, ed. Marc Manganaro (Princeton, NJ: Princeton University Press, 1990), 160.

21. Kaplan, *Zora Neale Hurston*, 97.

22. Using the camera as a visual notebook, taking it up as a mode of gathering and collecting, was precisely how early twentieth-century ethnographers approached the technology. As Jay Ruby has explained, film was not a standard technology or tool in anthropology until the second half of the twentieth century. While early motion pictures, movement studies, and the long history of photography set the disciplinary tone and created a grammar that shaped anthropology's visual economy, film was primarily a mode of gathering fieldwork.

23. Michael Boyce Gillespie, *Film Blackness: American Cinema and the Idea of Black Film* (Durham, NC: Duke University Press, 2016), 2.

24. Elaine Charnov, "The Performative Visual Anthropology Films of Zora Neale Hurston," *Film Criticism* 23, no. 1 (1998): 45.

25. For a foundational analysis of the regulatory function of early cinema, see Tom Gunning, "Tracing the Individual Body: Photography, Detectives, and Early Cinema," in *Cinema and the Invention of Modern Life*, ed. Leo Charney and Vanessa R. Schwartz (Berkeley: University of California Press, 1995). Gunning shows how in the midst of rapid demographic, geographic, and technical transformations, cinema produced the illusion of securing otherwise "fugitive physicality," and thus established a sense of security and stability in the midst of the feeling of chaos.

26. Wahneema Lubiano, "But Compared to What? Reading Realism, Representation and Essentialism in *School Daze*, *Do the Right Thing*, and the Spike Lee Discourse," in *Representing Blackness: Issues in Film and Video*, ed. Valerie Smith (New Brunswick, NJ: Rutgers University Press, 1997), 105.

27. Nicole Fleetwood, *Troubling Vision: Performance, Visuality, and Blackness* (Chicago: University of Chicago Press, 2011), 111.

28. Fleetwood, *Troubling Vision*, 16.

29. Kaplan, *Zora Neale Hurston*, 459.

30. Hurston's frustration that the camera cannot jump, that it cannot ultimately be as nimble as her own body, also anticipates Agamben's assessment that gesture is

both evacuated and restored by photographic technologies. Hurston's desire for the camera to capture embodied repertoire, the gestural archive of the church service, is thus emptied by the filmic technology that seeks to order and sync that which often exceeds the frame. Hurston also sees a future potential of film here, one in which the camera is an extension of the body. As it turns out, this is exactly the way she handled the camera in her early fieldwork.

31. Quoted in George Hutchinson, *The Harlem Renaissance in Black and White* (Cambridge, MA: Harvard University Press, 1995), 207.

32. For an account of the Opportunity dinner parties as an incubator for black artistic production, see Hutchinson, *The Harlem Renaissance in Black and White*.

33. For an account of Washington's black cultural life at the turn of the century, see Treva B. Lindsay, *Colored No More: Reinventing Womanhood in Washington, DC* (Urbana: University of Illinois Press, 2017).

34. Hurston, *Dust Tracks on a Road*, 138.

35. Gordon, "The Politics of Ethnographic Authority," 158.

36. Anne Cheng, *Second Skin: Josephine Baker and the Modern Surface* (Durham, NC: Duke University Press, 2010), 5.

37. This line of thinking is indebted to Cheng's provocations in *Second Skin*.

38. Lena Hill, *Visualizing Blackness and the Creation of the African American Literary Tradition* (New York: Cambridge University Press, 2014), 120.

39. Zora Neale Hurston, "How It Feels to Be Colored Me," 1928, reprinted in *I Love Myself When I Am Laughing: A Zora Neale Hurston Reader*, ed. Alice Walker (New York: Feminist Press, 2020), 147.

40. Zora Neale Hurston, "Drenched in Light," *Opportunity Magazine* 2, no. 24 (1924): 371.

41. Daphne Brooks, *Bodies in Dissent: Spectacular Performances of Race and Freedom, 1850–1910* (Durham, NC: Duke University Press, 2006), 5.

42. Hurston, "Drenched in Light," 372.

43. Hurston, "Drenched in Light," 372.

44. Hurston, "Drenched in Light," 372.

45. Hurston, "Drenched in Light," 373.

46. Hurston, "Drenched in Light," 373.

47. Hurston, "Drenched in Light," 374.

48. Hurston, "Drenched in Light," 375.

49. Valerie Boyd, *Wrapped in Rainbows: The Life of Zora Neale Hurston* (New York: Scribner, 2003), 91.

50. Boyd, *Wrapped in Rainbows*, 92.

51. Hemenway, *Zora Neale Hurston: A Literary Biography*, 13.

52. Hurston, *Dust Tracks on a Road*, 33.

53. Hill, *Visualizing Blackness*, 120.

54. Michael North, *The Dialect of Modernism: Race, Language, and Twentieth Century Literature* (New York: Oxford University Press, 1994), 170.

55. Deborah Poole, *Vision, Race, and Modernity: A Visual Economy of the Andean World* (Princeton, NJ: Princeton University Press, 1997), 10.

56. Cheng, *Second Skin*, 116.

57. Anthea Kraut, *Choreographing the Folk: The Dance Stagings of Zora Neale Hurston* (Minneapolis: University of Minnesota Press, 2008), 21.

58. Kraut, *Choreographing the Folk*, 21.

59. Hazel Carby, "The Politics of Fiction, Anthropology, and the Folk: Zora Neale Hurston," in *History and Memory in African American Culture*, ed. Genevieve Fabre and Robert O'Meally (New York: Oxford University Press, 1994), 32.

60. Carby, "The Politics of Fiction, Anthropology, and the Folk," 32.

61. Kraut, *Choreographing the Folk*, 43.

62. Hurston, *Dust Tracks on a Road*, 158.

63. Hurston, "Drenched in Light," 373.

64. Hurston, "Characteristics of Negro Expression," in *Sweat*, ed. Cheryl Wall (New Brunswick, NJ: Rutgers University Press, 1997), 59.

65. North, *The Dialect of Modernism*, 182.

66. Hurston, "Drenched in Light," 373.

67. Joseph Roach, *Cities of the Dead: Circum-Atlantic Performance* (New York: Columbia University Press, 1996), 25.

68. Kaplan, *Zora Neale Hurston*, 114.

69. Zora Neale Hurston, *Dust Tracks on a Road: An Autobiography*, ed. Robert Hemenway (1942; Urbana: University of Illinois Press, 1984), 17.

70. Zora Neale Hurston, "The Florida Expedition," 1937; Hurston, *Dust Tracks on a Road*, 145.

71. Kara Keeling, *The Witches Flight: The Cinematic, the Black Femme, and the Image of Common Sense* (Durham, NC: Duke University Press, 2007), 5.

72. Keeling, *The Witches Flight*, 5.

73. Keeling, *The Witches Flight*, 5.

74. Hurston, *Dust Tracks on a Road*, 43.

75. Hurston, *Dust Tracks on a Road*, 127; Kaplan, *Zora Neale Hurston*, 116.

76. Hurston, *Dust Tracks on a Road*, 143.

77. Griffiths, *Wondrous Difference*, 304, 305.

78. Griffiths, *Wondrous Difference*, 304, 305.

79. Jay Ruby, "Franz Boas and Early Cinema Study of Behavior," *Kinesics Report* (1989), 7.

80. Ruby, "Franz Boas and Early Cinema Study of Behavior," 8.

81. Zora Neale Hurston, *Mules and Men*, 1.

82. Rony, *The Third Eye*, 204.

83. Rony, *The Third Eye*, 207.

84. Such assessments describe Hurston as a filmmaker who arrived in the South with predetermined "representational method" that depended on creating an image of black life that would counter the construction of positivist knowledge that, as Kelly Wagers argues, is "about racial history and the division of this knowledge into distinct, mutually exclusive discourses that further negate African American experiences and history-making methods." Against this context, Hurston is read as actively and strategically working to "reformulate the subjects and practice of docu-

mentary study," in a way that anticipates the social documentary projects of Richard Wright and Ralph Ellison. See Kelly Wagers, "'How Come You Ain't Got It?': Dislocation as Historical Act in Hurston's Documentary Texts," *African American Review* 46, nos. 2–3 (2013): 210–16.

85. Jacqueline Stewart, *Migrating to the Movies: Cinema and Black Urban Modernity* (Berkeley: University of California Press, 2005).

86. Keeling, *The Witches Flight*, 5.

87. Boyd, *Wrapped in Rainbows*, 193. This reading of Hurston's camera work also resonates with Daphne Brooks's assessment of Hurston's sound recordings. For Brooks, Hurston's inexperience with sound technology and her lack of musical training provide the grounds for teasing out a radical, and indeed renegade, aspect of Hurston's gender politics. I am not making a claim regarding Hurston's gender politics here, but like Brooks I am interested in how approaching Hurston's artistry from the standpoint of experimentation by a nonprofessional is generative. See Daphne Brooks, "Sister Can You Line It Out? Zora Neale Hurston and the Sound of Angular Black Womanhood," *Amerikastudien/American Studies* 55, no. 4 (2010): 617–27.

88. See Rony, *The Third Eye*, esp. chaps. 1 and 2.

89. Rony, *The Third Eye*, 204.

90. Rony, *The Third Eye*, 204.

91. Tavia Nyong'o, *Afro-Fabulations: The Queer Drama of Black Life* (New York: New York University Press, 2019), 49.

92. Nyong'o, *Afro-Fabulations*, 49.

93. See Richard Dyer, *White: Essays on Race and Culture* (New York: Routledge, 1997).

94. Shawn Michelle Smith, *At the Edge of Sight: Photography and the Unseen* (Durham, NC: Duke University Press, 2013), 84.

95. Fleetwood, *Troubling Vision*, 11.

96. Shane Vogel, *The Scene of the Harlem Cabaret: Race, Sexuality, Performance* (Chicago: University of Chicago Press, 2009), 96.

97. Vogel, *The Scene of the Harlem Cabaret*, 96.

98. Zora Neale Hurston, "How It Feels to Be Colored Me" (1928), in *The Norton Anthology of African American Literature*, ed. Henry Louis Gates Jr. and Nellie McKay (New York: Norton, 2004), 1031.

99. Hurston, "How It Feels to Be Colored Me," 1031.

100. Hurston, "How It Feels to Be Colored Me," 1032.

101. Hurston, "How It Feels to Be Colored Me," 1032.

102. Hurston, "How It Feels to Be Colored Me," 1032.

103. Hurston, "How It Feels to Be Colored Me," 1032–33.

104. For an overview of these debates, see *The Psychic Hold of Slavery: Legacies in American Expressive Culture*, ed. Soyica D. Colbert, Aida Levy-Hussen, and Robert Patterson (New Brunswick, NJ: Rutgers University Press, 2016).

105. Hurston, "How It Feels to Be Colored Me," 148.

106. Hurston, "How It Feels to Be Colored Me," 148.

107. Kaplan, *Zora Neale Hurston*, 110.

108. Genevieve Sexton, "The Last Witness: Testimony and Desire in Zora Neale Hurston's Barracoon," *Discourse* 25, nos. 1–2 (Winter–Spring 2003): 190.

109. Zora Neale Hurston, "Barracoon," typescript, Morgan Spingarn Research Center, Howard University, 1931. See also Genevieve Sexton, "The Last Witness."

110. Kaplan, *Zora Neale Hurston*, 193.

111. Sexton, "The Last Witness," 191.

112. On July 10, 1928, Hurston sent a letter to Langston Hughes explaining that Lewis was not, in fact, the last living survivor of the Middle Passage. "OH! almost forgot. Found another one of the original Africans, older than Cudjoe about 200 miles up state on the Tombighee river. She is most delightful, but no one will ever know about her but us. She is a better talker than Cudjoe." Kaplan, *Zora Neale Hurston*, 123.

113. Elaine Charnov, "Performative Visual Anthropology Films of Zora Neale Hurston," 44.

114. Charnov, "Performative Visual Anthropology Films of Zora Neale Hurston," 44.

115. Darcy Grimaldo Grigsby makes a similar point in her reading of antebellum photography, specifically Sojourner Truth's famous portrait, captioned "I Sell the Shadow to Support the Substance." See "Negative Positive Truths," *Representations* 113, no. 1 (2011): 16–38.

116. Krista Thompson and Huey Copeland, "Perpetual Returns: New World Slavery and the Matter of the Visual," *Representations* 113, no. 1 (2011): 3.

117. Natalie Zemon Davis, *Slaves on Screen: Film and Historical Vision* (Cambridge, MA: Harvard University Press, 2000).

118. Giorgio Agamben, "Notes on Gesture," *Means without Ends* (Minneapolis: University of Minnesota Press, 2000), 68.

119. Christina Sharpe, "The Crook of Her Arm," in *Borrowed Lady: Martine Syms*, ed. Amy Kazymerchyk (San Francisco, CA: SFU Galleries, 2017), 35. I am grateful to Kemi Adeyemi for bringing this essay to my attention and for especially encouraging me to think about gesture as a black feminist praxis.

120. Agamben, "Notes on Gesture," 60, 68.

121. For a detailed analysis of the limits of Agamben and black cinema, see Rizvana Bradley, "Black Cinematic Gesture and the Aesthetics of Contagion," *TDR: The Drama Review* 62, no. 1 (2018): 14–30.

122. Sonya Postmentier, "Lyric Reading in the Black Ethnographic Archive," *American Literary History* 30, no. 1 (2018): 55–84.

123. Kaplan, *Zora Neale Hurston*, 115.

124. Elin Diamond, "Folk Modernism," 116.

125. Diamond, "Folk Modernism," 116.

126. Kaplan, *Zora Neale Hurston*, 115.

127. Kaplan, *Zora Neale Hurston*, 116.

128. Kaplan, *Zora Neale Hurston*, 116.

129. Zora Neale Hurston, "Characteristics of Negro Expression," in *Sweat*, ed. Wall, 55.

130. Hurston, "Characteristics of Negro Expression," 56.

131. Hurston, "Characteristics of Negro Expression," 56.

132. Hurston, "Characteristics of Negro Expression," 61.

133. Hurston, "Characteristics of Negro Expression," 59.

134. Diamond, "Folk Modernism," 114.

135. Cheryl Wall, *On Freedom and the Will to Adorn: The Art of the African American Essay* (Chapel Hill: University of North Carolina Press, 2018), 109.

136. Wall, *On Freedom and the Will to Adorn*, 10.

137. Jasmine E. Johnson, "Solange and Her Dance," *Aster(ix)*, October 25, 2016, https://asterixjournal.com/solange/.

138. Johnson, "Solange and Her Dance."

139. Kaplan, *Zora Neale Hurston*, 115.

Coda

1. Carla Kaplan, *Zora Neale Hurston: A Life in Letters* (New York: Doubleday, 2002), 134.

2. Charles Johnson, *The Negro in American Civilization: A Study of Negro Life and Race Relations in Light of Social Research* (New York: Henry Holt, 1930), v.

3. Johnson, *The Negro in American Civilization*, v.

4. Johnson, *The Negro in American Civilization*, vi.

5. Johnson, *The Negro in American Civilization*, vi.

6. There is a robust body of scholarship that unravels the vexed role of sociology and social science in African American literature. Such titles include Gene Jarrett, "Sincere Art and Honest Science: Richard Wright and the Chicago School of Sociology," in *The Cambridge Companion to Richard Wright*, ed. Glenda R. Carpio (New York: Cambridge University Press, 2019); Avery Gordon, *Ghostly Matters: Haunting and the Sociological Imagination* (Minneapolis: University of Minnesota Press, 2008); Heather Love, "Close but Not Deep: Literary Ethics and the Descriptive Turn," *New Literary History* 41, no. 2 (Spring 2010): 371–91; Roderick Ferguson, *Aberrations in Black: Toward a Queer of Color Critique* (Minneapolis: University of Minnesota Press, 2013).

7. Ruha Benjamin beautifully makes this point in her work on data, race, and ethics: *Race after Technology: Abolitionist Tools for the New Jim Crow* (New York: Polity Press, 2019).

8. Barack Obama, "Statement on the Ferguson Grand Jury's Decision," November 24, 2014, https://obamawhitehouse.archives.gov/blog/2014/11/24/president-obama-delivers-statement-ferguson-grand-jurys-decision/.

9. Campbell Robertson, "History of Lynching in the South Documents Nearly 4,000 Names," *New York Times*, February 10, 2015, https://www.nytimes.com/2015/02/10/us/history-of-lynchings-in-the-south-documents-nearly-4000-names.html.

10. Robertson, "History of Lynching in the South Documents Nearly 4,000 Names."

11. Campbell Robertson, "Over 2,000 Black People Were Lynched From 1865–1877 Study Finds," *New York Times*, June 16, 2020, https://www.nytimes.com/2020/06/16/us/reconstruction-violence-lynchings.html.

12. Saidiya Hartman, *Lose Your Mother: A Journey along the Atlantic Slave Route* (New York: Farrar, Straus & Giroux, 2008), 6.

13. Okieriete Onaodowan, "Hamilton Friday," interviewed by Alison Stewart, *All of It*, WNYC, August 7, 2020, https://www.wnyc.org/story/okieriete-onaodowan-hamilton-movie.

14. Jill Lepore, "American Exposure," *New Yorker*, July 16, 2016, https://www.newyorker.com/news/daily-comment/american-exposure.

15. "Philando Castile's Girlfriend Testifies: I Streamed Shooting for Fear I Would Die," *The Guardian*, June 6, 2017, https://www.theguardian.com/us-news/2017/jun/06/philando-castile-police-shooting-witness-diamond-reynolds.

16. Dawn Lundy Martin, "Looking for Language in the Ruins," University of Pittsburgh, October 29, 2020.

Index

Bold page numbers refer to figures.